Textbooks in American Society

SUNY Series
FRONTIERS IN EDUCATION
Philip G. Altbach, Editor

The Frontiers in Education Series draws upon a range of disciplines and approaches in the analysis of contemporary educational issues and concerns. Books in the series help to reinterpret established fields of scholarship in education by encouraging the latest synthesis and research. A special focus highlights education policy issues from a multidisciplinary perspective. The series is published in cooperation with the Graduate School of Education, State University of New York at Buffalo.

Class, Race, and Gender in American Education

—Lois Weis (ed.)

Excellence and Equality: A Qualitatively Different Perspective on Gifted and Talented Education

—David M. Fetterman

Change and Effectiveness in Schools: A Cultural Perspective

—Gretchen B. Rossman, H. Dickson Corbett, and William A. Firestone

The Curriculum: Problems, Politics, and Possibilities

—Landon E. Beyer and Michael W. Apple (eds.)

The Character of American Higher Education and Intercollegiate Sport

—Donald Chu

Crisis in Teaching: Perspectives on Current Reforms

—Lois Weis, Philip G. Altbach, Gail P. Kelly, Hugh G. Petrie, and Sheila Slaughter (eds.)

The High Status Track: Studies of Elite Schools and Stratification

—Paul William Kingston and Lionel S. Lewis (eds.)

The Economics of American Universities: Management, Operations, and Fiscal Environment

—Stephen A. Hoenack and Eileen L. Collins (eds.)

The Higher Learning and High Technology: Dynamics of Higher Education and Policy Formation

—Sheila Slaughter

Dropouts from Schools: Issues, Dilemmas and Solutions

—Lois Weis, Eleanor Farrar, and Hugh G. Petrie (eds.)

Religious Fundamentalism and American Education: The Battle for the Public Schools

—Eugene F. Provenzo, Jr.

Going to School: The African-American Experience

—Kofi Lomotey (ed.)

Curriculum Differentiation: Interpretive Studies in U.S. Secondary Schools

—Reba Page and Linda Valli (eds.)

The Racial Crisis in American Higher Education

—Philip G. Altbach and Kofi Lomotey (eds.)

The Great Transformation in Higher Education, 1960–1980

—Clark Kerr

College in Black and White: African-American Students in Predominantly White and in Historically Black Public Universities

—Walter R. Allen, Edgar G. Epps, and Nesha Z. Haniff (eds.)

Critical Perspectives on Early Childhood Education

—Lois Weis, Philip G. Altbach, Gail P. Kelly, and Hugh G. Petrie (eds.)

Textbooks in American Society

Politics, Policy, and Pedagogy

Edited by
Philip G. Altbach
Gail P. Kelly
Hugh G. Petrie
Lois Weis

State University of New York Press

Some of these chapters have appeared in *Educational Policy,* Volume 3, Number 2 (1989). They have been reprinted with the permission of the publisher. The chapter by J. Dan Marshall appeared in a different form in the *Capstone Journal of Education* and is reprinted here with the permission of the journal. The chapter by Howard Mehlinger appeared in the *Phi Delta Kappan* and is reprinted with the permission of the author and editor. We are indebted to Butterworth Publishers, a division of Reed Publishing (USA) Inc. for their permission to reprint the articles from *Educational Policy.*

Published by
State University of New York Press, Albany

Printed in the United States of America

For information, address the State University of New York Press,
State University Plaza, Albany, NY 12246

Library of Congress Cataloging-in-Publication Data

Textbooks in American Society : politics, policy, and pedagogy /
edited by Philip G. Altbach . . . [et al.].
p. cm. — (SUNY series, frontiers in education)
Includes bibliographical references and index.
ISBN 0-7914-0669-5 (alk. paper).—ISBN 0-7914-0670-9 (pbk. : alk. paper)
1. Textbooks—United States. 2. Textbooks—Publication and distribution—United States. I. Altbach, Philip G. II. Series.
LB3047.T49 1991
379.1′56—dc20 90-43397
CIP

10 9 8 7 6 5 4 3 2 1

Table of Contents

PHILIP G. ALTBACH

Introduction

Until very recently, one of the key elements in American education attracted scant attention. Textbooks are a central part of any educational system. They help to define the curriculum and can either significantly help or hinder the teacher. The "excellence movement" has directed its attention to textbooks in the past few years. American textbooks, according to the critics, are boring and designed for the lowest common denominator. They have been "dumbed down" so that content is diluted and "readability" is stressed. Textbooks have evolved over the past several decades into "products" often assembled by committees in response to external pressures rather than a coherent approach to education. Most important to many of the critics, textbooks do not provide the knowledge base necessary for American schools in a period of reform, renewal, and improvement.

It has been belatedly recognized that textbooks are a key part of any effort to reform America's schools. And there are few parts of the educational system that would seem easier to fix. Textbooks are a relatively small part of any school budget—the average school district spent about $4,000 per child in 1986, of which only $34.17 was spent on instructional materials. Even doubling the average expenditure on textbooks would only marginally increase school expenditures—from 0.85 percent to 1.7 percent.[1] Even in an age of high technology, the "oldest technology" in education, the textbook, remains very important.

It is often difficult to assess blame in America's decentralized educational structure. In the case of textbooks, critics have pointed in several directions. The publishers, they argue, have been only too willing to pander to fads, succumb to pressures from a variety of interest groups, and debase standards in their efforts to ensure a profit in an increasingly difficult marketplace. Many educators have stressed readability formulas rather than content in textbooks, and have contributed to the decline in both coherence and standards in textbooks. The centralized adoption system, prevalent in almost half of the states, including such key states as Texas, California, and Florida, gives tremendous power to textbook boards, which must approve books for use statewide. These boards are frequently both overworked and undereducated. School administrators have rarely made a stand for high quality in textbooks. And the scholars in schools of education who are frequently involved in writing and evaluating textbooks have been seen as remiss for not sounding the alarm. In short, the complex system that creates, publishes, selects, and distributes textbooks for America's schools is in disarray. Virtually no one involved in the textbook enterprise has defended the status quo. And as Harriet Tyson-Bernstein points out, the situation is a "conspiracy of good intentions."[2] Textbook development is expensive, and publishers are naturally concerned with the bottom line of immediate profits in a highly competitive marketplace. In the past two decades, educators have been more concerned with ensuring that young people stayed in school during a period of declining budgets and seemingly intractable problems.

This is an opportune time for us to focus attention on textbooks. Change is taking place in tandem with the excellence movement. In California, Superintendent Bill Honig has been at the forefront of criticism, and he has also taken action by rejecting many of the textbooks offered for adoption in California schools. Honig and others have demanded books that will stimulate a desire for reading rather than simply imparting linguistic skills. When California — the largest single centralized textbook market in the United States—speaks, the publishers listen.

The textbook debate takes place in a broader social and educational context. In the 1960s and 1970s, politicians stressed the importance of access to schooling and the importance of equality of educational opportunity. Textbooks, not surprisingly, reflected this emphasis by lowering standards to ensure that they were understandable to an evermore diverse, and sometimes poorly prepared, student population. The pendulum has taken a swing, and the emphasis now is on higher academic standards, "cultural literacy" and the need for skills in a competitive world economy. The special interest groups that earlier were able to demand that textbooks include material on creationism, specific historical interpretations, and other sometimes rather odd topics have lost some of their power. Textbooks are now seen to be an important part of the excellence movement. We are in the midst of a significant change in the American approach to school textbooks.

It seems clear that textbook standards will improve, that more emphasis will be placed on content as opposed to method, and that publishers will pay more attention to quality. Yet, there are many voices and many demands in the highly complex textbook debate. The excellence advocates have a very strong voice and states like California play a key role. There are also countervailing forces, including special interest groups, the opinions of school boards and others throughout the country, and resistance to the expenditures required for the development of new textbooks. At the moment, the advocates of higher academic standards, coherence, and quality have the strongest position.

The story of America's textbook dilemma has yet to be fully told. Analysts and critics such as Harriet Tyson-Bernstein, Frances FitzGerald, and Paul Gagnon have discussed key issues and analyzed specific elements of the highly complex nexus.[3] Authors in this volume extend the story. This book looks at textbooks in historical perspective with a perceptive discussion by Michael Apple, who argues that there has been a link between political factors and state control over textbook decisions. He focuses on the South in his analysis. Sherry Keith and Kenneth Wong and Tom Loveless all add to this discussion from several different perspectives. They deal directly with the complex political equation of textbook selection. Two of the essays in this book focus on basal reading textbooks, a very important segment of the textbook business. In these essays Allan Luke and Patrick Shannon both grapple with issues of legitimacy, control, and the nature of reading texts. Many of the ideological and curricular debates are played out in the arena of reading texts. Bill Honig and Harriet Tyson-Bernstein and Arthur Woodward, from rather different perspectives, discuss the role of textbooks in the current educational reform movement.

Two insightful essays consider the textbook industry from the "inside." Naomi Silverman writes as a college textbook editor. She discusses how textbook publishers at the postsecondary level operate, and focuses on some of the constraints involved. Joel Spring, author of several widely used college textbooks in the field of education, writes about his experiences as an author and links the contemporary situation with the historical difficulties of textbook authors. This book concludes with several essays that deal with textbooks in a comparative and international framework—bringing a perspective that is seldom available.

Several authors consider the textbook industry itself, although a full-scale analysis of the economics, politics and culture of textbook publishing remains to be done. The unprecedented amalgamation of publishers that has occurred in the past decade will inevitably have an impact on American textbooks, although the scope and nature of that impact remains to be seen. Textbooks have always been seen by their publishers as a commodity, and commercial considerations have been of primary importance. Now, with textbooks published by multinational media conglomerates, it is likely that the bottom line will become even more crucial. As the structure of publishing changes, the nature of professional work in the industry will very likely undergo alteration as well. We know very little about the role of editors and others in textbook publishing. Naomi Silverman provides some insights from college publishing. We attempted without success to locate an editor to write about elementary and secondary school textbooks for this volume.

We know very little about many of the most important people involved in the development and publication of textbooks. The role of "experts" also needs analysis. How do curriculum specialists, reading scholars, and others exercise influence on textbook decisions? We know how the textbook adoption process works in states with centralized mechanisms—and the picture is not a pretty one. However, we have very little data on how textbook decisions are made in decentralized states and at the school district level. The list could go on. It is surprising that such an important part of the American educational enterprise has been so badly neglected by researchers.[4]

This volume presents a variety of perspectives on the topic. We have assembled an articulate group of educators, publishers, policymakers, and scholars to consider the textbook dilemma from a range of perspectives. We cannot hope to provide solutions to complex problems. However, we are convinced that textbooks deserve much more attention from educational policymakers and from the educational community than they have hitherto received. It is for this reason that we devote this book to a consideration of textbooks.

This volume stems from an issue of *Educational Policy* (Vol. 3, No. 2, 1989). We are indebted to Butterworths Publishers for permission to reprint six of the articles from that issue.

NOTES

1. Harriet Tyson-Bernstein, *A Conspiracy of Good Intentions: America's Textbook Fiasco* (Washington, D.C.: Council for Basic Education, 1988), p. 13.

2. Ibid.

3. Ibid; Frances FitzGerald, *America Revised: History Schoolbooks in the Twentieth Century* (Boston: Little Brown, 1979); Paul Gagnon, *Democracy's Untold Story: What World History Textbooks Neglected* (Washington, D.C.: American Federation of Teachers, 1987).

4. For an overview of textbook issues, see Paul Goldstein, *Changing the American Schoolbook* (Lexington, Mass.: Lexington Books, 1978).

Part 1

Social and Political Issues

MICHAEL W. APPLE

Chapter One

Regulating the Text: The Socio-Historical Roots of State Control

The connections between education and the relations of economic, political, and cultural inequality in the larger society is a subject I have examined in a series of volumes.[1] I have urged us to think about curriculum and teaching not psychologically, but socially, as embodiments and the results of the class, race, and gender dynamics that organize society. In this way, we can see the curriculum not as a neutral set of "thats, hows, and tos," but as knowledge related to conflicts and compromises over power and control.[2]

THE POLITICS OF OFFICIAL KNOWLEDGE

The textbook is uniquely qualified to help us understand these complicated relationships. It is an economic commodity, bought and sold in the United States and in many other countries under the conditions of a capitalist market. Because of this, it is subject to intense competition and to the pressures of profit. However, the text is not only an economic artifact, but is through and through political as well. It is a *regulated* commodity.

I would like to thank Bukwon Park for his assistance on the research for this article. Further thanks go to the two anonymous reviewers and to the Friday seminar at the University of Wisconsin, Madison.

Decisions concerning it are usually conditioned by government policies, policies that are part of the political process of adjudicating among the claims of different class, race, gender, and religious groups. Finally, the text is cultural as well. It embodies the visions of legitimate knowledge of identifiable groups of people.[3] In most cases, it also becomes the real curriculum that is filtered through the lived culture of teachers and students as they go about their day-to-day lives in classrooms. Yet, while the textbook dominates the classroom,[4] while it by and large structures what becomes official knowledge, it is one of the things we know least about.[5]

Because of this, it is essential to understand even more about the political process by which some groups' knowledge becomes "official knowledge." How does the government intervene and regulate what counts as legitimate content? In the United States, the politics of state adoption policies plays an exceptionally important role in this.

Nearly half of the states in the United States have some process by which curricular materials, usually textbooks, are evaluated and endorsed at the state level. Publishers differentiate between two kinds of states. In what is called "open territory"—most of the East, Midwest, and Far West—publishers sell directly to school districts or individual schools. In "closed territory"—mostly in the South and Southwest—centralized adoption policies prevail. Currently, twenty-two states have such centralized policies, a figure that has remained relatively stable over the years.[6]

The influence of such state adoption policies should not be underestimated. The sheer economics of it is quite important. Texas, for example, spends nearly $70 million on instructional materials and has a rather narrow policy of approving five textbooks or less (the minimum is two) for each subject. This puts it in an exceptionally strong position to influence the content of texts as publishers compete over what is obviously a lucrative market.[7]

"INCOMPETENT" TEACHERS, "UNETHICAL" PUBLISHERS

State adoption policies and the overall tendency to centralize control of educational policy and content did not spring full grown. They have a distinctive history and grew out of a multitude of social and educational conditions. This essay will focus largely on the larger socio/historical conditions that led to such a tendency. But first, it is important to understand the overt educational arguments for such policies.

Historically, the arguments for state adoption policies and for statewide uniformity in texts centered around four basic points: (1) Such policies tend to ensure that books will be purchased at the lowest price; (2) instead of the all too real dangers of selecting poor textbooks that are associated with local school district control, state adoption guarantees that selections will not be done by relatively naive people but by experts; (3) state adoption of uniform texts ultimately lowers the costs associated with a mobile population, in which parents (often looking for work) move their children from district to district; and (4) uniformity of textbooks at a state level enables the establishment of a minimum and standard course of study throughout the state.[8]

Certain historical themes emerge here: the overpricing of texts due to what were seen as profit-hungry publishers, control by experts, a particular vision of school populations, and a statewide curriculum. As we shall see, each of these had its roots in wider social movements and conflicts.

Yet this history of internal problems does not fully explain the reasons for turning to statewide solutions in the South. The perception on the part of some government officials that teachers themselves were by and large incompetent played a part here as well. Speaking in 1874, the superintendent of schools of South Carolina, for instance, complained vociferously that county examiners awarded teaching certificates "to persons whose ignorance was glaringly apparent to the most careless observer." As he went on to say, "our schools never will and never can become deservedly popular so long as the evil of employing so many incompetent, inefficient and worthless teachers continues." All too many teachers taught "from motives of personal convenience, and in many instances, from a consciousness of being unfit for anything else."[9] Though similar complaints were heard throughout the country,[10] their effects in the South were more powerful.

The "incompetence" of teachers was a continuing concern that supported the power of state textbook commissions. Summarizing decades of criticism of teachers and reviewing the status of the state adoption policy in Kentucky, one educator stated, "We must recognize that our teachers are not . . . well prepared professionally . . . ." Given such a "poorly prepared corps of teachers," the report concluded that the only hope was to place the best textbooks possible in the hands of the students. "The poorer the teacher, the better the textbooks need to be."[11]

To the claim that teachers were poorly prepared was added the claim that they were too easily influenced by textbook agents who worked their way through the state. "Disinterested" experts, not naive teachers, were required. Commenting on the situation in 1918, when state adoption policies initiated in the late nineteenth and early twentieth centuries were being questioned, Charles Judd laid out this part of the case for the policies:

> It is because teachers are showing so little wisdom in the selection of books that the public has in many states safeguarded the situation by laws removing from the teacher all power of choice. The writer recalls a letter from a public official responsible for the choice of text-books who was moved by criticisms made of his selections to a sharp retort. He said that there was no justification for criticisms of the state selections, that school people were for the most part wholly unreliable in their choices. He asserted that it was entirely possible to map out the route followed by certain book agents through the state by the stream of letters recommending certain books that came to the state text-book commission.[12]

Linked to the distrust of teachers was a concern that is of great significance here—the vision of textbook publishers as more than a little rapacious and corrupt; money motivated them, not educational issues. And while many publishers expressly argued against such stereotyping,[13] this view of textbook publishers was still widespread even as late as the 1930s. It had its beginnings much earlier.

For example, from the late nineteenth century through the early twentieth century, serious questions were raised about "the control of text-books by private individuals and commercial publishing houses."[14] As long as the textbook was produced by commercial firms whose motive was profit and as long as teachers had such limited educational experience, the textbook unfortunately was "removed from institutional control."[15]

Such concerns continued to be widespread and influenced the development of state adoption policies. This can be readily seen in a questionnaire sent out to school superintendents, other educators, and representatives of textbook publishers by J. B. Edmonson, in preparation for his chapter on "The Ethics of Marketing and Selecting Textbooks" in the famous National Society for the Study of Education (NSSE) Yearbook on the textbook. Among the questions about the ethics of publishing and publishers' representatives were the following:[16]

1. Would it be ethical for a representative to try to influence the election or appointment of persons to teaching or administrative positions in order to secure adoptions of certain books?
2. Would it be ethical for a representative to try to stimulate dissatisfaction among teachers with the textbooks adopted for use in schools?
3. Would it be ethical for a representative to bring to the attention of a board of education unethical practices of a superintendent in the selection of textbooks?

4. Would it be ethical for a representative to bring to the attention of the superintendent unethical practices of a committee in the selection of textbooks?
5. Would it be ethical for a representative to try to secure confidential information regarding secret committees for textbook adoption?
6. Would it be ethical for a representative to circulate criticism of superintendents who have made decisions adverse to the representative's company?
7. Would it be ethical for a representative to take an active interest in the election of school board members in a community other than his own?
8. Would it be ethical for a representative to circulate petitions among teachers calling for changes in textbooks?
9. Would it be ethical for a textbook company to employ attorneys to influence the adoption of textbooks?
10. Would it be ethical for a representative to influence the appointment of persons to selecting committees?

The fact that questions such as these had such prominence documents the fear that the politics and economics of textbooks had been and could again easily get out of control. The answer across the South was to regulate and centralize to keep this from happening.[17]

However, there are a multitude of ways to respond to this situation. One response could be to heighten accountability through enhanced local control, as many northern and midwestern states did. Another would be to simply bring the sales practices of publishers under the ethically regulated codes of state departments of commerce and industry or leave it up to the Better Business Bureau. These and other solutions may not be adequate, but it is not preordained that the *state* should set up an elaborate machinery to specifically "police" the practices of publishers and the content of textbooks. Yet this is exactly what many southern states did.

What conditions caused such a response? The roots lie not in the immediacy of decisions to regulate texts but further back, in the establishment throughout many areas of the South of strong centralized regulatory dynamics that set that region apart historically from the North. Without a more thorough understanding of these dynamics we would miss the larger social movements that generated such centralizing responses, for as I shall show, these regulatory urges came not only from above but from *below* as well. Finally, we would miss the role the government has played in forming accords or compromises that incorporate certain progressive tendencies over knowledge and power while at the same time not threatening the overall basis of power over culture and economy.

TOWARD A REGULATORY STATE

From the late nineteenth century to the early twentieth century, American governance went through a fundamental transition. As Robert Weibe has described it, what emerged was "a government broadly and continually involved in society's operations."[18] Instead of a government dominated by the legislature, the executive branch enlarged its power. Even more importantly, power became increasingly vested in what was essentially a new branch of government made up of administrative boards and agencies. Through these administrative mechanisms, government agencies became increasingly involved in mediating clashing interests. These agencies assumed greater responsibility for mitigating conflicts through planning, administration, and regulation. At the end of the nineteenth century, government was not yet deeply involved in "recognizing and adjusting group differences." Yet, by the end of the second decade of the twentieth century, "innumerable policies committed officials to that formal purpose and provided the bureaucratic structures for achieving it."[19]

Scandals at local, state, and national levels had created a furor against politico-business corruption. Among the most glaring offenses uncovered were the many ways corporations corrupted politicians to secure government subsidies, public privileges, and benefits.[20] In California, legislative hearings uncovered fresh scandals. In many southern states, the divided Democratic party and other less powerful parties and alliances brought their rivalries into the public eye by extolling their own virtues and telling tales of each other's corruption by business interests.[21] Muckraking helped, of course, to bring these scandals center stage, and business corruption of politics soon became a leading theme in public discourse, in local newspapers, in party rhetoric, and in legislative halls.[22]

Out of this situation emerged a commitment to a particular type of government, one that would restrain privileged corporations, protect the weaker elements of the community, establish formal mechanisms for new interest groups to have a voice in government, and "acknowledge and adjust group differences."[23] At the state level in particular, the late 1890s and early 1900s were years characterized by experiments with a variety of methods of regulation and administration.[24] These experiments soon solidified into a body of practices and a particular approach to reform.

While these types of scandals were not new to the American political and economic system by any means and while many people had a vague understanding of the pervasiveness of some of the corrupting practices, there was an important new element. A new understanding had begun to emerge, one in which an awareness of the *process* of corruption was central. No longer was corruption seen largely as the result of a few "bad men." Rather, the problem was seen as *systemic* and could only be solved by enlarged government action that altered the system itself.[25] An onslaught of legislation ensued, regulating lobbying, outlawing special favors given by business to public officials, and establishing and/or strengthening the regulatory and administrative arms of government in a wide array of areas from commerce and transportation to health, welfare, and education.[26]

In the process, government involvement and direction shifted. The forces of localism and opposition to government authority (forces that were very strong in the South) slowly but surely lost ground to the forces of centralization, bureaucratization, and expanded governmental authority.[27] This had a special impact on education in general and ultimately on the state regulation of texts. Throughout the South, a coalition of businessmen, professionals, and the urban middle class — assisted, as we shall see, by turmoil and pressure from below—pushed for greater state responsibility. These efforts were aimed at efficiency combined with limited social reforms in education and social welfare.[28]

Progressive reformers from dominant economic groups and within the upwardly mobile new middle class sought to promote more efficient and effective schooling throughout the South by relying on objective information, on "the facts," and by employing experts in public administration for dealing with social problems.[29] Industrialization, economic development, material progress, the transformation and conservation of elements of southern culture, the "race problem," and the social conflicts that were threatening stability throughout the region—all of these could be addressed through limited social reforms.[30] The public sphere must be organized around knowledge, expertise, and efficient administration. The disinterested expert could be counted upon to promote the general interest. While municipal and countywide reforms were focused upon as well, it was in the growth of state functions that one saw the largest changes. As a commentator argued in 1912, "A realization of the greater efficiency that central state departments have . . . has, during the past decade, caused the people to delegate all new functions, and some old ones, to state departments or commissions."[31] In all of this, however, the most striking development of state services and state authority occurred in education.

Other actors were important here besides the spokespeople for the "new South" such as modernizing businessmen, professionals, and the urban middle class. Given the largely agrarian nature of the South, movements among farmers were also significant in focusing attention on areas crying out for reform—from credit and monetary policy to elections and education. The "old South," with its history of a powerful landed, planter class, had already established a tradition of educational reform *from above,* and the newer calls for reform by small farmers and others often moved in the direction of reform from above, as well.[32]

Small farmers in the South, who were being squeezed by sagging prices, mounting interest charges, and unfavorable laws, joined together to form organizations such as the Farmers' Alliance, which soon began searching for answers to their problems.[33] With their way blocked by policies within the resurgent Democratic party in southern states such as Texas, agrarian movements spawned calls for reform.[34] While adult education centering around radical political and economic issues played a very strong part in their program, public education and the kinds of knowledge taught (and not taught) to farmers and their children in schools were important areas of interest and political work for the alliance.[35] For alliance members, what was going on was *miseducation* in which "Those who labor are educated to be abject slaves and the rich are educated to be tyrannical, presumptuous, and vicious. . . . All the people have been educated to bow submissively at the feet of Mammon."[36] Since the capitalist controlled "the channels of information," only miseducation could result. In opposition to this, alliance spokespersons mounted attacks on newspapers, the publishing industry, and the public schools.[37]

Leaders of the alliance were not loath to criticize the public schools as being controlled by the exact same "plutocratic" groups that dominated other elements of government. They argued against both monopolies in textbook publishing and partisan political control of educational governance. At the same time, they advocated a more effective system of public education in Texas and in other southern states.[38]

In 1890, the national leadership of the Farmers' Alliance leveled charges against a group of textbook publishers. They accused the publishers of "conspiring to consolidate markets, control competition, and raise prices in the schoolbook market through the creation of a holding company, the American Book Company." For the alliance, this had the effect of raising the prices of texts, a cardinal sin for hard-pressed southern farmers. Just as bad, however, was the fact that the textbooks themselves seemed to teach exactly those ideological perspectives strongly opposed by the alliance—the virtues both of industrialization and the industrial giants. At the same time, the alliance argued that this publishing "trust" had guaranteed its economic and ideological power "through an intricate and secret system of kickbacks to local and state superintendents."[39]

These arguments about education and about the economic and political situation of small farmers and workers struck a responsive chord throughout the region. The fact that many of the dominant economic, political, and cultural interests originated in the North helped bind the supporters of these arguments together; but it also helped bind together groups opposed to such democratic policies within the South as well.

The strength of sentiment against the North was something that united most white southerners of all stations. The waving of "the bloody shirt"—the traditional symbol of white southern solidarity—wrapped race, party, and region tightly together, as the wounds of the Civil War and the Reconstruction period proved very slow to heal. This left a scar across the southern landscape uniting many southerners in a dislike and distrust of things northern.[40] What happened in school content was not immune from these emotions.

The issue of race also plays an important role here. Racism and racial antagonism helped determine a significant part of the cultural politics of the entire region at the same time as it so effectively shaped the consciousness of southerners,[41] including the small farmers. Racism, and racial politics, helped split the Populist movement and the Farmers' Alliance in the South. It divided people against each other and helped to obscure their common interest against dominant economic groups.[42] The ultimate result, as we shall see, was limited reform and a strong state dominated by conservative and "moderate" interests.

Other factors, too, split the Populist and alliance forces, a split that enabled centralizing reformers to take up some of the educational and social issues they raised and to transform these issues into problems to be solved not by the more radical proposals coming from the alliance but by the methods of "experts."

The defeat of the Populists in 1892 "broke the spirit of the Alliance."[43] As it became more and more difficult to maintain the alliance's status as a mass-based, grass roots organization, in later years many of its members were easily recruited into the educational crusade of the late nineteenth and early twentieth centuries to rebuild southern schools. The movement to bring them under the more centralized governance of a strong network of experts was sponsored by Rockefeller and other northern industrialists and strongly supported by many southern industrialists, a rising new middle class that was also interested in southern economic development, university intellectuals, and others. The alliance's faith in education later led many of its members to support policies that they would have been more than a little skeptical of earlier.[44] In the process, they too became actors in the historic dynamic to centralize and bring education under the control of "experts."

Expert regulation and administration had a number of advantages. They appeared sane and moderate while transferring responsibility out of the hands of the business and political figures who seemed to be at the root of the problems. This gave a (*limited*) voice to varied factions of the public. Even more important perhaps, it focused primarily on the *state* level, thereby effectively removing politically volatile elements from possibly exercising power. Thus by shifting the passion for reform from the local and often more insurgent level, the approach isolated groups that might have called for more radical solutions.[45] As Richard McCormick puts it, "In gaining a statewide hearing for reform, the accusations of politico-business corruption actually increased the likelihood that conservative solutions would be adopted."[46]

How and why did this happen? What were the economic, political, and ideological conditions that led to centralization in the South? This will require that we look again at the more general context in which education and the politics of symbolic control functioned.

THE CLASS AND RACIAL ROOTS OF CONSERVATIVE COMPROMISE

We need to understand that in the late nineteenth century, despite a regional trend toward diversification and industrialization, the South still retained important elements of what can only be called a colonial economy. It was characterized by undeveloped resources and an abundance of unskilled labor, low-wage industries, outside domination by railroads and large timber and mining interests, as well as external control of much of its banking and industrial wealth. Class resentments and racial antagonisms were exceptionally strong.[47] Poverty became increasingly institutionalized on both the farm and in the cities. And the schooling system of many states was more than a little underdeveloped and underfinanced. It was an inherently unstable and tense situation, one that fostered a concern for social order, stability, and efficiency among many groups.[48]

Because of this, across the South during the period, the state was increasingly looked upon as the source of regulatory action and as an important provider of new services.[49] The crusaders to improve schooling were influenced by the belief that it was essential to try to create a situation in which educational leaders were less vulnerable to pressure from an electorate and legislature often less than enthusiastic about spending large sums of money for education[50] or who would interfere in decisions better left to experts.

The reformers were bound together by a set of assumptions that favored increasingly centralized control to "balance" the tradition of local autonomy that was so powerful in the South. First, the educational reformers believed in the very correctness of their vision. Their own success as individuals gave them the right to lead. As Charles Dabney, one of the leaders of the educational crusade put it, "The people need leaders to show them the way."[51] In Theodore Mitchell's compelling words, these reformers "saw public opinion as a mass to be shaped and molded, convinced to accept their notions of education and schooling."[52] Second, their vision combined a progressive commitment to "clean government," one that was unpolluted by the taint of scandal and political interference, with an equally strong commitment to social control. The role of the public school in both its content and pedagogy was to "develop a broad and efficient system of drilling the children . . . to the habits of discipline and the customs of obedience which make for the public order." Sound moral training and obedience were to be combined with the third element—the reformers' belief that the South would only grow economically with the help of an enlarged and efficient school system, but again one that was insulated from political parties and politics in general.[53]

This was to be a society that was "democratic," but for whites only. However, while seeking to preserve white solidarity in the face of tensions and conflicts, not all whites were seen as being equal. All too many well-to-do and middle-class white southerners, including the bulk of the reformers, held a profound mistrust of the masses of people they were seeking to help. Because of this, mechanisms were developed that "cleansed" the governance of education and other services and at the same time limited participation in decision making to include only "those who were prepared for responsible citizenship."[54] State-level experts who could stand above the corrupt or overly political processes of educational governance and text and curriculum selection were clearly more responsible than others.

The evolving class structure of the South—"the presence of a depressed mass of rural and urban working people and an emerging middle class increasingly conscious of the need for social control and restraint"—is not an inconsequential element in this equation.[55] Yet, as I hinted at earlier, educational efficiency experts and reformers did not ignore the black population in their plans for centralization of authority over schools and texts. Their approach to what was called the "race problem" mixed paternalism, social efficiency, guidance, and protection in separate schools in exchange for the values of the new South that were emerging—thrift, industriousness, "self respect for the 'good negro'," and continued subservience.[56]

There were differences between states, of course. Texas, for instance, had a smaller black population and somewhat less of the tradition of corruption common to many southern regimes.[57] Yet, it is quite clear that behind certain of the reforms that the Democratic party enacted in the first decade of this century was a concern with the Hispanic and black citizens of the state.[58] Thus, as with all movements for reform in the South, the racial undercurrent here undoubtedly played no small part in the growth of centralized control over schooling and the text.

Both whites and blacks were focused upon by the reformers. For the more liberal reformers, a more efficient and effective school system —one organized by reformers and experts—was essential not just to "elevate the inferior race," but also to "save whites from the blighting influences of narrow mindedness, intolerance and injustice."[59] Rigid racial separation could be guaranteed by the state and fostered by state regulation and inspection of education and texts. Furthermore, educating the masses of poor whites and instilling in them "appropriate" morality and codes of behavior would make them more tolerant of blacks. Order and tranquillity would reign supreme.[60]

All of this was not only due to the politics of class and race. Gender politics played a role here as well. Thus, interestingly, added impetus for the educational crusade came from the involvement of women. Organized groups of mostly middle-class white women became deeply involved in social reform movements including prohibition, women's suffrage, the regulation of child labor, and the expansion of education.[61] These all required an expansion of the role of the state. And while the women's movements ultimately helped spawn processes that over the next decades solidified state control over education and the text, they also led to major gains in the self-formative power of women.[62]

Given these kinds of contradictory class, race, and gender pressures, in the largely one party politics of the region, southern Democrats in many states themselves increasingly accepted what had originally been an idea generated out of the Populist movement—the concept of the positive state, in which government played a much more active role in promoting growth and stabilizing and protecting the economic, cultural, and moral fiber of society.[63] And these movements dovetailed easily with some of the anticorporate and proregulatory sentiments I mentioned earlier in this essay.

When the anticorporate attack came as expected from farmers and labor, it also included small manufacturers, warehousemen, local merchants, and others who supported public regulation of large business concerns,[64] thereby creating quite complicated alliances among groups. Texas provides a good example of the complicated social alliances and ideologies that stood behind the movement toward more state regulation and control in a number of areas.

In Texas, the major campaign in the early years of the century concerned efforts to deal with corporate wealth and with the fact that the foremost corporations were of "foreign" (i.e., northern) origin. The rapaciousness of capital and the influence of foreign corporations fed into the other concerns. Not only was there foreign control of the economy through northern railroads, banks, and so on, but anger at foreign ideas —an anger that had been simmering since the Civil War—was unleashed again northern publishers as well, not only by the Farmers' Alliance but by many groups. The same regulatory impulse that was now impacting on banking, food, medicine, and so many other areas ultimately worked its way out in the state regulation of textbooks.[65]

In Texas, organized labor and farmers' unions were more influential than elsewhere and for a time at the beginning of the century they were able to work together to try to enlist the state's support for their cause. Support for increased state power again came from professional groups and organized businessmen, whose own influence grew as well.[66] Texas reforms, probably to a greater extent than those in other southern states, represented a response to the state's very diverse economic, physiographic, and cultural interests. This very diversity fostered the formation of groups to pressure the state. The pattern of Texas reforms was highlighted by "well-organized urban middle-class pressure groups loosely coordinated at times with farmer, labor, business, or professional organizations."[67] Thus, this newly emerging middle class played a major part. It was this group from which experts employed within the state would be drawn. Support for increased state intervention in education and elsewhere would guarantee their own mobility and give them a controlling interest in an expanded state. Motivated by a contradictory bundle of factors including altruism, optimism, expanding economic opportunity, social control, and a search for order and efficiency in a time of very real uncertainty, the new pressure groups provided important support for the power of the expert. As members of a reforming coalition, their increasing power within the emerging state bureaucracy helps explain the historic pattern of tight state control of texts in Texas.

Politicians were not blind to these issues. In fact, in many states they were quick to sense the advantages to be gained in supporting (and leading) campaigns against corporations. No matter what their commitments, which may or may not have been quite laudatory, many state politicians were astute enough "to capture the liveliest issues in sight."[68] In the first decade of the century, campaigns to establish regulatory commissions quickly grew. They soon extended beyond transportation and commerce and into other areas such as education. In the context of these concerns, the state assumed more and more of the functions of resolving and regulating conflicts, business practices, and social behavior.[69]

Yet, it is important to realize that many southern conservatives feared that the anticorporate sentiments would discourage northern economic and cultural investment in the region. The answer was not to drive northern corporations out but to regulate them so that they would help economic development in the South.[70] Education was part of this program of economic development, and textbooks — organized around southern but less overtly regional and more *modernizing* themes — were essential to such progress.

Dewey Grantham provides one of the most coherent summaries of the ideological tendencies that lay behind much of the centralizing movement. The southern reformers that ultimately led the movement for state control:

> shared a yearning for a more orderly and cohesive community. Such a community, they believed, was a prerequisite for economic development and material progress. Its realization depended upon the effective regulation of society in the interest of ethical business practices and good government, and in the elimination of political corruption, machine politics, and the insidious power of large corporations and other special interests. This meant that the regulatory power of the state must be expanded. Social controls were also indispensable for the preservation of moral values, for the purification of social institutions, and for the protection of men and women from their own weaknesses. Underlying this coercive reformism was a substantial vein of self-righteousness and moral apprehension. Optimistic about future prospects but alarmed by the tensions and conflicts that pervaded the South in the late nineteenth century, southern [reformers] looked toward the creation of a clearly defined community that would accommodate a society differentiated by race and class, but one that also possessed unity, cohesion, and stability.[71]

The result was what I have elsewhere called an *accord,* a historic compromise in which dominant groups maintain much of their economic, political, and cultural power by incorporating under their own leadership parts of the perspectives of competing or dispossessed groups.[72] Top-down models *would* incorporate greater public control. They would offer new services to the poor, the farmer, and the laborer. They would cleanse the government in general and the control of education and texts from the taint of corruption and would expand schooling extensively. Yet, they would also effectively depower the more democratically inclined movements for public control of economic, political, and educational institutions by keeping them in the hands of experts and elites.

> There was room in this [compromise] for material progress, efficiency, ethical standards, social order, a more vigorous regulatory state, social justice, public services, and especially the vision of a

> revitalized southern community. The [reformers] were able to effect a synthesis of the antithetical approaches of the Bourbons and populists. They attracted support from diverse social elements, including the section's civic-commercial elites and upwardly mobile urban groups. But [they] also drew on the swirling protest of the 1890s, and agrarian radicalism flowed in a somewhat attenuated but distinct current into the politics of the progressive era, helping to account for the anticorporation sentiment, party insurgency, and morality oriented campaigns that followed. In the early twentieth-century setting the [reformers] were able to function both as agents of modernization and as guardians of southern tradition.[73]

There was progress to be sure. But the reforms were still characterized by paternalism and a hierarchical view of society, by a class consciousness that distrusted the masses of people in the South, by basic acceptance of racial stereotypes and a racist social order, and by a search for social consensus and social stability that would be guaranteed by a "disinterested" state.[74] The politics of state regulation, then, is the politics of the South as a whole, in microcosm.

CONCLUSION

In this article, I have explored what is seemingly a simple question—Why the South? What made the South more inclined to accept state-centered solutions to the regulation and control of textbooks in particular and education in general? In answering this question, I have purposely focused our attention on larger social movements and on economic, political, and ideological forces that differentiated the South from other areas, rather than on the internal educational justifications given by educators at the time.[75] Not that I believe that such internal arguments had no weight. Of course they did. However, they would not have been made or accepted if these larger social movements and forces had not been so powerful. The justifications for state educational control did not stand alone, isolated either from the conflicts in the larger society or from attempts to solve these conflicts on terms acceptable to groups with power.

While I have highlighted the complex nexus of historical forces out of which the centralizing tendencies arose in the South, this story should interest us not only because it is a fascinating part of the history of the growth of educational regulation in this country. The story says something of great import to those interested in the politics of educational policy. It was large-scale social movements, organized groups, stimulation from above *and below,* that made a difference. State regulation and control came about because of a complicated politics of social ferment. *Altering what we now have will undoubtedly require the same.*

How something becomes "official knowledge" is always a political process. If we are to understand how the primary carrier of such official knowledge—the textbook—evolved and if we are to understand how to alter it, we cannot afford to ignore the historic politics of social movements. History has a way of not always remaining in the past.

NOTES

1. See Michael W. Apple, *Ideology and Curriculum* (Boston: Routledge and Kegan Paul, 1979); *Education and Power* (Boston: Routledge and Kegan Paul, 1982); and *Teachers and Texts: A Political Economy of Class and Gender Relations in Education* (Boston: Routledge and Kegan Paul, 1986).

2. For representative examples, see Michael W. Apple and Lois Weis, eds., *Ideology and Practice in Schooling* (Philadelphia: Temple University Press, 1983).

3. See John W. Meyer, "Types of Explanation in the Sociology of Education," in *Handbook of Theory and Research for the Sociology of Education,* ed. John G. Richardson (New York: Greenwood Press, 1986), p. 356, for an argument that we actually have few studies that examine how content actually gets to be "legitimate."

4. See Paul Goldstein, *Changing the American Schoolbook* (Lexington, Mass.: Lexington Books, 1978), p. 1.

5. Apple, *Teachers and Texts.*

6. "The Textbook Selection Process," *Interracial Books for Children Bulletin* 14, no. 5 (1983): 17. See also M. David Bieber, "Textbook Adoption Laws, Precensorship, and the First Amendment," *The John Marshall Law Review* 17 (1984): 167–194. For a complete listing of the states and the differences in their specific state level policies, see Michael A. Tulley and Roger Farr, "The Purpose of State Level Textbook Adoption: What Does the Legislation Reveal?," *Journal of Research and Development in Education* 18, no. 2 (1985): 1–6. I shall focus on the South here; the history of states such as California is even more intricate. For further, more detailed discussion of the economics of textbook publishing, see Apple, *Teachers and Texts.*

7. "Texas Battles Over Evolution," *EPIE gram* 12 (May 1984): 6.

8. Guy M. Whipple, "The Selection of Textbooks," *The American School Board Journal* 80 (May 1930): 51.

9. Quoted in Edgar Wallace Knight, *The Influence of Reconstruction on Education in the South* (New York: Teachers College, Columbia University Contributions to Education, no. 60, 1930, Arno Press reprint, 1969), p. 80.

10. Ibid., p. 97.

11. H. L. Donovan, "How to Select Textbooks," *Peabody Journal of Education* 2 (July 1924): 2. It would be important to know whether the teachers being attacked here were women. Often, gender relations underpin the mistrust of teachers. See Apple, *Teachers and Texts*.

12. Charles Judd, "Analyzing Textbooks," *The Elementary School Journal* 19 (October 1918): 145–146.

13. See John Franklin Brown, "Textbooks and Publishers," *The Elementary School Journal* 19 (January 1919): 382–388.

14. Judd, "Analyzing Text Books," p. 143. This theme is echoed in a vast array of literature and in the press and professional publications from the middle of the nineteenth century onwards.

15. Ibid.

16. J. B. Edmonson, "The Ethics of Marketing and Selecting Textbooks," in *The Textbook in American Education,* ed. Guy Montrose Whipple (Bloomington, Ill.: Public School Publishing Co., 1931), pp. 208–215.

17. See Clyde J. Tidwell, *State Control of Textbooks With Special Reference to Florida* (New York: Bureau of Publications, Teachers College, Columbia University, 1928) and Whipple, ed. *The Textbook in American Education*.

18. Robert H. Weibe, *The Search for Order 1877–1920* (Cambridge, Mass.: Hill and Wang, 1967), p. 160.

19. Richard L. McCormick, "The Discovery That Business Corrupts Politics," *American Historical Review* 86 (April 1981): 251.

20. Ibid., p. 255.

21. Ibid., p. 262.

22. Ibid., p. 60.

23. Ibid., p. 257.

24. Ibid., p. 259.

25. Ibid., p. 265.

26. Ibid., p. 267.

27. Ibid., p. 268.

28. Dewey W. Grantham, *Southern Progressivism: The Reconciliation of Progress and Tradition* (Knoxville: The University of Tennessee Press, 1983), p. 416.

29. Ibid., p. 275.

30. Ibid., p. 276.

31. Ibid., pp. 301–302. For further discussion of regional differences, see John G. Richardson, "Historical Sequences and the Origins of Common Schooling in the American States," in *Handbook of Theory and Research.*

32. Richardson, "Historical Sequences," p. 47.

33. Theodore Mitchell, *Political Education in the Southern Farmers' Alliance 1887–1900* (Madison: The University of Wisconsin Press, 1987), p. 25.

34. Ibid., p. 40.

35. Ibid., p. 46. This was not limited to agrarian movements. In California, for instance, the Workingmen's Party—also resentful of the power of the railroads and of corruption—won nearly one-third of the delegates to the second constitutional convention in 1878. Among other things, the delegates proposed state printing of free textbooks and weekly school lectures on the importance of labor. They, too, like the alliance later on, attacked the "textbook ring" and the "unethical practices" of publishers. By 1884, their position had influenced all major parties and an amendment was passed—the Perry Schoolbook Amendment—that established state printing and regulation of textbooks. For further discussion of California, see James A. Lufkin, "A History of the California State Textbook Adoption Program" (unpublished Ph.D. diss., University of California, Berkeley, 1968).

36. Ibid., p. 70.

37. Ibid., p. 71. In the process, the alliance also built its own educational materials, in essence a series of "countertexts," organized around its own sense of class politics. For further examples of such countertexts in, say, the socialist movement, see Kenneth Teitelbaum, "Schooling for Good Rebels" (unpublished Ph.D. diss., University of Wisconsin, Madison, 1985).

38. Mitchell, *Political Education in the Southern Farmers' Alliance*, p. 123.

39. Ibid., pp. 128–129.

40. Ibid., p. 74. Anger over northern textbooks was widespread as well and had a long history. See Marjory R. Kline, "Social Influences in Textbook Publishing," *Educational Forum* 48 (Winter 1984): 224.

41. Mitchell, *Political Education in the Southern Farmers' Alliance*, p. 76.

42. Ibid., p. 77.

43. Ibid., p. 170.

44. Ibid., p. 148.

45. McCormick, "The Discovery That Business Corrupts Politics," pp. 272–273.

46. Ibid., p. 273.

47. Grantham, *Southern Progressivism,* p. 4.

48. Ibid., p. 7.

49. Ibid., p. xxi.

50. Mitchell, *Political Education in the Southern Farmers' Alliance,* p. 186.

51. Quoted in ibid., p. 190.

52. Ibid.

53. Ibid., pp. 190–192.

54. Grantham, *Southern Progressivism,* pp. xvii–xviii.

55. Ibid., p. 176.

56. Ibid., pp. 231–233. The historic struggles by Afro-Americans against these pressures is discussed in Vincent Harding, *There Is a River: The Black Struggle for Freedom in the United States* (New York: Vintage, 1981).

57. Alwyn Barr, *Reconstruction to Reform: Texas Politics, 1876–1906* (Austin: University of Texas Press, 1971), p. 74.

58. Ibid., pp. 241–242.

59. Grantham, *Southern Progressivism,* p. 31.

60. Ibid., pp. 125–126.

61. Ibid., p. xx. See also William Reese, *Power and the Promise of School Reform* (New York: Routledge and Kegan Paul, 1986) for his discussion of women's political activity in educational and social reform movements. See also Barr, *Reconstruction to Reform,* p. 230.

62. This is an important point. There were contradictory results from the movement to centralize authority. What may have often been retrogressive in class and race terms could at one and the same time have been partly progressive in gender terms. See Cameron McCarthy and Michael W. Apple, "Class, Race, and Gender in American Educational Research," in *Class, Race, and Gender in American Education,* ed. Lois Weis (Albany: State University of New York Press, 1988), pp. 9–39.

63. Grantham, *Southern Progressivism,* p. 13.

64. Ibid., p. 145.

65. Ibid., p. 155. There *were* differences among the southern and southwestern states in the political, cultural, and economic dynamics that led to such a regulatory impulse. Yet the overall patterns are similar.

66. Ibid., pp. 99–100.

67. Ibid., p. 103.

68. Ibid., p. 146.

69. Ibid., p. 14.

70. Ibid., p. 157.

71. Ibid., p. xvii.

72. Michael W. Apple, "Social Crisis and Curriculum Accords," *Educational Theory* 38 (Spring 1988): 191–201.

73. Grantham, *Southern Progressivism,* pp. 418–419.

74. Ibid., p. 421.

75. I have not gone into the role played by organized groups of *teachers* here in the debates over state regulation. This would be essential if we were to more completely understand the internal dynamics and the politics of state regulation of education.

KENNETH K. WONG
AND TOM LOVELESS

Chapter Two

The Politics of Textbook Policy: Proposing a Framework

The process by which textbooks move from publishers to students is exceedingly complex. In examining the issues this process spawns, some researchers have focused on the books themselves, analyzing their quality of content,[1] their role in cultural and social reproduction,[2] their race and sex bias in presentation,[3] and the effects of censorship. Other analysts have focused attention on the procedures of textbook adoption, including differences between adoption procedures at the state and local level,[5] the criteria employed in review and selection,[6] and the influence of pressure groups in textbook adoptions.[7]

Using this rich and diverse literature that has come out of this research, we shall focus on the politics of textbook policy in the United States. Indeed, from publisher to student, textbooks move through a political world. Unlike the market forces defining the producer-consumer relationship in general publishing, the publisher–classroom-user relationship in textbooks is mediated by the decisions made by actors whose function is to intervene in the transaction. This essay shall provide a framework for analyzing the path from publisher to student in an effort to better understand the political context of the textbook policy decisions made by key actors in the process. Though we recognize that the political landscape of textbooks is rife with variation (the particular book a student opens on a given day depends upon the classroom, school, district, and state in which the student is located), we seek to distill commonalities from the variations without sacrificing the unique blend of circumstances found in individual cases, commonalities that will serve to bring form to an otherwise amorphous set of phenomena.

Two kinds of politics govern textbook policy. We shall call the first and the more pervasive pattern the "institutionalized politics." The second pattern type, the "de-institutionalized politics," occurs less frequently. Both political patterns involve three key entities or sites of textbook policy, namely, publishers as suppliers of books, governmental agencies of selection that regulate text content, and classroom teachers and students as users. In both kinds of textbook politics, disagreements on the content may exist among key actors, and ways are found to resolve these conflicts. Yet, the two patterns differ significantly in terms of the relative importance of the key actors and their political environment in shaping adoption decisions, the visibility and intensity of disagreement, and the ways in which conflicts are addressed.[8]

In institutionalized politics, a stable network of key actors, consisting primarily of publishers, subject matter experts, and educational administrators, operates under a routinized set of procedures in designing, writing, revising, and adopting textbooks. Disagreements over content do occur, but they are not publicized and are readily resolved through compromise. In contrast, de-institutionalized politics are characterized by publicized challenges on textbook decisions from sources outside of the regular decision-making network. Outsiders' intrusion is facilitated by broad social and ideological movements, political leadership, changing socioeconomic context, organized interest groups with specific demands, and individual defiance on the part of teachers and parents. Disputes are highly visible and, in most cases, can only be reconciled through protracted litigation and legislative process. Nevertheless, in spite of overt disputes that occasionally disrupt the more routinized decision-making process, textbook policy is predominantly marked by institutionalized politics. Through a synthesis of the literature, we shall use our political typologies to categorize and illuminate textbook policymaking in this essay.

THE PERVASIVENESS OF INSTITUTIONALIZED POLITICS

Dominance of Expert Network and the Publishers

The textbook adoption process occupies a central role in institutionalized politics. The governmental role legitimizes decisions on book selection.

It imposes regulatory guidance on what the publishers should print for public school pupils. The North Carolina Board of Education, for example, recently announced that publishers must fully comply with the new curricular standards. In virtually all states, expectations of what is required in a book are typically communicated to publishers prior to adoption, often in the form of a subject matter scope and sequence or a curricular framework. At the state and district levels, book selection is made by the textbook selection commission, which, in effect, is made up of layers of committees of administrators, experts, educators, and public representatives.

The expert network dominates the entire selection process. Subject area experts and educational administrators write the curricular framework that governs the scope and content of the text. Curricular guidelines usually follow complex administrative rules and legislative provisions. Even when given the opportunity to offer comments on the framework, parents and lay organizations seldom have the specialized knowledge or the organizational resources to effect major regulatory changes. Although teachers who are not in the selection committees are sometimes polled as to their choice for adopted text,[9] the expert network decides on its own terms. For example, in his study of California textbook adoption policy, Kirst found that the state's textbook commission relied heavily on a small group of subject matter specialists for recommendations.[10] At the national level, the physical qualities of the text are determined by decisions made jointly by powerful interest groups that represent publishers (the Association of American Publishers), state administrators (the National Association of State Textbook Administrators), and the production companies (Book Manufacturing Institute).

The extent to which the power of selecting books is concentrated in the expert-publisher network has raised a great deal of concern. To be sure, there are selection agencies that operate effectively — current research is read and discussed, the reactions of teachers who have piloted the materials are considered, and curricular specialists and administrators express their views. Yet, more often than not, the review process becomes a formal exercise and fails to contribute much to improve the quality of textbooks. In Indiana, a state that has statewide adoption procedures, reviewers were said to have paid more attention to appearances than to quality of the materials covered.[11] Subject to local community influences, members of the selection committees lacked sufficient time to perform a more thorough examination. Consequently, the institutionalized selection process often leads to decisions that are simultaneously exclusive and inclusive in regards to content — selecting books that contain no materials that may offend users but include topics fulfilling curricular requirements. Selected books are also likely to be inclusive in matters of pedagogy, with each of the educational philosophies represented on review committees finding something to support in the adopted text.

Varieties in Adoption Practices

The agency of selection may be at the state or district level or a system with shared powers at both levels. The degree to which policy is formulated at the state level distinguishes the twenty-two adoption states from the twenty-eight nonadoption states. The former group of states, which encompasses half of the nation's market, exhibits considerable differences in centralization. Texas, the most centralized of the adoption states, approves a list of no less than two and no more than five textbooks from which local districts may make their K–12 selections. California approves a broader list of texts for K–8 adoption, and high school texts are adopted at the district level.[12]

Consistent with institutionalized politics, the history of centralized state textbook adoption has remained remarkably stable for the last hundred years. As Farr and Tulley observed, "Legislation creating these state-level practices was developed during a relatively short period of time—from the last few years of the nineteenth century through the early years of the twentieth century."[13]

Geography and political culture are salient to the adoption choices made by states, with nearly all twenty-two adoption states located in the South and West. Far from the eastern publishing houses, these states' centralized systems appear to have evolved from a mixture of regional distrust, a desire to ensure adequate supplies of books, and a political environment supporting the tradition of strong state governance of a uniform educational system.[14] For example, Tidwell reports that the 1917 law strengthening state control over textbook adoptions in Florida was in response to county superintendents' complaints that many children were going without books.[15] Cubberly attributes the victory of the 1884 constitutional referendum in California that established state publication and control of textbooks to "an anti-book-trust movement that swept the state, and for which the practices of certain publishers' agents of that period were probably responsible."[16] On the contrary, Colorado, a nonadoption state, enjoys a strong tradition of local autonomy. The Colorado Association of School Executives has often succeeded in circumscribing legislative actions on curricular matters.[17] Indeed, the proposition that a state's control of textbook adoptions may be embedded within a broader predilection for centralized governance of schools finds contemporary support in Wong's analysis of school finance. Of the twenty-five states with state dominance of school funding, seventeen are adoption states; of the twenty-five states with fiscal patterns of state-local parity, only five are adoption states.[18]

More important, the site of selection agency (i.e., state or district) seems not as critical in understanding the institutionalized politics of textbook policy.[19] As Goldstein points out, "It is easy to attach too much weight to the adoption and non-adoption categories."[20] The two levels create textbook selection systems that operate in a similar manner and include a similar set of actors working within the institutionalized politics of the two systems.[21] Similar adoption practices are found in big-city districts in both "open territories" and adoption states.[22] Moreover, even among the adoption states, no state selects only one textbook. Thus a final selection process is required at the local level—albeit one that adopts a textbook from a subset of the books considered by the state, but a selection process nevertheless. Indeed, this structural redundancy inherent within state adoption systems has been questioned by critics of state adoption.[23]

Publishers' Role in Pre-empting Controversy

To be sure, publishers exercise a great deal of influence through both formal and informal channels during the selection process. While 80 percent of the nation's textbook market is controlled by only seven major publishing firms, competition for a greater market share remains very intense. Lobbying directed at governmental bodies is well organized. In Texas, the Merrill Publishing Company spent $300,000 to lobby state legislators for a change of schedule in the adoption of math textbooks. Other competing firms, as soon as they learned of Merrill's activities, spent at least as much to counter the company's influence.[24] At times, the methods used by publishers to consolidate their influence in the selection process raise serious ethical questions. In California, publishers entertained scores of teachers and administrators who served on the district selection committees.[25] In Texas, contacts between publishers and members of the adoption commissions are prohibited only two weeks prior to making the selection. Members of review committees often receive free equipment, supplies, and discounts on publications.

At a more formal level, publishers make presentations to and work closely with the selection committees. The selection agency typically selects books by subject on an adoption cycle (usually five or six years) and is thus constrained by the textbooks available at the time of selection. This time constraint makes it more optimal for selection commissions to communicate curricular goals to publishers long before a textbook is adopted. Indeed, publishers have recently asked states to specify curricular guidelines at least a year and a half in advance, and the rigidity of adoption cycles has been reformed in some states, including California.[26]

The relatively low level of overt controversies in institutionalized politics is sustained in large part by pre-emptive strategies on the part of the publishers. In anticipation of potential criticism and possible rejection of the text, publishers have in effect employed a variety of mechanisms to enhance adoption by the selection committees. As Chall explains, publishers "exist in a symbiotic relationship with teachers and schools, with textbook selection committees, with educational researchers and curriculum specialists, and with each other."[27] These forces combine to provide powerful constraints on the process of creating a text. Goldstein has commented on the inherent conservative bias of this influence: "Orthodoxy in outlook and preference sets the tone for the instructional materials marketplace. . . . In competing for school sales, publishers cannot be expected to introduce products that take off in new directions of instructional efficiency."[28] Consequently, publishers have to make judgments on the content of future texts on the basis of anticipated reactions from selectors and users. This anticipation compels a concern with the past history of other actors' reactions to similar content in past adoptions, leading to pre-emptive strategies during the creation of texts. An example is the readability formula. One publisher attributes the domination of readability formulae in textbook preparation to this concern: "If only one set of materials is used for all children, regardless of reading ability, the choice is likely to be a textbook comprehensible to the poorest reader in the class . . . successful textbooks feature reading levels below the grade for which they are intended."[29]

The omnipresence of readability formulae is not the only issue on which publisher sensitivity to narrow demands of the marketplace has been criticized. The publishers' self-censorship of potentially controversial content has been exposed and condemned by several researchers.[30] However, as Woodward and Elliot have pointed out in their analysis of variation in the treatment of evolution and creationism in biology texts, this anticipation of controversy does not necessarily result in a uniform outcome.[31]

Book selectors and user groups are not the only forces anticipated and accommodated by publishers in the institutionalized politics. The well-known California Effect and Texas Effect, for instance, describe the shaping of textbook content at the publishing house to maximize adoption chances in these two large markets.[32] A comparison of readers in 1975 and 1986 in Texas found that 25 percent of the textual changes were attributed to mandates passed in Texas and California.[33] More importantly, in anticipating the reactions of educators and users, the texts are constructed with pedagogical elasticity. By creating materials that can be used by teachers of varying instructional philosophies, styles, and strategies, instructional manuals for teachers provide "the kitchen sink" in teacher-centered, child-centered, cooperative-learning, ability-grouped, open-classroom, traditional-classroom, mastery-learning, individualized, and whole-class lessons.[34] Indeed, Durkin has provided a trenchant description of how one elementary basal reading series accommodated the conflicting instructional recommendations of Chall and Fries by incorporating both experts' methods within its teachers' edition.[35] Moreover, recognizing the onus of instructing classes with vast diversity in ability, publishers provide textbooks that come complete with suggestions for providing for gifted and remedial students, resulting in teacher's manuals that are overwhelming compendiums of fragmented activities, instructional tools characterized by Durkin as "heavy in weight but light in substance."[36]

Thus, we see that textbooks are shaped at the publisher level by two forms of institutionalized input—the direct input of members of the textbook-expert network and the indirect input of anticipated reactions from users, adoption agencies, and educators. In matters of content, these influences tend to be simultaneously exclusive and inclusive, leading the publishers to omit anything that might offend, and to include, often without depth in coverage, any topic demanded.[37] In matters of pedagogy, these influences tend to be inclusive, leading the publishers to include a wide variety of teaching strategies for a wide variety of students. By offending no one politically and pleasing everyone educationally, textbook publishers attempt to produce books that will make everyone happy, and thus ensure a market for their products.

Coping Strategies of Classroom Teachers

The textbook represents a critical element in the connection between pupils and the school system. The teacher's instructional role becomes critical. As argued by Dreeben and Barr, teachers organize "their instruction around the content presented in the adopted textbooks and design their instruction so that some amount of the material becomes the agenda for the school year."[38]

In this classroom context, teachers seldom openly challenge and reject the adopted textbooks. The sheer complexity of the review-adoption process, the administrative bent toward standardization of curriculum, and the linkages made between textbooks and standardized tests all undergird the likelihood of teacher acceptance of the selected textbook. Indeed, Rogers found in a sample of Connecticut teachers that 88 percent of the teachers disagreed with the belief that textbook quality was declining, and 80 percent disagreed or strongly disagreed with the assertion that textbook writing is choppy and stilted.[39]

An absence of overt defiance does not mean that teachers are passive actors in textbook usage. In the classroom setting, teachers enjoy a great deal of discretion—to the extent that they can dissipate any discontent with particular texts. Teachers can employ particular instructional strategies in teaching the text, emphasizing or undermining certain topics or sections within the text, skipping parts, diminishing the text's dominance by introducing supplementary materials, or reordering topics so as to present them in a sequence different from that in the book. These instructional strategies vary across individual schools and classrooms, as contexts vary regarding several constraints: (1) time allowed for a subject, (2) student abilities and interests, (3) parental and community input, (4) teacher competence and values, and (5) visibility of standardized test results and the value placed on them by the community.[40] Thus, the teacher emerges not only as one who acts upon textbook policy, but also as one acted upon by the policies of others within the dynamics of institutionalized textbook politics.

DE-INSTITUTIONALIZED POLITICS

Institutional stability in textbook policy can be transformed into de-institutionalized politics, which are characterized by an intrusion of outside influences, highly visible disputes over adoption rules and book content, and the engagement of higher authorities in conflict resolution. In this section, we shall discuss three important sets of circumstances that have contributed to de-institutionalized politics.

Challenge from Organized Interest Groups

Organized interest groups are the most visible actors shaping the textbook policy of the agency of adoption and represent a prominent "outside" source of influence that may upset the mutual agreement otherwise present in the institutionalized adoption process. Groups often rally around issues addressing ideology, beliefs, or values, issues sure to gain public reaction and media coverage.[41]

Complaints from organized interest groups focus on omissions or commissions within the textbook coverage. These protests are often embedded in broader social and ideological movements. The civil rights and equal rights movements of the sixties and seventies generated many criticisms on the treatment of race and gender. History, social studies, and literature textbooks have been criticized for the inadequate coverage of women in history, an insensitivity to the victims of racism in the United States, and the underrepresentation of the literary accomplishments of women and minority authors. At the same time, religious rights groups have criticized textbooks for expurgating religious teachings or traditional values in their presentation.[42] These critiques of omission are directed at what textbooks do not include in their content, and agencies of selection are urged to reject potential textbooks that do not include the desired materials.[43]

Interest groups also complain about the inclusion of certain issues in a textbook's coverage. Evolution, human secularism and bias that is detected to be probusiness or antibusiness, or gender, race, or ethnic bias have all been targets of textbook watchdog groups' scrutiny and complaint. These critiques are directed at what textbooks include in their content, and agencies are urged to reject the textbooks that contain the offensive materials.

Whereas the attacks on textbooks due to omission require persuading the agency of selection that the omitted material is of such importance that to leave it out renders a textbook inadequate, the challenge of a textbook due to inclusion is far more potent. Quotations from the textbooks can be used as documentation of indictment and as a means of whipping up a maelstrom of public outrage, as most dramatically evidenced in the 1974 Kanawha County, West Virginia, textbook protest that led to school boycotts, miners' strikes, school bombings, and police-escorted school buses fired upon with shotguns.[44] At the heart of the prolonged confrontation, as Hillocks's analysis of the books' content suggested, was "a conflict between diametrically opposed beliefs about the nature of truth and human behavior." While the protestors shared an "unquestioning faith in revelation," the published texts were guided by the "Western traditions of reason and empiricism."[45]

Organized protests can be triggered by individual parents who express public dissatisfaction with a particular text. Often the battles we read about in the national news media begin when a particular textbook used by a particular teacher arouses complaints. Beall describes examples of teachers in Florida and Michigan being attacked for using books accused of being offensive, and Fleming explains the existence of taboo topics in the classroom as "generally because of the fear of drawing the wrath of a special interest group down upon the head of the teacher or school system."[46] Subsequently, to deal with sources of discontent within the school system, Weil has reported the establishment of procedures in many schools to handle challenges to textbook decisions, an institutional response to the potential for de-institutionalized conditions.[47]

Conflict Emerges from Changing Economic and Social Context

Competition among advocacy groups on textbook issues can be intensified in a changing economy. In these circumstances, the routinized, expert-dominated selection process no longer performs its policymaking function. This is illustrated by the prolonged dispute over the adoption of a fourth grade social studies text, *Get Oregonized,* in the adoption state of Oregon during 1985 and 1987.[48] The text was written by teachers from around the state, but funding was provided by timber and agricultural industries. The environmentalist groups charged that the book exhibited a pro-industry bias. The confrontation finally reached the Oregon Court of Appeals, which rejected the suit filed by the environmentalists. The dismissal was a victory for Oregon industries.

The Oregon case can be understood in terms of the broader economic and political context in the state. The confrontation between environmentalists and progrowth interests came at a time when the state economy stood at a crossroads. The long and deep recession in the state during the early 1980s has posed a serious challenge to its traditionally strong preservation policy. Consequently, the textbook dispute was rooted in the conflict between two competing visions, namely progrowth versus preservation, that would shape the future direction of the state economy. Politics becomes even more polarized when these policy differences are split along partisan lines and regional cleavages, i.e., the more urbanized Willamette Valley versus rural Eastern Oregon.

Visibility Due to Political Leadership

The state legislature, the state school board, and state school superintendents have become more actively involved in curricular reform because of heightened public concerns for educational performance. In this regard, the political salience of textbook policy can be understood in the context of recent legislative efforts to restructure schools. To be sure, the current back-to-basics movement has been going on for more than a decade. During the 1970s, citizen concerns for minimal competency in students' reading, writing, and calculating skills prompted dozens of state legislatures to adopt new school requirements. With the publicity of the 1983 federal report, *A Nation At Risk,* the reform movement has gathered new momentum and taken on a broader agenda. The policy debate of the mid-1980s has gone beyond the basic skills of graduating seniors, and has quickly moved into areas of teaching competency and training as well as comprehensive curricular reform.[49]

This reform-accountability climate has enabled the political leadership to assume a more visible role in textbook and curricular matters. California Senator Gary Hart and the state school superintendent, Bill

Honig, for example, are strong reform advocates. As the chief executive of the nation's fourth largest state, Governor Bob Martinez of Florida wants textbooks to include more information about his own state than "the armadillos of Texas or California condors."[50] While enhancing their electoral profile, political leaders' involvement is likely to contribute to de-institutionalized politics.

Conflict Resolution by Higher Authorities

Because de-institutionalized politics involve more fundamental disagreements among actors, the resolution of conflicts often requires the active participation of higher authorities. Judicial rulings on constitutional disputes over textbooks are well documented.[51] The state board of education and the state legislature are also important arbitrators. In California, for instance, evolution emerged as a highly controversial topic in the adoption of the 1990 state science framework, with the state board finally striking language describing evolution as "a scientific fact" in favor of the more muted statement—"the theory of evolution is the accepted scientific explanation." State Superintendent of Public Instruction Bill Honig was reported to have argued that the change made the document "less argumentative."[52] Finally, other authorities occasionally serve as arbitrators. For example, the Texas state attorney general helped resolve a decade-old conflict over a controversial state board of education requirement—textbooks should mention evolution as "only one of several explanations" of human origin.[53] In response to the attorney general's opinion that the board's rule had allowed for religious influence in state affairs, the board reluctantly eliminated the requirement.

CONCLUSION

A review of the literature on textbook policy may lead one to conclude that textbook issues are idiosyncratic and seamless, with unique sets of processes, actors, and textbooks dictating chance, and often deplorable, outcomes. In this essay we propose a framework in understanding the politics of textbook policy. In reviewing and synthesizing the literature, we find textbook decisions largely operate under institutionalized politics, where the expert-publisher network functions as an autonomous decision-making entity and where disagreements are less publicized and can be resolved through compromise. We also find that de-institutionalized politics occur. Under these circumstances, text decisions become politically salient, and controversies are prolonged and require arbitration from higher authorities.

NOTES

1. F. FitzGerald, *America Revised: History Schoolbooks in the Twentieth Century* (Boston: Little, Brown and Company, 1979); G. T. Sewall, "American History Textbooks: Where Do We Go from Here?" *Phi Delta Kappan* 69, no. 8 (1988): 553–558; A. Woodward and D. L. Elliott, "Evolution, Creationism, and Textbooks: A Study of Publishers' Perceptions of Their Markets" (Paper presented at the Annual Meeting of the American Educational Research Association, New Orleans, April 23–27, 1984).

2. A. Luke, "Making Dick and Jane: Historical Genesis of the Modern Basal Reader," *Teachers College Record* 89, no. 1 (1987): 91–116; M. W. Apple, "The Culture and Commerce of Textbooks," *Journal of Curriculum Studies* 17, no. 2 (1985): 147–162; S. B. Palonsky, "Political Socialization in the Schools," *Elementary School Journal* 87, no. 5 (1987): 493–505.

3. M. B. Kane, *Minorities in Textbooks: A Study of Their Treatment in Social Studies Texts* (Chicago: Quadrangle Books, 1970).

4. M. L. Beall, "Censorship and Self-censorship: A Problem in the Schools," *Communication Education* 36 (1987): 313–316; F. Parker, "Textbook Censorship and the Religious Right: Rise or Decline?" ERIC Document ED 292 715, 1987; M. H. Kamhi, "Limiting What Students Shall Read. Books and Other Learning Materials in Our Public Schools: How They Are Selected and How They Are Removed" (Chicago: American Library Assocation, 1981).

5. R. Farr and M. A. Tulley, "Do Adoption Committees Perpetuate Mediocre Textbooks?" *Phi Delta Kappan* (March 1985): 467–471; C. R. Duke, "A Look at Current State-wide Text Adoption Procedures" (Paper presented at the Annual Meeting of the National Council of Teachers of English Spring Conference, Houston, March 28–30, 1985); D. A. Powell, "Selection of Reading Textbooks at the District Level: Is This a Rational Process?" *Book Research Quarterly* 1 (1985): 23–35.

6. S. Keith, "Choosing Textbooks: A Study of Instructional Materials Selection Processes for Public Education," *Book Research Quarterly* 1 (1985): 24–37; J. A. Dole, T. Rogers, and J. Osborn, "Improving the Selection of Basal Reading Programs: A Report of the Textbook Adoption Guidelines Project," *The Elementary School Journal* 87, no. 3 (1987): 283–298.

7. D. Tanner, "The Textbook Controversies," pp. 122–147 in *Critical Issues in the Curriculum,* Eighty-seventh Yearbook of the National Society for the Study of Education, pt. 1 (Chicago: University of Chicago Press, 1988); J. R. Squire and R. T. Morgan, "The Elementary and High School Textbook Market Today," in *Textbooks and Schooling in the United States,* Eighty-ninth Yearbook of the National Society for the Study of Education, ed. D. L. Elliott and A. Woodward, pt. 1 (Chicago: University of Chicago Press, 1990).

8. Other typologies have been used by political analysts. Among these are T. Lowi, "American Business and Public Policy, Case Studies, and Political Theory," *World Politics* (July 1964): 677–715; P. E. Peterson, B. Rabe, and K. Wong, *When Federalism Works* (Washington, D.C.: Brookings Institution, 1986); M. Derthick, *Policymaking for Social Security* (Washington, D.C.: Brookings Institution, 1979). Also see K. Wong, "Policy-making in the American States: Typology, Process, and Institutions," *Policy Studies Review* 8, no. 3 (1989): 527–548.

9. P. Goldstein, *Changing the American Schoolbook* (Lexington, Mass.: Lexington Books, 1978).

10. M. Kirst, *Who Controls Our Schools?—American Values in Conflict* (New York: W. H. Freeman, 1984).

11. R. Farr, M. A. Tulley, and L. Rayford, "Selecting Basal Readers: A Comparison of School Districts in Adoption and Nonadoption States," *Journal of Research and Development in Education* 20, no. 4 (Summer 1987): 59–72.

12. R. English, "The Politics of Textbook Adoption," *Phi Delta Kappan* (December 1980): 275–278.

13. Farr and Tulley, "Do Adoption Committees Perpetuate Mediocre Textbooks?" p. 468.

14. J. Barna, "The Texas Textbook Controversy," Special Legislative Report to the House Study Group, Texas House of Representatives, Austin, Texas, 1984.

15. C. J. Tidwell, *State Control of Textbooks* (New York: Teachers College, 1928).

16. E. P. Cubberly, "The State Publication of Textbooks," pp. 235–248 in *The Textbook in American Education,* Thirtieth Yearbook of the National Society for the Study of Education (Bloomington, Ill.: Public School Publishing Company, 1931).

17. K. Hamm, "The Role of 'Subgovernments' in U.S. State Policy-making: An Exploratory Analysis," *Legislative Studies Quarterly* XI, no. 3 (1986): 321–351.

18. K. Wong, "Fiscal Support for Education in the American States: The 'Parity-to-Dominance' View Examined," *American Journal of Education* 97, no. 1 (1989): 329–357.

19. For comparison of influences as perceived by members of the book selection committees at the district and state levels respectively, see Powell, "Selection of Reading Textbooks at the District Level"; and J. D. Marshall, "The Politics of Curriculum Decisions as Manifested Through the Selection and Adoption of Textbooks for Texas" (unpublished Ed.D. diss., University of Texas, 1986).

20. Goldstein, *Changing the American Schoolbook,* p. 39.

21. J. Armstrong and J. Bray, *How Can We Improve Textbooks?* (Denver: Education Commission of the States, 1986).

22. Squire and Morgan, ''The Elementary and High School Textbook Market Today.''

23. Farr and Tulley, ''Do Adoption Committees Perpetuate Mediocre Textbooks?''

24. *Education Week* May 31, 1989.

25. *Education Week* May 24, 1989.

26. *Education Week* May 17, 1989.

27. J. S. Chall, ''Middle and Secondary School Textbooks,'' pp. 24–26 in *The Textbook in American Society,* ed. J. Y. Coyle (Washington, D.C.: Library of Congress, 1981).

28. Goldstein, *Changing the American Schoolbook,* p. 55.

29. R. Follett, ''The School Textbook Adoption Process,'' *Book Research Quarterly* 1 (Summer 1985): 19–23.

30. Parker, ''Textbook Censorship and the Religious Right''; Beall, ''Censorship and Self-censorship''; J. K. Bradford, ''To Be or Not to Be: Issues on Changes in Literature Anthologies,'' *English Journal* 75, no. 6 (1986): 52–56.

31. Woodward and Elliott, ''Evolution, Creationism, and Textbooks.''

32. B. Crane, ''The 'California Effect' on Textbook Adoptions,'' *Educational Leadership* (January 1975): 283–285; M. Bowler, ''Textbook Publishers Try to Please All, but First They Woo the Heart of Texas,'' *The Reading Teacher* (February 1978): 514–518.

33. J. C. Comas, ''Adaptations: Award-winning Children's Literature Found in Basal Textbook Readers'' (unpublished Ph.D. diss., Indiana University, 1987).

34. Goldstein, *Changing the American Schoolbook.*

35. D. Durkin, ''Influences on Basal Reader Programs,'' *The Elementary School Journal* 87, no. 3 (1987): 331–341.

36. Follett, ''The School Textbook Adoption Process''; Durkin, ''Influences on Basal Reader Programs.''

37. P. A. Gagnon, *Democracy's Untold Story* (Washington, D.C.: American Federation of Teachers, 1987).

38. R. Dreeben and R. Barr, ''An Organizational Analysis of Curriculum and Instruction,'' pp. 13–39 in *The Social Organization of Schools,* ed. M. T. Hallinan (New York: Plenum Press, 1987).

39. V. Rogers, ''School Texts: The Outlook of Teachers,'' *Education Week,* August 3, 1988.

40. For a discussion of classroom constraints on teachers, see D. Lortie, *Schoolteacher* (Chicago: University of Chicago Press, 1975).

41. Keith, ''Choosing Textbooks''; C. Cody, ''The Politics of Textbook Publishing, Adoption, and Use,'' in *Textbooks and Schooling in the United States;* Kamhi, ''Limiting What Students Shall Read.''

42. M. and N. Gabler, ''Moral Relativism on the Ropes,'' *Communication Education* 36 (October 1987): 356–366.

43. P. C. Vitz, *Censorship: Evidence of Bias in Our Children's Books* (Ann Arbor: Servant Books, 1986).

44. J. Moffett, *Storm in the Mountains: A Case Study of Censorship, Conflict, and Consciousness* (Carbondale: Southern Illinois University Press, 1988).

45. G. Hillocks, ''Books and Bombs: Ideological Conflict and the Schools—a Case Study of the Kanawha County Book Protest,'' *School Review* 86, no. 8 (1978): 632–654.

46. Beall, ''Censorship and Self-censorship''; D. Fleming, ''Ethical Issues in the Classroom,'' *The Clearing House* 61, no. 2 (1986): 85–87.

47. J. S. Weil, ''Policy and Procedures: Dealing with Censorship,'' *Social Education* 51, no. 6 (1987): 448–449.

48. *Oregonian,* January 30, 1986 and February 14, 1986.

49. See K. Wong, ''State and Local Government Institutions and Educational Policy in the Western States,'' in *Politics in the American West,* ed. C. Thomas (University of New Mexico Press, Forthcoming).

50. *Education Week,* May 18, 1988, p. 3.

51. See Edward J. Larson's essay in this volume. Also see Cody, ''The Politics of Textbook Publishing.''

52. As quoted in *Chicago Tribune,* November 10, 1989, p. 4.

53. *New York Times,* April 15, 1984.

SHERRY KEITH

Chapter Three

The Determinants of Textbook Content

INTRODUCTION

School children in the United States are one of the largest captive reading audiences in the world today and textbooks account for at least three-quarters of their in-school exposure to the written word. Textbooks are frequently the student's major source of information on a particular subject taught in school, and may even constitute the only exposure the student receives on a given topic within a subject area. Playing such a central role in the dispensation of knowledge, the content of textbooks becomes a critical issue. The exclusion and inclusion of specific content, such as evolutionary theory or human sexuality, the portrayal of historic events such as the Vietnam War and the civil rights movement, or the discussion of contemporary issues such as East-West relations or the changing role of women in American society, spark intense battles among civic groups (as well as among educators, themselves) aligned with opposing viewpoints.

Likewise, the process of determining which books are used in public school classrooms across the United States is, and has historically been, controversial. Textbooks are significant economically, as well as ideologically and pedagogically. They represent a substantial market to the publishing industry, and a significant budgetary expense when new books are purchased by a state or school district.

What are the factors that influence the content of textbooks? Is content determined by authorship? Are textbooks influenced by the concerns of teachers who instruct from them? Are they responsive to the characteristics and interests of students who read them? Research suggests that none of these are indeed primary factors. This essay explores several alternative factors that have a major influence on the content of elementary and high school textbooks sold by the millions across the United States: the organizational and operational practices of the textbook publishing industry; the structure, process, and criteria used by state and local authorities to select specific books from the array offered in the marketplace; and the influence of special interests of citizens' groups which monitor and dispute the content of books. Together these constitute the prime forces pressing to include or remove ideas, facts, and theories from the nation's schools.

THE TEXTBOOK PUBLISHING INDUSTRY

Although a debate over the content and selection of appropriate textbooks can be traced to the last century, a flutter of public and scholarly concern with the selection and content of school textbooks surged in the early 1970s.[1] A parallel concern with the book publishing industry did not appear until nearly five years later. The importance of understanding the organization and functioning of book publishing or the process of determining textbook content cannot be underestimated. As Lewis Coser indicated, book publishers are the gatekeepers of ideas and knowledge.[2] The publishing industry as a cultural as well as economic enterprise plays a critical role in the shaping, production, and dissemination of ideas.

Elementary and high school textbook publishing has a special significance within the book publishing industry. Until the 1960s elementary and high school book publishers were largely independent publishing houses—Ginn & Company; Addison-Wesley; Holt, Rinehart and Winston—each with its own orientation and attention to a particular segment of the elementary and/or high school and instructional materials market. Since the late 1960s, a new trend within the publishing industry as a whole accelerated, and textbook publishing was carried along in its wake. This was the trend toward mergers and the absorption of traditionally independent publishing houses by larger publishing firms and by large conglomerate firms—particularly media and data processing conglomerates like IBM, Xerox, RCA, and others.

Why were these conglomerates attracted to independent publishing houses and textbook publishers in particular? The main reason is that textbooks offer a mass market, steady turnover, and relatively stable profits to present to the stockholders. Within the publishing field, textbooks had become the bread and butter of the industry.

The educational system as a unit is the key consumer of printed materials in the United States. Thirty percent of all books sold are purchased by the education system and the elementary school/high school market accounts for approximately 16 percent of total annual sales. While textbooks are not a particularly high profit item (averaging approximately 12 percent net income), they offer a large pressrun. Typically an elementary textbook run may be one million copies or more, with a secondary textbook, depending on subject matter, rising to several million copies. Publishers can also depend upon a fairly stable sales rate for textbooks over a five to seven-year cycle—sometimes longer. Distribution of textbooks is relatively simple because the education system acts as the intermediary between the publishers and the consumer—in this case, the classroom student.

Government-Financed Instructional Materials

During the 1960s there was a tremendous expansion of public and private funding for education as a social enterprise. The cold war in schooling originally spurred by Sputnik in 1957 was felt in all corners of the educational establishment and certainly no less in the areas of instructional materials and curriculum development than in other facets of the schooling process. The federal government through the Office of Education, National Science Foundation, and the National Institute of Education all offered sizeable grant and contract funds for the planning and development of instructional materials — curriculum packages which frequently attempted innovative approaches to learning by extending their efforts far beyond the scope of the textbook approach. Private foundations, such as Ford, Rockefeller, and Carnegie, were also generous in encouraging the experimentation with new instructional technology "media," as the innovations came to be called.

Instructional technologies range from computer-programmed learning to a wide range of audio-visual materials, accompanied by textbooks and individualized programmed instruction workbooks.[3] The race to develop new instructional materials, including the textbook but ranging beyond the printed word, attracted interest beyond the scope of traditional textbook publishing houses. In fact, the structuring of grant monies generally prohibited publishers and other commercial agents from participating in the development of new learning programs. However, they were allowed to participate as the publishers of instructional materials packages—including textbooks—once these materials had been developed and tested. An example was the S-APA (Science — A Process Approach), receiving approximately $2,250,000 from the National Science Foundation between 1962 and 1969 Once developed, S-APA was transferred to the Xerox Corporation for publication. According to Paul

Goldstein, "the role of Xerox in the development of S-APA consisted of refining the materials produced by AAAS's (American Association for the Advancement of Science) summer workshops as well as promoting and distributing the finished product."[4] Even though Xerox was allowed only five-year copyright control, Goldstein comments that S-APA worked. It achieved widespread acceptance in the nation's schools, satisfied its sponsors, and probably earned a profit for its publishers."[5]

The availability of funds for the development and purchase of new instructional materials stimulated new economic interest in textbook publishing activities. It was probably one of the most important factors attracting large, high-technology conglomerates like Xerox to buy up the small, traditionally independent school book publishers. What are the implications, however, of this trend for the production of school books? This issue can be examined in both quantitative and qualitative terms.

A Growing Market, A Growing Business

In quantitative terms, the push was for larger markets and larger press-runs which could yield more profits. Thus the scale of educational publishing became increasingly attractive to larger corporations. As Theodore Sizer, former dean of Harvard Graduate School of Education stated, "companies like IBM, Xerox, and General Electric know there is a big, growing market in education. These companies bought the educational houses to find out what they did. The real big change will come when they decide what to do."[6] The decision to undertake the development and publication of a new textbook has become increasingly based upon economic rather than educational considerations, especially projected demand within the elementary and high school market for a particular series in a given time frame. (Textbooks are often produced in series, for example kindergarten through grade eight science or social studies series, rather than in single grade-level, subject-specific editions. Large single-subject sellers for the high school level, U.S. history and biology, are, of course, important exceptions.) Book publishers do careful market studies of the buying trends of states with large school enrollments to plan their program of instructional materials development. The interface of the publishers' economic preference to tailor instructional materials to the large-scale educational markets with the educational preferences of these markets is a salient factor in the content determination process.

In this respect, the educational preferences of large elementary/high school book consumers give these groups some leverage and influence over the type and content of the books publishers print. The ability to sell the textbook once it has been developed is of utmost concern to the publisher. Since the actual production of a textbook series is a long and relatively costly process (anywhere from two to five years, costing up to several million dollars), publishers want to minimize their risk by tailoring the product to expected market preferences.

Concentration and Conglomeration in Textbook Publishing

Since the mid-1960s the publishing industry, like many sectors of the economy, has been transformed. The small, independent publishing house dedicated to producing textbooks has become an endangered species. Most of these companies have been purchased by larger publishing houses, which have themselves been purchased by even larger conglomerate corporations. This transformation put more pressure on the educational houses to produce principally for profit. In interviews with executives of houses integrated into larger corporations, executives reported that parent companies are not concerned with the quality or content of the books published. The parent company provides expertise and places emphasis on such activities as the control of cash flow, planning, and annual balance sheets rather than on the technical or educational aspects of textbook writing.

Frances FitzGerald notes in *America Revised,* a critique of how and why U.S. history textbooks have changed so dramatically in the past decades, that these changes in the publishing industry seem to have had an impact on editorial policies:

> . . . few people in the textbook business seem to reflect on their role as truth givers. And most of them are reluctant to discuss the content . . . The reticence of the textbook people derives, one soon discovers, from the essential ambiguity of their position. On one hand, they are running what amounts to Ministries of Truth for children, and on the other, they are simply trying to make money in one of the freest of free enterprises in the United States, where companies often go under. The market sets limits to the publishers' truth giving powers.[7]

The Change in Textbook Authorship

Generally, books are closely identified with their authors as the products of individual scholars or the collaborative work of a small group of scholars. Elementary and high school textbooks were authored traditionally by individual writers. These writers were most frequently identified as authorities in the particular field which the book's content covered—say, human biology, mathematics, or U.S. history — and/or proven and respected educators, who through years of direct teaching had developed both pedagogical mastery and subject area expertise.

The trend has been toward a new process of textbook creation referred to as the "managed" text. The managed text has become especially popular at the elementary school level but is also found among secondary school books and even most recently at the university level. To produce a managed textbook, the publisher contracts a writing team to author a series of textbooks. The writing team is usually managed by an editor of the publishing company.[8] In most instances, however, this is a writing team in name alone, rather than in working style. Team members may include practitioners in the field: classroom teachers, district-level curriculum specialists, scholars, even administrators. It is rare for these individuals to meet or function in any coordinated fashion. Coordination is the editor's job: to pull together all the parts which may include a teacher's guide from one author, or even several, depending on grade-level span; the texts from several different authors, again depending on subject area and grade level; the workbooks from still another writer; comments and criticism from field testers, usually targeted school districts. It is a very complex and disparate set of inputs which go into completing the textbook series package. If there is a real writer, it is most likely to be the publisher's in-house editor and not the identified editor on the book's title page. All in all, the writing of textbooks is a long, expensive, synthetic process. Currently the process follows a series of stages including the following:

- Determining demand. Publishers determine the demand for a new series based on the field market representatives' contacts with state and local curriculum planners and departments of education which deal with instructional materials selection.
- Contracting Authors. Based on the projected demand for a new series of elementary texts or a particular high school text, the publisher contracts with two or more leading authorities in the field—usually a subject area expert and an educator. Also, there may be a number of specialists contracted to write special elements such as teaching editions, workbooks, tests, etc. These authors produce a skeletal manuscript which is submitted to the publisher's editors.
- Editing. This manuscript is edited for a variety of factors: reading level according to carefully prescribed vocabulary lists; its relative emphasis on different aspects of content; its political orientation; its stand on any controversial issues which may potentially spark outcry from special interest groups within the public; its adequacy in meeting state-specified legal compliance requirements such as nondiscriminatory representation of men, women, and various ethnic groups, and other factors which some states demand.
- Pilot testing. With an edited text in hand, most publishers will print a pilot run of books and contract with a school district or set

of school districts to pilot test their program before trying to sell it on a mass scale.

- Marketing. This is perhaps the most critical phase from the publisher's perspective. Marketing requires an extensive network of sales representatives who keep in close touch with the educational establishment in critical stages, or key market areas. The marketing phase has several stages of its own, including the distribution of books to key educators in the field; the display of books at resource centers, book fairs, teachers' conventions; and managing of the state or local-level adoption procedure for textbooks.

Publishers devote a considerable proportion of their textbook development budgets to the marketing aspects of the production process. Information is sketchy on the relative costs of each facet of textbook preparation, publication, and distribution. However, it is known that textbook promotion is far more costly and extensive than trade-book promotions. Not only do these books require a large number of exemplar copies, but also a battery of salespersons throughout the nation to present them to potential consumers.

Free Market and Editorial Censorship

On the one hand, the publishing industry as part of the printed media industry has a reputation for strong advocacy of the First Amendment with respect to freedom of speech. However, with regard to the publication of textbooks, by contrast with trade books, freedom of expression seems to be guided by criteria other than the principles embodied in the U.S. Constitution. Censorship of any controversial issue or literary work in an attempt to avoid alienating a potential segment of the market is standard practice. Examples include the systematic exclusion of a play like Shakespeare's *Othello* "because publishers are convinced that they would lose part of the southern market which would reject a school book that had a play about 'miscegenation'."[9] The opposing, or rather different view with which publishers and educators approach instructional materials, is capsulated by FitzGerald as follows:

> From the publisher's point of view, the educational system is a market but from the point of view of the schools it is a rough kind of democracy. If a state or a school district wants a certain kind of textbook—a certain kind of truth—should it not have it? . . . In fact, it might be argued that it is less oppressive, that, given the size of the United States, the texts reflect the values and attitudes of a society at large much more accurately than they would without decentralization.[10]

In this respect, the question needs to be asked: How do publishers find out what schools want and who in fact determines, from the educational side of the equation, what is appropriate or inappropriate as textbook content?

There is practically no information, other than word of mouth, to document how decisions to include or exclude materials are made by publishers. The impact of instructional materials litigation such as the Kanawha County case, which put a series of textbooks being recommended for language arts on trial for being "disrespectful of authority and religion, destructive of social and cultural values, obscene, pornographic, unpatriotic or in violation of individual and familial rights of privacy," is not taken lightly by the publishing industry.[11] The attempts to ban school textbooks—either through formal litigation or informal political pressure—has had an impact on the editorial policies and practices. It may be responsible for a "self-censorship" rule of thumb based on the publishers' worst fears rather than explicit policy directives coming from the educational system itself.

TEXTBOOK SELECTION

While noticeable changes in the structure of the educational publishing industry and practices relative to the production of elementary and high school textbooks have taken place in recent decades, formalization of the procedures for selecting textbooks appeared during a much earlier epoch. A study of the purpose of state-regulated textbook adoptions found that most state adoption regulations and procedures were legislated during the period 1890–1920.[12] The legislation has survived a persisting debate since that time over the respective merits of state versus local control of textbook choice. The same study concluded, from a content analysis of the legislation in twenty-two states which regulate the textbook selection process, that the intent of state-level textbook adoption may be primarily a tool to control the marketing practices of the publishing industry. While the intention to control the marketing practices may be one important objective, the formalization of textbook selection procedures at both state and local levels has other implications as well. These encompass efforts by local and state-level administrators to put some distance between the ideological battles over content and the schoolhouse door, as well as the continuous effort over the past sixty years to professionalize all aspects of education, thereby removing its many and varied aspects from the hands of the lay public. The following section of this essay describes the varied ways in which the state and educational establishment have attempted to secure control over the selection of textbooks and suggests how these controls have functioned to shape the content and form of the contemporary American textbook.

There are several factors that define the parameters of the selection process for instructional materials. Each factor has an important influence on the content of educational materials selected for use in public schools and influences the content of instructional materials produced by publishers for classroom use. One overarching dimension is the degree of centralization or decentralization of the actual selection process. A second feature is the specification of criteria that must be used to evaluate instructional materials and determine which will be selected. Another aspect is the composition of persons involved in selecting the materials. A final factor is the external interests and pressures that are brought to bear on the selection process. Each of these factors is discussed in turn.

Centralization vs. Decentralization

One of the salient aspects of the relative decentralization of the American educational system, with each state having the autonomy to define an almost complete range of educational practices — from qualifications of teachers to definition of the elementary and high school curriculum — is the decentralization of the instructional materials' selection process. There are no federal regulations or specifications regarding what a state is to teach or not to teach in the public school curriculum. Nor are there guidelines for the way in which educational materials used in public schools should be selected. This being the case, each state has the power to define how it will select instructional materials.

It is relatively easy to make a typology of state adoption procedures throughout the United States on the basis of the degree to which these procedures are centralized or decentralized. There are two basic variants of the selection procedure: those states categorized as nonadoption states and those categorized as adoption states. A nonadoption state uses a decentralized approach to selection. Instructional materials are selected by local school districts in accordance with procedures and criteria that are locally established. Twenty-eight states, concentrated in the Northeast and Midwest regions of the country, practice decentralized or nonadoption methods of selection. These states (with the notable exception of New York) tend to be smaller in terms of school-age population and relatively more homogenous in the ethnic and cultural characteristics of their population. The nonadoption approach allows maximum flexibility to the school district in defining its choice of materials. Because the school district is a small market (including even a large district like Chicago or New York), possibilities of economies of scale in buying are limited. Similarly, leverage to influence the content of instructional materials produced by the publishing companies is negligible.

Adoption states tend to be concentrated in the South and Southwest regions of the country (California and Oregon being the exceptions), and tend to have heterogeneous populations with respect to ethnic and cultural characteristics. Adoption states are distinguished from the nonadoption states by varying degrees of centralization in the processes used for selecting textbooks and other instructional materials. Fundamentally, adoption states select one or more textbooks for each subject area to be used on a statewide basis. There are several variants of the centralized adoptions approach. The most common is the fully centralized model where several subject area textbooks series are adopted for the entire state by a single state-level selection committee. School districts then select one of the several series available on the state list for classroom use. Seventeen of the adoption states use this model. Among them is California, the largest instructional materials market in the United States, with a school enrollment exceeding 4.5 million students in 1990. In his book *The American School Book,* Hillel Black states, "if one state provides a large enough market for a textbook, it can ask and sometimes get a publisher to change the content of the school book if the state decides to buy. Because publishers find it less costly to issue a single, nationwide edition, they will frequently incorporate these changes in future printings sold throughout the country. In short, it is possible for one state to determine the content of textbooks used from Maine to Oregon."[13] Texas and Florida, along with California, are currently in this influential position.

There are many specific characteristics of the selection process used in adoption states that make it either more centralized at the state level or more within the domain of local school district preference. The state of California, the largest textbook market in the United States, preselects several series at the K–8 levels (usually five to ten depending on grade level and subject area) and provides each school district with a per student subsidy, based on average daily attendance statistics, to purchase preselected books or other books of the district's preference. Under this system there are clear financial incentives to use state-selected textbooks that may (though not always) be purchased at a lower unit cost, therefore allowing a district to get more material for its allotment than if it were to buy directly from publishers.

Centralization and size give a general indication of the potential power the state wields with respect to textbook content. If a state is highly centralized in its adoption procedure and represents a substantial market for publishers, it can be quite a powerful determinant of textbook content. Centralized states also have considerable control over the production standards for books (i.e., paper, printing, binding, the timing of adoption cycles, and legal requirements with respect to content). The degree of centralization or decentralization is not, however, closely associated with the selection criteria used for evaluating textbooks or the specification of persons who actually screen the materials.

A survey conducted in 1984 by the California State Department of Education on textbook evaluation and adoption processes revealed that of the adoption states, instructional materials reviewers are appointed by the state board of education in ten states, by the state superintendent of public instruction in five states, and by textbook commissions in another five states. In only one state are appointments left to the discretion of local school districts. The reviewer committees always include professional educators, and in nine states laypersons (either parents, the general public, or, in one instance, pupils) are included on review panels. Without exception, reviewers are organized into subject area committees (mathematics, language arts, etc.) to study submissions from publishers. As a rule only a single subject is handled each year, with the adoption cycle for a given set of materials in a particular subject running from four to six years. The length of the review process may be as little as one week or as long as one year; however, it averages four to seven months in the adoption states, and similar patterns are observed in nine school districts surveyed in nonadoption states. In addition to review panels appointed specifically to evaluate textbooks, each of the adoption states has a limited number of professionals (between one and twelve) who make up the state department of education's textbook unit. While professional educators do predominate in the selection process, they are either uniformly paid or allowed release time. The state of California, for instance, has a one-week intensive review period during the summer and two days of release time during the school year for teachers participating on review panels. While formalized and comprised of professionally qualified evaluators, the review process still in some ways resembles a volunteer activity.

Selection Criteria

The criteria used for the evaluation of instructional materials are by no means homogenous from state to state or school district to school district. Farr and Tulley reviewed seventy criteria sheets from school districts in adoption and nonadoption states and found only one common item among them.[14] Besides their lack of uniformity, these criteria can be examined from several perspectives: (1) how they are formulated; (2) how they are used by the selection committee reviewers; and (3) their adequacy in terms of evaluating the quality of the materials being reviewed.

In a study conducted by the Educational Research Service (ERS) in 1976, it was found that over 86 percent of the local school districts surveyed in nonadoption states had formulated written evaluation criteria to be used by selection committees in screening instructional materials. Responsibility for formulating the criteria was not investigated. It is known, however, through the California Department of Education's recent survey that content criteria in adoption states are generally formulated by the state curriculum commissions/committees or state textbook committees themselves. These committees frequently refer to subject area curriculum frameworks (when they exist) in developing instruments to be used by reviewers in the evaluation process.

In addition to content review, all adoption states and nine nonadoption districts included in the California study review instructional materials for social content. This is usually referred to as a legal compliance process whereby either the state legislature has established as statute, or the department of education has established as policy, social content criteria for instructional materials. In general, the review focuses on racial and sexual biases in textbooks. Some states have more extensive criteria that include depiction of the disabled, the aged, ecology, religion, etc. In many states this social content review is conducted as part of the educational content review process, in others it is a separate process with an independent set of reviewers.

The criteria specified for evaluating the content of textbooks and other materials tend to focus on the presentation of subject matter rather than the quality and accuracy of the information covered. The most recent instrument used by the state of California for evaluating social studies/history texts was overwhelmingly weighted towards pedagogical and physical aspects of the books. This may reflect an assumption that textbooks are written by subject area authorities (an increasingly disputable assumption) and that selection committees do not have sufficient expertise to pass judgment on these aspects. In some ways, it appears as if the educational establishment is ducking one of its fundamental responsibilities and passing this on to publishing house editors.

Choosing Reviewers

Historically, the district superintendent selected textbooks, often with the assistance and approval of the local school board. This practice no longer prevails. Superintendents have long since been replaced by review committees and commissions. Among the adoption states, the reviewers are appointed by the state board of education in ten states, by the state superintendent in five states, by textbook commissions in another five states, and by local school districts in only one state. In the ERS study of nonadoption states, the most common method of selecting reviewers is to allow the school district superintendent to appoint selection committee members (17 percent of the cases). Other relatively common practices include requesting volunteers for committees and allowing the curriculum coordinator to appoint committee members.

The composition of these committees varies greatly from state to state and from district to district. However, in nine of the adoption states laypersons participate on committees along with professional educators. In the district-level study conducted by ERS, nearly 24 percent indicated that students also participate in selection committees; while in the adoption states only one instance of student participation is reported. The characteristics of the professional educators who review materials is at this point unstudied. It is, however, in the larger centralized adoption states, a political process due to the influence that these states exert on the national textbook market. Textbook committees may well be selected with the implicit intent of coalescing a consensus of views on the materials rather than promoting a diversity of opinions. Although examples of changes made in textbooks have been cited in the literature, committees seem to primarily influence materials in future rounds of adoptions, because it is difficult to exact major changes in a book once it has already been developed and presented for review.

In addition to review panels appointed specifically to evaluate textbooks, each of the adoption states has a limited number of professionals employed in the state department of education's textbook unit. These professionals frequently handle the logistical work with regard to the selection process and also may be involved in drawing up the criteria or elaborating the specific instruments to be used by selection committee members.

EXTERNAL PRESSURES ON THE SELECTION PROCESS

Any discussion of the process of instructional materials' selection without mention of the external pressures brought to bear on that process would be incomplete. It is indeed rare to hear of a teacher asking a school district to censor a particular text or going to the school board with complaints about instructional materials selected for the classroom. Criticism of instructional materials' content has almost always come from outside the educational system itself. This is not to imply that teachers are satisfied with any or all materials that pass their way. Their reactions and the ways in which they mediate instructional materials that they as individual instructors find objectionable for whatever reasons, however, are another issue.

It is quite possible that almost anyone who reads a U.S. history textbook today would find something objectionable. However, it is not everyone who eventually translates that objection into a formal complaint. Over the past three decades there has been considerable controversy regarding the content of instructional materials. One survey showed that 26 percent of the four hundred school districts throughout the nation reported that there has been a recent challenge to textbooks or instructional materials. While these challenges seemed to reach their peak in the years 1975 to 1976, other studies have shown a steady stream of the same groups presenting their objections over the last fifteen to twenty years.

Objections to instructional materials have frequently begun with the reaction of a student's parent to allegedly objectionable materials. In some cases organized interest groups have arisen to monitor instructional materials for a particular aspect of content. These groups are extremely varied in terms of the viewpoints and issues represented. They range from the Interracial Council on Children's Books formed in 1965 with the objective of identifying racism and sexism in children's books, including textbooks, to the American Educational Association (AEA) with a committee formed in 1938 to "combat the inroad by PEARL [Public Education and Religious Liberty] which seeks to destroy all godly religion in education and denies aid to private and parochial schools." The first project of the Joint Committee of the AEA was to expose and remove "atheistic sex education" from the classroom. All groups have a common emphasis: excluding from the curriculum what is objectionable—according to their own specific criteria—rather than advocating the discussion of controversial issues as part of the learning process. Nonetheless, there are a number of ongoing organizations either independently formed or adjuncts of other political interest groups that scrutinize textbooks for content. What is important about these groups, however, is not the particular issues upon which they focus, but the ways in which they attempt to influence the content of instructional materials.

There are several strategies used by civic interest groups that wish to make an impact on instructional materials. The first is to set up a process parallel to the school system's instructional evaluation procedure. Groups either informally or formally take it upon themselves to monitor instruction materials in accord with their own interests and criteria. These special interest groups do not as a rule focus their criticism on the selection process itself. In some respects it seems reasonable to hypothesize that such groups would prefer to conduct independent reviews than be incorporated into the system's review process.

A second strategy of pressure groups is to address themselves to political rather than bureaucratic structures within the educational system. It is relatively common for an organized interest group to address itself directly to a board of education rather than to an appointed instructional materials review committee. While the pressure group tries to politicize the question of textbook content in an effort to further its cause, the instructional materials review committees act to depoliticize instructional materials' selection. This may be one important factor contributing to the emphasis on pedagogical criteria rather than content criteria found in evaluation instruments.

In addition, special interest groups rely on moral and value-specific arguments to bolster their perspective on instructional materials that should be excluded from the school curriculum. The use of moral and value positions on issues such as patriotism, sexual behavior, religion, and family life tend to politicize the instructional materials in question and draw sharp lines within the educational system between those who are "for" and those who are "against." This has a further politicizing effect, which the selection process is designed to dampen. Excessive politicization threatens the legitimacy of an educational system that presents itself as above ideology and above the particular interests of any one group within that society. However, neutralizing special interest groups in the selection process has also contributed to the process of expurgating controversy, debate, and intellectual vitality from textbooks.

CONCLUDING REMARKS

The concern with factors determining the content of textbooks is ultimately a concern for educational quality. Given the prominence of textbooks in the context of current pedagogy, the debate is an important one. The foregoing analysis suggests that improvement in textbook quality could result from several sources. First, and possibly foremost, we should recognize that in the current climate publishers are unlikely to be the leaders of change. The force for improvement must come from the state and local committees involved in the selection of materials. Members of selection committees need to develop expertise in the selection process. Criteria and their application to concrete examples must be clearly and commonly understood by all. This involves a training process for committee members rather than the ad hoc approach which has been widely employed. Since the mid-1980s the state of California has been attempting to generate the necessary force for change. As they've learned, this requires several measures: more time, greater simplicity, greater expertise, and more political will.

- *Time*. Selection committees need adequate time to evaluate textbooks. This means that people involved in selection committees must be giving their full attention to the task at hand. The voluntaristic approaches should be abandoned. Members of selection committees should be compensated and/or released from other professional responsibilities while serving on selection committees. Moreover, they must also be trained for the task of evaluating books.

- *Greater Simplicity.* Selection criteria need to be simplified. As Farr and Tulley have noted, adoption committees should focus their attention on those factors that are most likely to identify effective textbooks. Evaluation instruments that elaborate twenty to forty criteria for reviewers to consider are unrealistic and ineffective.[15]
- *Greater Expertise.* Selection committees may need to embody greater expertise, particularly with respect to subject matter and research on teaching and learning. This may mean the inclusion of scholars and specialists, who by no means should dominate the committees, but who can work with the teachers and members of the community who also comprise the committees' membership.
- *Political Will.* Committees need to have the political will and the political mandate to reject all possibilities, if none of the books submitted meet the specified criteria to satisfactory standard. Selection should not be the process of choosing among the lesser of evils. This is a difficult position, but it is a major force that selection committees can wield.

Of course these suggestions for reform in the textbook selection process beg another question. What about moving away from the textbook as the primary instructional resource? There is a growing chorus from within the educational establishment calling for a more fundamental solution. This call is not falling altogether on deaf ears. We are witnessing the revival of literature-based reading programs; the use of more varied materials for the teaching of history and social sciences; and a strengthening of the laboratory approach to learning science. The educational impact of these alternatives will need to be monitored carefully for their motivational and educational potential. But even if such dramatic changes were to appear, it is unlikely the issues surrounding what is to be used in schools for instruction and how materials are to be selected will disappear.

NOTES

1. C. J. Tidwell, *State Control of Textbooks* (New York: Columbia University Press, 1928).

2. Lewis Coser, "Publishers as Gatekeepers of Ideas," *Annals of the American Academy of Political and Social Science* 421 (September 1975), pp. 14–22.

3. Paul Goldstein, *Changing the American Schoolbook* (Lexington, Mass.: Lexington Books, 1978).

4. *Ibid.*

5. *Ibid.*

6. Hillel Black, *The American School Book* (New York: Morrow, 1967).

7. Francis FitzGerald, *America Revised* (Boston, Mass.: Little Brown, 1979), pp. 27–28.

8. Mike Bowler, "The Making of a Textbook," *Learning* (March 1978).

9. Black, *American School Book,* p. 55.

10. FitzGerald, *America Revised,* pp. 31–32.

11. Edward B. Jenkins, *Censors in the Classroom* (Carbondale, Ill.: Southern Illinois University Press, 1979), p. 18.

12. Michael Tulley and Roger Farr, "The Purpose of State Level Textbook Adoption: What Does the Legislation Reveal?" *Journal of Research and Development in Education* 18, no. 2 (1985).

13. Black, *American School Book.*

14. Roger Farr and Michael Tulley, "Do Adoption Committees Perpetuate Mediocre Textbooks?" *Phil Delta Kappan* (March, 1985).

15. *Ibid.*

GILBERT T. SEWALL
AND PETER CANNON

Chapter Four

The New World of Textbooks: Industry Consolidation and Its Consequences

---

During the 1980s a broadly based macroeconomic phenomenon changed permanently the conditions of production and trade. Companies accustomed to regional and national markets discovered that products from computers to cantaloupes were competing in global networks. Multinational corporations that had emerged over several decades continued to integrate and reorganize in order to link and control diverse enterprises. In industry after industry, small firms led by aggressive entrepreneurs likewise found special opportunities and grew into global forces. Telecommunication and high-technology data transfer revolutionized how information and wealth moved across national boundaries. Actual distribution of products and the investment banking that provides the fuel for capital growth became fully international.

This new economic environment generated impressive profits. It fostered the efficient production of goods, many of them once considered luxuries, which reached untold millions of consumers worldwide, most spectacularly in the Pacific Rim. Marketing in the 1980s and 1990s emphasizes mass-market goods that will attract, please, and captivate everyone from the South Korean steel worker to the American housewife. Successful product development and revenue expansion emphasize niche-building, whereby a company secures a comfortable if not impregnable position in a specialized market. So it is with books.

Numerous independent publishers that once comprised a large part of the field of elementary and high school textbook publishing have become arms of much larger media operations whose central activities are noneducational. Since these companies produce entertainment products, surface is apt to overshadow substance in the textbooks they publish. In some cases autocratic, glitz-oriented individuals with little understanding of textbooks and instructional materials may formulate company policy for textbook subsidiaries.

In the 1990s printed educational materials issue not from traditional publishing houses but from oligopolies where products are designed so as not to compete, overlap, or, in textbook industry jargon, "cannibalize" one another. Weaker "products" must be phased out and dropped. A smaller publishing pool means fewer titles in each subject area, with distinctions among them increasingly cosmetic and superficial.

Throughout publishing, nearly everyone, including authors, benefits from the economies of scale that produce savings in areas such as warehousing, printing, and paper. "For an author to say that he doesn't want to be published by a conglomerate is almost like a homeowner saying that he doesn't want his electricity provided by Con Edison," is how one New York literary agent puts the situation today. Consolidation allows publishers to integrate their title lines and sales forces, making them more efficient distributors.

Basal readers comprise at least 40 percent of elementary-level textbook purchases, and mathematics books constitute perhaps another 25 percent. Social studies texts are also integral through the elementary and secondary curriculum. In these subjects, a new generation of textbook titles has begun to appear, bearing 1990 and 1991 copyrights.

These books will be the standard printed curriculum for public school teachers and schoolchildren over the next five to ten years. Curricular reform in social studies will turn on this set of facts. Macmillan, Harcourt Brace Jovanovich, Silver Burdett and Ginn, Houghton Mifflin, and Scott, Foresman now dominate school publishing, offering a full menu of textbooks in all basic curricular areas. A national field of five or so publishers with a continental reach compares now with a dozen or more major educational book suppliers in the basic subject disciplines in the 1960s and 1970s. The likelihood of mid-size, regional, or boutique publishers unexpectedly bringing to market serious new competition is remote. For example, instead of developing social studies texts, which may be too expensive and chancy, smaller publishers interested in self-preservation might turn toward less demanding subject areas, such as vocational education or teen living.

Signals of niche-awareness on the part of leading textbook companies abound. That is to say, publishers who don't think that they can create a "best-seller" are choosing not to compete in major markets. In Texas, for example, the elementary-level basal reading and social studies submissions dropped by half during the 1980s, according to one Scott, Foresman executive.

Those worried about the changing nature of textbook publishing fear that fewer books in the marketplace will undermine efforts to improve an area of curriculum and instruction long overdue for reform. Some educators argue—with some justification—that restraint of trade and enforced product sameness will inevitably result from the consolidation of the industry during the 1990s. How valid are these changes?

THE TEXTBOOK MARKET

In some ways textbooks are no different from other consumer products. For major publishers, a national or international audience is essential. But textbooks are different from other consumer durables because they comprise the de facto curriculum for any nation's elementary and secondary schools. Teachers and students assume that learned researchers exercise extreme pedagogical care to produce authoritative, even canonical, tomes. But textbook content and format fall far short of the ideal, as shown by diverse studies by Paul Gagnon, Gilbert Sewall, Harriet Tyson-Bernstein, and others during the late 1980s.

A few aggressive regional publishers have established lucrative niches, with strong but limited lines in one subject, such as geography, or one genre, such as state histories. Small companies cannot as a rule field large enough staffs to sell a product line effectively over a wide area. Smaller publishers that concentrate on supplementary materials aimed at a particular audience can come out with outstanding products that contrast with the one-size-fits-all approach of mass-market publishers. But their market share remains minimal when compared to large-scale corporate publishers.

Book publishing is a vast enterprise, and one now linked to global concerns. The total U.S. market for textbooks and all other instructional materials exceeded $4 billion in 1988, of which almost $2 billion represented elementary and high school materials. About $13 billion was spent on all books in the United States the same year. In 1988, the ten leading textbook publishers controlled 70 percent of the market; the top three about one-third. While this indicated continuing competition in the industry, such concentration was not the case ten or twenty years earlier. During the 1980s the number of competing book lines diminished sharply. By 1990, after Macmillan's aggressive joint venture with McGraw-Hill and purchase of Merrill, what some editors referred to as the "Big Three"

—Macmillan, Harcourt Brace Jovanovich, and Simon and Schuster—had about a 45 percent share. The five largest textbook publishing companies—including Scholastic and Houghton Mifflin—collectively held a 58 percent share.

THE ATTRACTIONS OF TEXTBOOK PUBLISHING

One attraction of educational publishing in the 1990s is that established companies will probably not have to worry about new companies entering the field. For example, Silver Burdett and Ginn, which in the late 1980s developed a new national basal reading program, estimates that the cost of any such program for kindergarten through sixth grade can reach up to $40 million, a front-end investment that can take years to recoup. At worst such an investment can lead to huge losses. Even single volumes and smaller programs require millions of dollars to launch.

Forbidding barriers to market entry are compounded by the complications of warehousing and mobilizing a sales force that necessarily numbers in the hundreds. According to one leading media properties banker, any company that plans to compete nationally in school publishing has to be in the basal textbook business. It must also offer ancillary study guides, workbooks, and other related products, often through premiums and other teacher enticements.

Because textbooks occupy a nondiscretionary, mandated sector of the market with predictable earning flows, they differ considerably from regular trade books, which are sensitive to buyer whim and economic fluctuation. A successful book or program can provide many years of revenues, and in capturing a large share of a market, ring up huge profits over time. The plumiest profits stem from the mass-market volume that goes into more than one edition and has a ten-year-or-more shelf life. Such national textbooks represent by far the most lucrative segment in book publishing, with margins estimated in the late 1980s at 10 and 20 percent, and for a few, much more.

The premier high school U.S. government text, *Magruder's American Government,* for example, has been in print since 1918, sells at least 100,000 copies annually, and comes out in revised editions every election year. *Magruder* is a dream title, of course. It enjoys "brand name" recognition and has no initial investment to recapture, its authors and consultant receiving a flat fee for updates. Successful texts like *Magruder* make the field dependable and of keen interest to those seeking to build communication networks.

Textbooks are here to stay. Many innovators are exploring custom-made books, though such books have limited applications to elementary and high school courses outside of literature. While desktop publishers are creating a plethora of supplementary materials, by no means are the bulk of these new materials promising.

New technology poses no immediate threat to established publishing houses, and much software remains more in the realm of gimmickry than curricular advancement. "Despite the growing use of computers, textbooks remain the foundation for as much as 90% of classroom learning," noted the 1988 Paramount corporate report. The standard textbook is and will continue to be the workhorse of educational publishing.

The long-term outlook for textbooks is bright. The postwar generation's children are now going to school, and many Americans from President Bush on down have identified education as a vital area for improvement. School budgets for instructional materials are increasing in response to bipartisan calls. On top of this, instructional materials continue to be a relatively small expenditure in U.S. schools, and provide a relatively low-cost opportunity for curricular reform.

Children's trade sales are booming. Nearly a billion dollars was spent in 1989 on hardback books for children and more than $500 million on paperbacks, according to the Book Industry Study Group. This represents a 115 percent climb in revenues for hardbacks and 156 percent for paperbacks compared with 1984. In one example, Harcourt Brace Jovanovich saw a 27 percent increase in the sales of its children's titles in 1988 and was adding two new book lines.

A VOLATILE MARKET IN THE 1980s

The educational publishing industry of the 1980s, no longer distinct from media, communications, and entertainment, was clearly in a volatile state. This instability was taking a toll, as companies posted lost earnings, agonized over research and development costs, and seemed generally indecisive about their future. In 1989, Macmillan's joint venture with McGraw-Hill and purchase of Merrill, followed by Time Warner's precipitous sale of Scott, Foresman, capped a decade that saw many small and medium-sized independent textbook — and trade — publishers cease to exist, or rather become brand lines and imprints in divisions of vast, diversified, horizontally integrated communications empires with transnational aspirations.

The corporate transformation of Macmillan during the 1980s gives an idea of how swift and substantial changes in school publishing were. The formerly independent American publisher Macmillan was taken over by British communications entrepreneur Robert Maxwell. In 1989, the increasingly aggressive Macmillan and McGraw-Hill formed a joint textbook company. McGraw-Hill, whose elementary and high school lines had grown stale, paid $190 million for the privilege. Just a year earlier,

McGraw-Hill had bought the assets of the college and school divisions of Random House, the largest American trade-book publisher, for about $200 million in cash. This addition, however, did not stop the continuing erosion of McGraw-Hill's basal series in elementary and high school markets. After considering an independent move to develop new textbook programs, the company decided to give up publishing basal series. Starting with a new social studies series carrying a 1990 copyright, Macmillan is doing it for both of them. What had been two independent, competing lines became one. Having acquiring Merrill for $260 million, Macmillan/McGraw-Hill/Merrill, with estimated annual sales of $550 million by 1990, seems to have edged out Harcourt Brace Jovanovich as the nation's largest primary and secondary school publisher.

What had been for most of the decade the largest educational publisher, Harcourt Brace Jovanovich, was in trouble. In 1986, Harcourt Brace Jovanovich bought Holt, Rinehart and Winston from CBS for about half a billion. Harcourt Brace Jovanovich carried enormous debt, inspired first by its expansion and second by a hostile bid from Maxwell, the British communications giant that then went on to buy Macmillan in 1988. Its $2.5 billion debt severely restricted expenditures to develop new texts. In 1989, the new president, Peter Jovanovich, identified elementary and secondary publishing as an area where the company particularly needed to improve performance. But how he and the company planned to capitalize such efforts in the highly leveraged company remained unclear.

Also unclear was the future of Scott, Foresman, once a part of Time Inc., but at the end of 1989, sold to become a subsidiary of Harper and Row, a publishing company controlled by the Australian press magnate Rupert Murdoch. A few months after merging with Warner Communications, Time sold Scott, Foresman for $455 million, about 30 percent less than its putative value advertised during negotiations. Time Warner representatives categorized educational publishing as marginal, even incompatible with the new company's prevailing interest in entertainment, before taking a $175 million loss on Scott, Foresman.

Simon and Schuster — the second largest school publisher before the Macmillan/McGraw-Hill/Merrill venture — has been on a buying spree. In 1985 what is now Paramount purchased Ginn, a venerable publisher of elementary readers, from Xerox for about $500 million. The next year it acquired Silver Burdett, a major math and science textbook company. From these acquisitions, it created Silver Burdett and Ginn, dedicated to elementary school publishing, while leaving Prentice-Hall, purchased in 1984, to concentrate on the high school and college markets. Simon and Schuster's Follett, Allyn and Bacon, and Globe lines have become imprints of Prentice-Hall, where they are bound to lose whatever individual characteristics they may once have had.

At the end of the 1980s, Simon and Schuster had to take a write-off of $140 million against earnings of its publishing operations, largely because of sharp increases in textbook development and marketing costs. "Cost pressures are from the increasingly competitive environment because of industry consolidation," said Michael S. Hope, a senior Paramount executive to the *New York Times*. "People are putting more money into their products to ensure that they get into the marketplace."

Houghton Mifflin remains one of the last independent players in the textbook field. In 1988, it earned $24 million on sales of $368 million, two-thirds of which represents school revenues. Houghton Mifflin has been aggressive in maintaining its independence, as demonstrated by its 1989 purchase of Britain's Gollancz and by its gamble to push its literary-based curriculum developed mainly for the California market. In spite of critical acclaim, the Houghton Mifflin basal readers have not been a financial success. Houghton Mifflin's situation indicated that even carefully devised, innovative, educationally sound texts might not return the needed earnings, and that concentrated competition might put companies in very unstable positions. In this decade the readers will face stiff competition from Silver Burdett and Ginn and other new elementary-level programs.

In 1988, Pearson, a British conglomerate, became the first foreign company to make a direct acquisition of an American school publishing house when it bought Addison-Wesley. Pearson, together with Maxwell, which owns Macmillan, and the Murdoch empire, which controls Scott, Foresman, now have a significant portion, albeit English-language based, of the U.S. textbook market. Not long ago, some education observers forecast that this could not happen, assuming that state education committees and local school boards would raise objections to foreign control of national curricula. None have to date.

Up until now, the two largest publishers in the world, Bertelsmann (West Germany) and Hachette (France), at least until the creation of the Time Warner colossus, have exhibited no interest in the U.S. textbook market. But the global reach of multinational companies and the relentless move toward an international framework of communication cannot be discounted.

THE OUTLOOK

The current consolidation of the textbook industry is not unprecedented. In 1890, five large houses, including A. S. Barnes, Appleton and Co., and Harper and Bros., combined their textbook lists to form the American Book Company, which controlled 75 to 80 percent of the market at the height of its influence. Besides publishing the legendary McGuffey lines of readers and spellers, this trust gained a virtual monopoly in certain subjects like geography, producing no new books in that field for many years. But competition also increased from the 170 smaller textbook firms then in operation. Exposures of favoritism and even bribery in connection with state adoptions worked to the advantage of the independents, who were also bringing out texts that were more up-to-date, fresh, and responsive to emerging curricula than those put out by the American Book Company. Product quality and the changing tastes of teachers made a difference.

What differs from the market control of the century-old publishing trust is, first, the increased barriers to market entry and survival, both in production (e.g., printing costs) and distribution (e.g., sales costs). What differs secondly are the universal aspirations of American education, aimed at an entire population rather than a fraction of it, meaning that textbooks are not tailored for an elite or college-bound audience. They are directed at the largest possible number of consumers. As a result, academically rigorous or inventive books risk rejection in wide markets alongside losses for their makers.

The subjugation of educational publishers to communication giants more interested in MTV and Nintendo games than in Thomas Jefferson or quadratic equations is a serious problem. Textbook publishers' lack of enthusiasm for investing money in new products is obvious, especially at a time when makers have yet to see the long-term financial benefits of reduced competition. Textbook companies are profit driven as never before. When educational publishing falls into the hands of individuals who cannot afford quality if it doesn't pay out, the curriculum is at grave risk.

The new world of textbooks may portend a thin universe of very similar texts, dumbed down, fatuous, and so undistinguished that special funds will be raised locally, where possible, to explore and fund alternatives. Yet this remains unlikely. The collateral pressure of educational leaders and parents for curricular quality, combined with the relative low cost of textbook improvement, makes the development of better instructional materials one area where substantial gains are likely to occur during the coming decade.

SOURCES

This essay is compiled in large part from data reported between 1985 and 1990 in the *New York Times, Wall Street Journal, Value Line,* and Book Industry Study Group yearbooks. Of special interest are current estimates of industry share and sales in 1989 issues of *Educational Marketer* and *BP Report,* trade newsletters published by Knowledge Industry Publications. Recent studies that document conditions in the textbook industry include Paul Gagnon, *Democracy's Untold Story* (American Federation of Teachers, 1987), Gilbert T. Sewall, *American History Textbooks: An Assessment of Quality* (Educational Excellence Network, 1987), and Harriet Tyson, *A Conspiracy of Good Intentions* (Council for Basic Education, 1988). For further information, see Gilbert T. Sewall and Peter Cannon, "Textbook Consolidation: How Big a Menace?" *Social Studies Review* (Fall 1989) and Robert Rothman, "Critics Warn Mergers In Textbook Industry Could Hurt Quality," *Education Week* (December 6, 1989). For a history of the early textbook industry, see Hellmut Lehmann-Haupt, *Book Publishing in America* (R. R. Bowker, 1939).

EDWARD J. LARSON

Chapter Five

Constitutional Challenges to Textbooks

Recent court rulings have reaffirmed local school board control over textbook choices within broad constitutional limits. These rulings typically involve lawsuits brought by disgruntled parents offended by public-school instruction. Textbooks often become the focal point of such disputes because texts usually provide parents with their best available evidence of what is actually being taught in public-school classrooms. Parents become offended by texts for a variety of reasons, including concerns about quality and content. The disputes that most often end up in court, however, arise when material presented in a textbook offends parents' deeply held moral or religious beliefs. Then parents mount a crusade to protect their children, and other children, from the objectionable material. These crusades occasionally wind up in court, with parents raising constitutional objections to the offending textbooks.

This essay examines constitutional challenges to the use of textbooks adopted by local public schools. First, selected legal disputes of the past are used to trace the emergence of the constitutional doctrines invoked in these challenges. Focus then shifts to three recent federal court rulings upholding school district authority over textbook choices. Finally, the essay places these decisions within a broader trend toward judicial restraint in constitutional matters involving public schools.

The author wishes to acknowledge the research support provided by the William Pendleton Lamar Archival Research Fund of the University of Georgia.

COMMON SCHOOLS AND THE CONSTITUTION

Although the constitutional ground for fighting textbook controversies has shifted over time, the disputes themselves are not new. Indeed, they are as old as the common-school movement, which arose during the last century in part as a means to assimilate the increasingly diverse immigrant groups then entering the United States in steadily multiplying numbers. Prior to this movement, schooling took place in private or religious institutions. In contrast, the nineteenth century common school offered nonsectarian, public elementary education to all local school-age children regardless of their economic class or religious belief.

The new common schools were not devoid of religious influences, however. For example, one of the most prominent early leaders of this movement was Horace Mann, secretary of the Massachusetts Board of Education from 1837 to 1849. Mann was strenuously opposed to using sectarian textbooks in common schools but not to using books (including the Bible) that promoted religiously based moral values. He summarized this view in his final annual report to the Massachusetts Board of Education in 1848:

> I believed then (1837), as now, that sectarian books and sectarian instruction, if their encroachment were not resisted, would prove the overthrow of the schools.
>
> I believed then, as now, that religious instruction in our schools, to the extent which the Constitution and the laws of the State allowed and prescribed, was indispensable to their highest welfare, and essential to the vitality to moral education. . . .
>
> Our system earnestly inculcates all Christian morals; it founds its morals on the basis of religion; it welcomes the religion of the Bible, and in receiving the Bible, it allows it to do what it allowed to do in no other system, to speak for itself.[1]

Mann envisioned using the Bible, devoid of sectarian commentary, as a means to teach moral values in common schools. His only stated legal concern was to stay within the bounds imposed by *state* constitutional and statutory law. At the time, provisions in the U.S. Constitution respecting the separation of church and state only applied to the federal government, not to local school districts.

The allegedly nonsectarian use of the Bible in Massachusetts common schools led to controversy. During much of the last century, minority Roman Catholics objected to the public-school use of both Protestant versions of the Bible and Protestant-leaning textbooks. When Catholics took over the school committee of heavily immigrant Boston in the 1880s, it was the Protestants' turn to complain. A nationally publicized controversy arose when the new school committee removed an allegedly anti-Catholic history textbook from the public schools. The Protestant-backed Boston Evangelical Alliance responded with a public campaign protesting the school committee's actions as reflecting wrongful sectarian control over public education and advocating public-school instruction in nonsectarian Christian principles. Petitions circulated by the alliance also endorsed a federal constitutional amendment preventing local public schools from promoting sectarian religious beliefs.[2]

Such an amendment was first proposed on the national level by President Ulysses S. Grant a decade earlier. In a message to Congress in 1875, Grant stated, "I suggest for your earnest consideration—and most earnestly recommended—a constitutional amendment making it the duty of each of the several States to establish and forever maintain free public schools . . . [and] forbidding the teaching in said schools of religious, atheistic, or pagan tenets."[3] Efforts to adopt such a constitutional amendment continued for decades, in part because advocates did not believe that existing federal constitutional provisions adequately addressed local school textbook controversies. Indeed, the Boston textbook controversy only ended when protesters achieved a political solution that restored Protestant dominance over the school committee.[4]

State political intrusion into the local school curriculum led to the most famous American textbook controversy—the 1925 prosecution of John T. Scopes for violating Tennessee's newly enacted statute against teaching human evolution in public schools. That law was adopted largely in response to religiously motivated concerns about the impact of evolutionary teaching on the moral values and spiritual beliefs of school children. Since Scopes taught physics rather than biology, he doubted whether he had ever violated the law. However, he had once conducted a review class for the biology final exam using an assigned textbook that prominently featured evolution. On this basis, Scopes agreed to participate in a test case of the new statute.[5] In the ensuing trial and appeal, top defense attorneys assembled from around the country by the American Civil Liberties Union repeatedly tried to raise constitutional objections to the statute. That these attempts failed revealed the limited impact of constitutional constraints on textbook controversies prior to midcentury.

The constitutional arguments raised in Scopes's defense challenged the reasonableness of the statute. For example, defense cocounsel Arthur Garfield Hays, a prominent Wall Street lawyer and founding ACLU national committee member, argued at trial, "My contention is that no law can be constitutional unless it is within the right of the state under the police power, and it would be within the right of the State to pass it if it were reasonable, and it would only be reasonable if it tended in some way to promote public morals.'' This argument correctly summarized the applicable limits then placed on state action by the U.S. Constitution. Hays proceeded to compare the antievolution statute to a hypothetical law against teaching that the earth revolves around the sun. Surely the hypothetical law would be unconstitutionally unreasonable, Hays reasoned, and the antievolution statute should be, too. "The only distinction,'' Hays argued, ''is that evolution is as much a scientific fact as is the Copernican theory, but the Copernican theory has been more fully accepted.''[6]

In reply, the prosecution maintained that the law did not infringe upon individual freedom because it only applied to persons who chose to teach at public schools. Of course the legislature could not constitutionally proscribe private evolutionary teaching, the prosecution acknowledged, but it had authority ''to direct the expenditure of the school funds of the state, and through this act to require that the money shall not be spent in teaching of theories that conflict or contravene the Bible story of man's creation.''[7] The trial court sided with the prosecution and upheld the statute on the basis of several controlling federal and state supreme court decisions generally affirming legislative control over public education.[8]

Scopes's resulting conviction was appealed to the Tennessee Supreme Court. Comparing Scopes's conviction to the execution of Socrates, lead defense counsel Clarence Darrow closed his emotional appellate argument by proclaiming that ''we are once more fighting the old question, which after all is nothing but the question of the intellectual freedom of man.''[9] Not so, declared the prosecution's brief: ''It is not part of anyone's 'liberty' to perform labor for the state.''[10] In oral arguments, the prosecution went on to describe the law as the ''deliberate thoughtful enactment of a sovereign people, which was designed to protect their children in their own public schools in their beliefs in the divine origin of man, which in turn measures their responsibilities to God and their fellow-man.''[11] The prosecution thus saw the key freedom issue as being the right of parents to use political means to protect their children from evolutionary teaching rather than the constitutional ''liberty of mind and of thought and of education'' identified by the defense.[12] Although these serious issues of parental rights, democratic control over public education, and academic freedom were obscured both by the hoopla surrounding the trial and in subsequent dramatized accounts (such as *Inherit the Wind*), they remain the issues driving current textbook controversies.

The elected Tennessee Supreme Court sought middle ground in addressing these issues by overturning Scopes's conviction on a technicality while upholding the statute. In particular, the court found ''little merit'' in the contention that the statute violated constitutional liberties, ruling instead that Scopes ''had no right or privilege to serve the State except on such terms as the State prescribed.''[13] In this way, the court affirmed democratic control over public high schools at a time when compulsory secondary education was still somewhat new in the South. Further, this resolution illustrates the lack of meaningful federal constitutional limits then imposed on a state's power over the content of public-school instruction or textbooks.

LAYING DOWN THE LAW

This situation began to change around midcentury. The First Amendment of the U.S. Constitution begins with the two-part guarantee that ''Congress shall make no laws respecting an establishment of religion or prohibiting the free exercise thereof.'' During the past three decades, the legal controversies surrounding public-school textbooks have focused on the interpretation of these two constitutional clauses, which together serve to protect religious freedom, including the right not to believe in any religion. That neither clause figured prominently earlier bespeaks a changing interpretation of the Constitution.

The first of these clauses, the Establishment Clause, has undergone a complete reinterpretation by the U.S. Supreme Court in the past forty years. During the heyday of the antievolution crusade in the 1920s, no court would have seriously considered a legal argument that state antievolution statutes violated the Establishment Clause. The clause traditionally barred only an American state church, such as the Anglican Church in England.[14] Since the federal government never established a state church, the Supreme Court did not directly encounter the clause until 1947, when the landmark case of *Everson v. Board of Education* questioned the constitutionality of a state's providing public transportation for parochial school students.[15] The court chose this case to declare that the Establishment Clause precludes government from aiding religion generally, as well as simply establishing a particular denomination.

Even more significant for public-school textbook issues, the *Everson* decision, written by Justice Hugo Black, applied this newly recognized constitutional ''wall of separation'' between religion and government to the states.[16] The declaration that ''Congress shall make no laws respecting an establishment of religion'' expressly limits only *federal* action. States were left free to establish state churches, and many states did so during the first half-century of the republic. The 1868 Fourteenth Amendment to the U.S. Constitution barred *states* from depriving ''any person of life, liberty, or property, without due process of law.'' In its historical context, this language obviously was intended to facilitate the abolition of human slavery—for example, by preventing the jailing of former slaves without trial. It does not as clearly indicate what other types of personal liberty are protected against state encroachment. Over the years, the U.S. Supreme Court gradually incorporated many of the Constitution's limits on federal action into the individual ''liberty'' protected from state interference by the Fourteenth Amendment. The First Amendment right of free speech was so incorporated in 1927, followed by the First Amendment freedoms of press, assembly, and petition during the 1930s. The Court then used this mechanism to apply the Free Exercise Clause to the states in 1940, followed by the Establishment Clause seven years later in *Everson*.[17] Only then were the constitutional principles in place for the federal judiciary to address many of the most difficult textbook controversies.

Public education first felt the effect of the Establishment Clause in 1948, when the Supreme Court, in *McCollum v. Board of Education,* struck down a school program conducted by local churches to provide classroom religious instruction using sectarian texts. ''Here not only are the State tax supported public school buildings used for the dissemination of religious doctrines,'' Justice Black wrote for the Court. ''The State also affords sectarian groups an invaluable aid in that it helps to provide pupils for their religious classes through use of the State's compulsory public school machinery. This is not separation of Church and State.''[18]

The Supreme Court carried this principle a step further in 1962, when it outlawed state-sponsored prayer in public schools. At the time, eighteen widely scattered states authorized classroom prayer, which in many instances continued a tradition dating back to the earliest days of public schooling in those states. Yet the Court, again speaking through Justice Black, found even the nondenominational and noncompulsory New York State school prayer ''wholly inconsistent with the Establishment Clause.''[19] A year later, the Court in *Abington School District v. Schempp* overturned statutes and practices mandating Bible reading in public-school classrooms. In his majority opinion, Justice Tom C. Clark wrote ''that to withstand the strictures of the Establishment Clause there must be a secular legislative purpose and a primary effect that neither advances or inhibits religion.''[20] This became the test applied when the Supreme Court finally struck down the antievolution statutes in 1968.

At that time, the Court voided an Arkansas antievolution statute on the grounds that it was enacted with a wrongful religious purpose in violation of the Establishment Clause. The case, *Epperson v. Arkansas,* arose after a committee of local biology teachers in Little Rock, Arkansas, selected an evolutionary textbook as the assigned reading for biology classes in the public schools.[21] Backed by the leading state teacher's association, a Little Rock biology teacher named Susan Epperson then sued to test the legality of using the assigned textbook and to challenge the constitutionality of the antievolution statute. In striking down the statute for violating the Establishment Clause proscription against promoting religion in public schools, the Supreme Court wrote, "It is much too late to argue that the State may impose upon the teachers in its schools any conditions that it chooses, however restrictive they may be of constitutional guarantees."[22] Under this holding, and in marked contrast with the *Scopes* era, the state could not exclude evolution from public-school textbooks for religious reasons. During the *Scopes* era and before, federal constitutional protections against the establishment of religion simply were not applied to actions by state and local governments, including their actions relating to public education. This approach changed by 1968, especially with the Supreme Court's school-prayer decisions of the early 1960s, so that in *Epperson* and thereafter the constitutional concept of religious freedom counterbalanced the right of political control over public education.

The reach of *Epperson* has been repeatedly tested in a variety of cases involving the use of creationist and evolutionary textbooks in public schools. Two cases from the 1970s are particularly instructive. In one, a federal appellate court struck down as "patently unconstitutional" a 1973 Tennessee statute mandating that all public-school textbooks presenting a theory of origins give "equal space" to other theories "including but not limited to, the Genesis account of the Bible." The court viewed this restriction as clearly violating the Establishment Clause by promoting a religious doctrine in public schools.[23]

A somewhat different situation emerged in 1976, when the Indiana Textbook Commission adopted a creationist text as one of seven biology textbooks approved for use by public schools within the state. Since all of the other texts presented a traditional evolutionary perspective, the commission viewed the creationist alternative as a fair way "to inculcate in the student an open and questioning mind on all subjects of inquiry."[24] This academic rationale of acquainting students with a variety of ideas broke down when one local school district adopted only the creationist textbook. After reviewing the text in a suit brought by the Indiana ACLU, a state trial-court judge then rejected *any* public-school use of the book—either alone or in conjunction with evolutionary materials. Finding the textbook a transparent attempt to clothe the Genesis account in scientific garb, the court wrote, "The question is whether a text obviously designed to present *only* the view of Biblical Creationism in a favorable light is constitutionally acceptable in the public schools of Indiana. Two hundred years of constitutional government demand the answer be *no*.''[25] Under the Establishment Clause, material promoting religion could not be included in public-school textbooks. This barrier still stands.

The centrality of the Establishment Clause to American textbook controversies is illustrated by a comparison to the current situation in Great Britain. England and Scotland have maintained established Christian churches for centuries and have required religious education and worship in public schools. Political pressure has mounted within some quarters in Great Britain, as in the United States, for the government to address social problems by enhanced moral education for students. While American public schools must follow the dictates of *McCollum*, *Epperson*, and other Establishment Clause rulings to avoid promoting or inhibiting particular religions in the teaching of moral values, British schools are not so limited. Noting that ''recently there have been great debates about religious education,'' British Prime Minister Margaret Thatcher declared in the spring of 1988, ''I believe strongly that politicians must see that religious education has a proper place in the school curriculum.''[26] Subsequently, legislation was enacted requiring that public-school pupils both participate daily in collective worship that is ''wholly or mainly of a broadly Christian character'' and receive religious education reflecting ''the fact that the religious traditions in Great Britain are in the main Christian.''[27] The Establishment Clause clearly precludes such government responses in the United States.

Although religious freedom has become the primary constitutional issue in American textbook controversies, partisans occasionally raise other rights as well. For example, antievolution statutes were originally challenged as unconstitutionally unreasonable in *Scopes*. More recently, in the 1982 case of *Board of Education v. Pico*, the U.S. Supreme Court suggested that a school board could not remove public-school library books as a means to suppress objectionable ideas. The case arose when a local school board in New York removed several library books that offended ''its conservative educational philosophy.''[28] Overturning a lower court ruling the school board's favor, a plurality of three liberal justices on a deeply divided Supreme Court wrote that ''the Constitution protects the right to receive information and ideas'' as a ''corollary of the rights of free speech and press that are explicitly guaranteed by the Constitution.''[29] The plurality opinion then concluded, ''If petitioners *intended* by their removal decision to deny respondents access to ideas with which the petitioners disagreed, and if this intent was the decisive factor in petitioners' decision, then petitioners have exercised their discretion in violation of the Constitution.''[30]

Although *Pico* expressly did not apply to textbooks or to the initial purchase of library books, the decision raised additional constitutional issues for school book controversies. *Pico* and the various Establishment Clause rulings involving textbooks show the dramatic change that has occurred in this area of constitutional law during the century since partisans in the Boston textbook controversy assumed that a constitutional amendment would be needed to roll back allegedly religiously motivated censorship of public-school textbooks. By the 1980s, existing Constitution provisions had become sufficient to address the subject.

JUDICIAL RESTRAINT

These developing constitutional doctrines provide a stage for current textbook controversies, and grounds for taking objections to court. Three recent federal appellate court decisions, all cut from the same cloth, illustrate the key constitutional doctrines at work. In particular, each decision shows a different federal court struggling to limit these doctrines from excessively restricting the authority of public-school educators over textbook choices. By doing so, these decisions reflect concern for the concept of judicial restraint, which encourages federal courts to defer to decisions by the elected branches of government in questionable or borderline areas of constitutional law.

The first of these three cases arose in 1983, when Cassy Grove was assigned *The Learning Tree* in her Washington State public-school sophomore English literature class. Cassy found the book offensive to her fundamentalist religious beliefs. Her mother also found the book offensive and asked that it be removed from the curriculum. Cassy was given an alternative assignment, but the book remained in the curriculum for other students. Carrying out a threat increasingly heard from the religious Right and advised by an attorney who was also state director for the Moral Majority, the Groves then filed suit contending that public-school use of the text violated the religion clauses of the First Amendment by burdening the free exercise of their religion and by establishing the religion of secular humanism in the schools.[31]

In *Grove v. Mead School District,* the Ninth Circuit U.S. Court of Appeals easily disposed of both contentions. Noting that the burden on Grove's free exercise of religion was minimal because Cassy was assigned an alternative book, the court stressed, "The state interest in providing well-rounded public education would be critically impeded by accommodation of Grove's wishes." To underscore this point, the court added that eliminating everything objectionable to any religious body from the schools would "leave public education in shreds." The court gave equally short shrift to Grove's Establishment Clause allegations by simply describing *The Learning Tree* as a religiously neutral book. "The central theme of the novel is life, especially racism, from the perspective of a teenage boy in a working class black family," the court noted. "Comment on religion is a very minor portion of the book."[32] A concurring judge found much in the book that "denigrates the figure of Jesus and casts doubt upon much fundamentalist doctrine," but approved it as part of an overall curriculum that was on balance objective.[33] The *Grove* court was clearly not inclined to let a student's sectarian religious beliefs govern a school's textbook choices. A similar attitude was later reflected in two 1987 federal appellate court decisions from the South.

The two cases developed independently but always seemed to follow a parallel course. The first case, *Smith v. Board of School Commissioners,* arose in Alabama, where ultraconservative jurist W. Brevard Hand tried to overturn the doctrine of incorporation by upholding a state school-prayer statute on the grounds that the Establishment Clause does not limit state (as opposed to federal) action.[34] After the U.S. Supreme Court reversed this ruling in 1985, Hand reorganized the lawsuit into a challenge against allegedly anti-Christian materials in the curriculum—leading to a decision banning the public-school use of over three dozen standard textbooks found to promote the religion of secular humanism in violation of the Establishment Clause.[35] Hand reasoned that if he were forced to apply the Establishment Clause against the state, then he would apply it with vengeance.[36]

Meanwhile, in neighboring Tennessee, seven fundamentalist families (supported by a conservative national religious group called Concerned Women for America) challenged the elementary school use of a popular series of basic reading textbooks published by Holt, Rinehart and Winston. They alleged that these texts undermined their children's religious beliefs by including stories containing themes such as telepathy, feminism, the occult, pacifism, and evolution. This, the suit charged, unconstitutionally burdened both the parents' and the children's rights to freely exercise their religion. After extensive judicial proceedings in the case, *Mozart v. Hawkins County Board of Education,* Judge Thomas Hull agreed. He ordered that the local public schools allow the children to opt out of classes using those texts.[37] Although Hull stressed that the remedy would not disrupt the overall education program, the school board strenuously disagreed. It appealed the decision.

The Sixth Circuit U.S. Court of Appeals reversed Hull's ruling in an opinion that reads like an ode in praise of local control over textbook choices. Quoting from a forty-year-old Supreme Court concurring opinion, the decision of the court written by Chief Judge Pearce Lively observed that eliminating everything objectionable to religious groups would "leave public education in shreds. Nothing but educational confusion and a discrediting of the public school system can result from subjecting it to constant law suits." After finding no Free Exercise Clause violation because the children were required neither to affirm nor deny any religious beliefs nor to participate in any religious practices, Lively cautioned that courts should be hesitant to "order changes in an educational program adopted by duly chosen local authorities."[38]

Both other judges on the three-judge panel reviewing *Mozart* filed concurring opinions. In the first, Judge Cornelia Kennedy stressed the disruptive effect of allowing some students to selectively opt out of such core courses as basic reading.[39] In the second, conservative Judge Danny Boggs concluded that federal courts should *never* interfere with politically controlled school systems to protect free exercise rights except to prevent schools from forcing students to participate in religious rituals contrary to their beliefs. The Supreme Court has never required more than this, Boggs reasoned, and "such a significant change in school law and expansion in the religious liberties of pupils and parents should come only from the Supreme Court itself, and not simply from our interpretation." Accenting this bow to judicial restraint, Boggs added, "schools are very important, and some public schools offend some people deeply. That is one major reason private schools of many denominations—fundamentalists, Lutheran, Jewish—are growing. But a response to that phenomenon is a political decision for the schools to make."[40]

Two days after this decision was issued, the federal Court of Appeals for the Eleventh Circuit followed suit by overturning Judge Hand's ruling in *Smith*. Although *Smith* involved an Establishment Clause challenge to textbook selection, for which there is more Supreme Court precedent than in a Free Exercise Clause challenge, deference was again paid to local control. In a unanimous opinion by Judge Frank Johnson, the appellate court cautioned that the context of public schools requires judicial sensitivity to "the broad discretion given school boards in choosing the public school curriculum, which mandates that courts not interfere in the resolution of conflicts arising in the daily operation of school systems unless basic constitutional values are directly and sharply implicated."[41] Although textbooks promoting sectarian religion would cross this barrier, the standard texts at issue in *Smith* did not.

EMERGING TRENDS

These three appellate court decisions follow an emerging trend in U.S. Supreme Court decisions against interfering in the policy decisions of local schools. While the Supreme Court's 1969 decision in *Tinker v. Des*

Moines School District allowed elementary and secondary students to wear antiwar arm bands over the objection of school officials, its 1986 ruling in *Bethel School District v. Fraser* permitted school officials to punish a student for lewd remarks made during a campaign speech at a student assembly, and its 1988 ruling in *Hazelwood School District v. Kuhlmeier* approved a principal's censorship of student articles in a school newspaper.[42]

Of course, these three cases involved significantly differing fact patterns, and *Tinker* has never been overruled. Yet a change in tone was apparent. The Court in *Tinker* suggested that school officials must "justify prohibition of a particular expression of opinion" by showing that "the forbidden conduct would 'materially and substantially interfere with the requirements of appropriate discipline in the operation of the school.' "[43] Conservative Justice John Harlan—a respected advocate of judicial restraint—dissented sharply, noting that "school officials should be accorded the widest authority in maintaining discipline and good order in their institutions. To translate that proposition into a workable constitutional rule, I would, in cases like this, cast upon those complaining the burden of showing that a particular school measure was motivated by other than legitimate school concerns."[44] Harlan's tone was reflected in *Hazelwood,* where the Supreme Court ruled that "the standard articulated in *Tinker*" did not apply to the situation at issue, which was described as determining "when a school may refuse to lend its name and resources to the dissemination of student expression." In that situation, the Court adopted a Harlanesque approach of permitting school officials to censor "the style and content of student speech in school-sponsored expressive activities so long as their actions are reasonably related to legitimate pedagogical concerns." Reiterating this point, the Supreme Court explained that "judicial intervention to protect students' constitutional rights" is required "only when the decision to censor . . . has no valid educational purpose."[45] This reflected a shift toward leaving public-school matters in the hands of local educators. *Grove, Mozart,* and *Smith* fit into this trend. Accordingly, the Supreme Court refused to review the appellate court rulings in *Grove* and *Mozart,* and the plaintiffs in *Smith* did not even ask for high court review.[46]

Some conservative leaders have suggested that antifundamentalist bias, not a faith in local school officials, underlay the recent textbook decisions. The words of Judge Boggs in *Mozart* suggested otherwise, however. "The rule here is not the rule just for fundamentalist dissenters, for surely the rule cannot be that when school authorities disagree with nonfundamentalist dissenters, the school loses, and when the school authorities disagree with fundamentalists, the school wins. Rather, . . . the democratic principle must prevail.''[47] That democratic principle gives elected school officials broad authority to choose textbooks, even in the constitutionally sensitive area of texts presenting concepts or events relating to religion, so long as basic constitutional values are not directly and sharply implicated.

Federal courts have repeatedly emphasized that public schools can constitutionally teach about religion provided that such teaching neither has the sole intent or principal effect of promoting belief nor excessively entangling the school with religion.[48] In upholding the public-school use of *The Learning Tree*, the *Grove* court observed, ''Not all mention of religion is prohibited in public schools.'' Stressing that this discretion is not limited to allegedly anti-Christian works such as *The Learning Tree*, the decision added, ''The Supreme Court has stated clearly that literary or historic study of the Bible is *not* a prohibited religious activity.''[49] A concurring opinion elaborated on this point. Even assuming that *The Learning Tree* was anti-Christian, the opinion noted that educational ''objectivity is to be assessed with reference to the manner in which often highly partisan, subjective material is . . . integrated into the school curriculum, where [even] the Bible may constitutionally be used in an appropriate study of history, civilization, ethics, comparative religion, or the like.'' The opinion went on to list Luther's ''Ninety-Five Theses,'' Greek mythology, *Paradise Lost*, *Pilgrim's Progress*, and *The Divine Comedy* as examples of obviously religious textual material that may be appropriate for public-school use in certain contexts.[50]

The U.S. Supreme Court has made similar observations on several occasions. In the landmark 1963 decision against mandatory public-school Bible reading, *Abington School District v. Schempp*, the Court wrote:

> It might well be said that one's education is not complete without a study of comparative religion or the history of religion and its relationship to the advancement of civilization. It certainly may be said that the Bible is worthy of study for its literary and historic qualities. Nothing we have said indicates that such study of Bible or of religion, when presented objectively as part of a secular program of education, may not be effected consistently with the First Amendment.[51]

In a concurring opinion, Justice William Brennan added, ''The holding of the Court today plainly does not foreclose teaching *about* the Holy Scriptures or about the differences between religious sects in classes in literature or history. Indeed, whether or not the Bible is involved, it would be impossible to teach meaningfully many subjects in the social sciences or in the humanities without some mention of religion.''[52]

The balance struck in *Schempp* still stands. In a 1987 decision striking down a Louisiana statute mandating balanced treatment for "creation-science" and "evolution-science" in public-school science classes, Justice Brennan wrote that "teaching a variety of scientific theories about the origin of humankind to schoolchildren might be validly done with the clear secular intent of enhancing the effectiveness of science instruction."[53] In his concurring opinion, Justice Lewis Powell added:

> As a matter of history, school children can and should properly be informed of all aspects of this Nation's religious heritage. . . . In fact, since religion permeates our history, a familiarity with the nature of religious beliefs is necessary to understand many historical as well as contemporary events. In addition, it is worth noting that the Establishment Clause does not prohibit *per se* the educational use of religious documents in public school education. . . . The Establishment Clause is properly understood to prohibit the use of the Bible and other religious documents in public school education only when the purpose of the use is to advance a particular religious belief.[54]

Of course, public-school textbooks are not required to include material about religion. Rather, courts have left broad discretion to local educators to determine the content of their public-school textbooks.

CONCLUSION

A variety of constitutional doctrines rooted in current interpretations of the First and Fourteenth amendments potentially impact public-school textbook decisions. These include restrictions against public schools promoting religious belief, inhibiting the free exercise of religion, and abridging basic freedoms of speech and press. Courts, however, appear increasingly cautious in applying these doctrines against public-school officials, absent a clear constitutional violation. Indeed, recent cases brought by fundamentalists against the use of allegedly antireligious texts resulted in decisive victories supporting local school board discretion over textbook choices in borderline cases that could have extended individual religious freedom at the expense of school authority. This fit the current judicial trend toward granting school officials broad authority over educational matters generally. Such authority carries a responsibility, however, because parents, students, and public interest groups on all sides stand ready to invoke existing constitutional doctrines as a means to fight objectionable texts. Yet, textbook choices conscientiously made for secular educational reasons have consistently withstood assault and should continue to do so as long as the federal judiciary maintains its current course.

NOTES

1. Mann's declaration is reprinted in Anson P. Stokes, *Church and State in the United States,* vol. 2 (New York: Harper & Row, 1950), p. 57.

2. *New York Times,* July 13, 1888, p. 1; Sept. 11, 1988, p. 1; and Oct. 10, 1888, p. 3. The petitions are in the records of the Senate Committee on Education and Labor, 50th Congress, at the National Archives, Washington, D.C.

3. 4 *Cong. Rec.* 175 (1875).

4. *New York Times,* Sept. 23, 1888, p. 4; Oct. 2, 1888, p. 5; and Dec. 12, 1888, p. 1.

5. John T. Scopes and James Presley, *Center of the Storm: Memoirs of John T. Scopes* (New York: Holt, 1967), pp. 56–62. The motivations underlying the Tennessee statute are examined in Edward J. Larson, *Trial and Error: The American Controversy Over Creation and Evolution* (New York: Oxford University Press, 1985), pp. 28–57.

6. *The World's Most Famous Court Trial: State of Tennessee v. John Thomas Scopes* (1925; reprint New York: Da Capo, 1971), pp. 56–57.

7. Ibid., p. 67.

8. Ibid., pp. 107–108.

9. "Argument of Clarence Darrow," *Scopes v. State,* 154 Tenn. 105, 289 S.W. 363 (1927) in Clarence Darrow Papers (Library of Congress, Washington, D.C.)

10. "Reply Brief," *Scopes,* 154 Tenn. 105, 289 S.W. 363, p. 16.

11. *New York Times,* June 1, 1926, p. 8.

12. Ibid.

13. *Scopes,* 154 Tenn. at 111, 289 S.W. 364.

14. E.g., *see* Joseph Story, *Commentaries on the Constitution of the United States* (Boston: Hilliard, Gray, and Co., 1833), p. 728.

15. *Everson v. Board of Education,* 330 U.S. 1 (1947).

16. Ibid., at 15.

17. Laurence H. Tribe, *American Constitutional Law,* 2d ed. (Mineola, N.Y.: Foundation Press, 1988), pp. 772–774 and 1155–1157.

18. *McCollum v. Board of Education,* 333 U.S. 203, 212 (1948).

19. *Engel v. Vitale,* 370 U.S. 421, 424 (1962).

20. *Abington School District v. Schempp,* 374 U.S. 203, 222 (1963).

21. "Proceedings" in *Appendix, Epperson v. Arkansas,* 393 U.S. 97 (1968), p. 40.

22. *Epperson,* 393 U.S. at 108.

23. *Daniel v. Waters,* 515 F.2d 485, 492 (6th Cir. 1975).

24. "Brief of Indiana Textbook Commission," *Hendren v. Campbell,* No. S577–0139 (Marion Co. Ind. Super. Ct. No. 5, April 14, 1977).

25. *Hendren,* slip op. at 19.

26. M. Thatcher, *Speech to the General Assembly of the Church of Scotland* 26 (May 21, 1988) (manuscript copy).

27. Education Reform Act, 1988, c. 40, secs. 6–8 (U.K.).

28. *Board of Educ. (Island Trees) v. Pico,* 457 U.S. 856, 860 (1982).

29. Ibid., at 868.

30. Ibid., at 872.

31. *Grove v. Mead School Dist. No. 354,* 753 F.2d 1528, 1531 (1985) *cert. denied,* 474 U.S. 826 (1985). The attorney, Michael P. Farris, also litigated *Mozart v. Hawkins County Board of Education.*

32. Ibid., at 1533–1534.

33. Ibid., at 1540–1541 (Canby, J., concurring).

34. *Jaffree v. Board of School Comm'rs of Mobile County,* 554 F.Supp. 1104, 1128–1129 (1983); *aff'd in part, rev'd in part sub. nom. Jaffree v. Wallace,* 705 F.2d 1526 (11th Cir. 1983), *aff'd.,* 472 U.S. 38 (1985).

35. *Smith v. Board of School Comm'rs of Mobile County,* 655 F.Supp. 939, 988 (S.D. Ala. 1987), *rev'd,* 827 F.2d 684 (11th Cir. 1987).

36. *Jaffree,* 554 F.Supp. at 1129, n. 41.

37. *Mozart v. Hawkins County Bd. of Educ.,* 647 F.Supp. 1194 (E.D. Tenn. 1986), *rev'd,* 827 F.2d 1058 (6th Cir. 1987), *cert. denied,* 108 S.Ct. 1029 (1988).

38. *Mozart v. Hawkins County Bd. of Educ.,* 827 F.2d 1058, 1069–1070 (6th Cir. 1987), *cert. denied,* 108 S.Ct. 1029 (1988).

39. Ibid., at 1071–1073 (Kennedy, J., concurring).

40. Ibid., at 1081 (Boggs, J., concurring).

41. *Smith v. Board of School Comm'rs of Mobile County,* 827 F.2d 684, 689 (11th Cir. 1987).

42. *Tinker v. Des Moines Comm. School Dist.,* 393 U.S. 503 (1969); *Bethel School Dist. No. 403 v. Fraser,* 106 S.Ct. 3159 (1986); and *Hazelwood School Dist. v. Kuhlemeier,* 108 S.Ct. 562 (1988).

43. *Tinker,* 393 U.S. at 509 (1987).

44. Ibid., at 526 (Harlan, J., dissenting).

45. *Hazelwood,* 108 S.Ct. at 570–571.

46. *Grove v. Mead School Dist. No. 354,* 474 U.S. 826 (1985); and *Mozart v. Hawkins County Bd. of Educ.,* 108 S.Ct. 1029 (1988).

47. *Mozart,* 827 F.2d at 1086 (Boggs, J., concurring) (citations omitted).

48. See *Lemon v. Kurtzman,* 403 U.S. 602, 612–613 (1971).

49. *Grove,* 753 F.2d at 1534.

50. Ibid., at 1540–1541 (Canby, J., concurring).

51. *Schempp,* 374 U.S. at 225.

52. Ibid., at 300 (Brennan, J., concurring).

53. *Edwards v. Aguillard,* 107 S.Ct. 2573, 2583 (1987).

54. Ibid., at 2589–2590 (Powell, J., concurring).

Part 2

Reform and Improvement

HARRIET TYSON-BERNSTEIN
and ARTHUR WOODWARD

Chapter Six

Nineteenth Century Policies for Twenty-first Century Practice: The Textbook Reform Dilemma

---

Textbooks are a ubiquitous part of schooling in the United States. Visit any elementary or secondary school classroom and the chances are that textbooks will be a prominent, if not dominant, part of teaching and learning. Indeed, as much as 90 percent of instructional time is structured by some sort of instructional material.[1] The extensive use of textbooks was documented as early as 1931 by William C. Bagley.[2] More recent studies of textbook use include those by Allen H. Barton and David E. Wilder, Richard E. Gross, and Gail McCutcheon.[3]

The heavy use of and dependence on textbooks suggest a relationship between the quality of textbooks, effective teaching, and student achievement. Given the central role played by textbooks in schooling, one would expect that they would be a focus of debate about how to improve schooling. Unfortunately, since the publication of *A Nation at Risk* the focus of these reports and of school reform efforts has been on the poor performance of students, the low expectations of student achievement, and the school curricula.[4] They have not focused on the importance of textbook quality in the reform process.

As a result of these reports, curriculum requirements have been strengthened (more science and foreign language, for example), graduation requirements increased, and tests introduced to track how well students and schools are doing. Now that the first phase of school reform has passed, reformers are discovering that all is still not well with American elementary and secondary education. The focus of the reform debate has shifted to the teacher and the institution, or to use current jargon, to "school restructuring." However, still missing from the reform debate is any acknowledgment that in many cases the textbook defines curriculum and the scope, sequence, and method of instruction. Also missing is the understanding that textbooks represent a nexus between institutional change, teacher professionalism, and improved student success.

This essay explores the issue of school restructuring and teacher professionalism in terms of the nature and role of textbooks. It argues that states and localities have constructed a system of rules, regulations, and practices concerning textbook selection and use that were once sensible and functional but are now obsolete and impede reform. It is claimed that textbooks play a crucial role in schools, and that the failure by reform advocates to deal with textbook issues will prohibit systemic change.

BUREAUCRACY AND THE ADOPTION OF TEXTBOOKS

That schools are entangled in a web of bureaucratic structures and regulations is obvious to anyone involved in any aspect of schooling. In many respects these structures and regulations mirror the image of schools as factories as described by Ellwood P. Cubberly in 1916:

> Our schools are, in a sense, factories in which the raw products (children) are to be shaped and fashioned into products. . . . The specifications for manufacturing come from the demands of the twentieth-century civilization, and it is the business of the schools to build its pupils according to the specifications laid down. This demands good tools, specialized machinery, continuous measurement of production to see if it is according to specifications, the elimination of waste in manufacture, and a large variety in the output.[5]

Yet, a number of individuals and groups argue the school system itself must be radically restructured — in other words changed from the factory model to a new model of organization. For example, the Carnegie Forum notes:

> We do not believe the educational system needs repairing; we believe it must be rebuilt to match the drastic change needed in our economy if we are to prepare our children for productive lives in the 21st century.[6]

What is it then about textbooks and the bureaucratic structure for their adoption and use that supports the status quo and inhibits reform?

All states and school districts have, to one degree or another, a system of textbook bid specifications and selection processes that exemplify the bureaucratic, factory model described by Cubberly. Indeed, while states such as Texas, California, Georgia, and Florida are the largest and most prescriptive textbook adoption authorities, accounting for almost 15 percent of the textbook market nationwide, other states and districts mirror their textbook systems.[7] These systems and the professionals who staff and sustain them seem to subscribe to a common set of assumptions about textbooks and schooling.

First, it is assumed that a textbook or a textbook series can and inevitably does reflect the state's or school district's curriculum in terms of content, instruction, and sequence. Hence, if teachers closely follow the textbook and teachers' guide, *ergo* the curriculum is being implemented. This assumption, of course, devalues curriculum and makes curriculum building an empty exercise. Such an assumption is fallacious, as research has shown how poorly textbooks are analyzed and selected.[8] Other textbook selection is based on superficial criteria such as aesthetics and tables of contents, and more substantive selection criteria are often ignored or only superficially attended to.

Second, it is assumed, especially at the elementary school level and for reading and mathematics, that the textbook provides a foolproof means of ensuring that students are successfully taught. Detailed lesson plans, elaborate management systems, and the like have locked teachers into certain ways of teaching. While it may be claimed that such textbook systems are merely "safety nets" for the new or long-tenured incompetent teacher, the effect of school- or districtwide adoption is to force all teachers to follow their textbooks closely. In a sense, reliance on elaborate basal systems reduces all teachers to the status of neophytes and incompetents. Recent research shows that between the 1930s and 1980s reading instruction became progressively more skill-based and "managed" and that the "image" of the teacher as reflected in the reading series teachers' guides changed from that of a professional exercising judgment and discretion to that of a manager or implementer of a predetermined lesson or unit plan.[9]

Third, it is assumed that demands for accountability—that is, for evidence of student achievement and school success—can be met by textbooks closely correlated to standardized achievement tests. Especially at the elementary level and for reading and mathematics this means that the textbook content children learn must be compatible with machine readable standardized achievement tests. Textbooks and tests, therefore, tend to emphasize easily measured content and skills. The emphasis on accountability has even crept into subject areas that are by no stretch of the imagination skill-based. Arthur Woodward and Kathleen

C. Nagel found that recently published elementary social studies textbooks have a high level of so-called skill content but that many of these skills are "low" order or "phantom" skills.[10]

Fourth, it is assumed that adoption authorities can ensure the proper reading level of textbooks by matching a textbook's score on a readability formula with the average statewide scores of student reading attainment at each grade level. Consequently, publishers produce textbooks whose readability level corresponds to the grade they are intended for. The result is stilted prose, short sentences, unclear referent, and bad writing.[11] The use of readability formulas is often enshrined in state law or regulation; the uninformed use of such formulas, while enabling officials to claim that those textbooks selected clearly and objectively meet student needs, also results in textbooks that are harder for children to read.

Fifth, it is assumed that new textbooks are better than old textbooks. Many states and localities have either formal or informal policies that consider only those textbooks published within the previous three years. The rationale for such a policy is unclear, although its consequences are crystal clear. As Woodward and Nagel have shown in an analysis of changes in elementary textbooks from one copyright date to the next, publishers make cosmetic not substantive changes in their books.[12]

Sixth, it is assumed that a good textbook organizes its contents in modules that can be covered during the standard class period. Continuity is provided by end-of-unit summaries.

Seventh, it is assumed that central selection of textbooks is more efficient, resulting in the discounts or leverage to extract "free" materials from the publisher. This view prevails despite the fact that the cost of free materials is simply added to the price of a textbook.

TEXTBOOK SELECTION AND THE DEVELOPMENT OF NATIONAL PUBLISHING

Concomitant with the development of elaborate state and local control of textbook selection has been the growth of national publishers. These publishers produce what have been called national consensus textbooks.[13] These textbooks are as acceptable in Los Angeles as in New York, New Orleans, or Chicago. They reflect the implicit and explicit policies that undergird the bureaucratic model of education and at the same time manage to appeal, however superficially, to the actual users of these materials.

Textbook selection policies and perceptions of the role of textbooks have resulted in a demand for books that "cover" the curriculum with up-to-date content amenable to and congruent with standardized achievement tests. At the same time, the market demands textbooks that have as high a production and aesthetic quality as do coffee-table books. Not surprisingly, textbooks are expensive to produce, market, and distribute. The costs associated with publishing textbooks to these standards means that only companies able to compete and sell nationally have any hope of recouping their investment. Inexorably, this leads to the concentration of textbook publishing in the hands of a small number of companies and the development of national textbooks with sales to justify the investment in production and marketing.

Ironically, textbooks are produced by a few national publishing companies for numerous states and localities, all of whom consider their textbook guidelines and curriculum to be unique to them. This would lead one to expect that states and localities would find textbooks produced for a national market unacceptable. That there exists a consensus between publishers and the adoption authorities on the acceptable qualities of textbooks means that fundamental issues about curriculum, learning, and scholarship from the state and local perspective are ignored.

In order to demonstrate that states and localities are receiving different, better and more up-to-date textbooks, textbooks are revised frequently. This revision usually consists of elaborate changes in artwork with minimal changes in content and instructional design.[14] Thus, publishers can point to "new" materials, and adoption agencies can say they have chosen different and better textbooks. In other words, the philosophy of "new is better" obscures objective analyses of textbooks.

"New is better" as an overarching rationale for textbook selection can only work if selectors do not take time to review textbooks carefully. It has been found that those who serve on selection committees have little time to devote to the task and little training.[15]

There are, however, a number of issues, in addition to readability and copyright date, that are litmus tests for textbook adoption. One issue is the importance of breadth of coverage compared to depth of coverage. This, of course, makes sense given that textbooks, as national documents, must meet regional, state, and local needs. When adoption committees peruse textbooks they often rely on tables of contents and indexes to show which topics are covered and whether the selection agency's guidelines and curriculum are also fully covered. Unfortunately, the mere mention of a topic is enough to warrant an entry in a textbook table of contents or index. Thus, unless selection committees read the content in question they will be satisfied that their curriculum needs are well met.

Another litmus test is the issue of minorities and women in textbooks. This criterion is often codified as part of state and local regulation, and selection committees or their staff usually expend tremendous energy in making sure that textbooks include appropriate numbers of previously excluded or underrepresented groups. Ironically, these professionals probably spend more time analyzing textbooks for coverage of minorities and women than in examining them for the actual quality of content. Certainly, there is evidence that these groups have been excluded from textbooks both in terms of their intellectual and historical contributions and their representation in society (through illustrations, etc.).[16] Publishers now include numerous photographs, illustrations, biographies, and "sidebars" of blacks, Hispanics, and women in recent textbooks. There are, however, two problems. First, acceptance of a book can be based on its relatively high inclusion of pictures of women and minorities, regardless of whether the representation is good, poor, or indifferent. Second, by focusing only on certain groups, other groups may be slighted. As Woodward has noted, high school civics textbooks contain numerous photographs of minority groups and women, many of which do not have any instructional relationship to the text.[17] We must draw the conclusion that these photographs were responses to a perception by the publishers that selection committees would simply count the number of photographs of minorities.

A final litmus test is the aesthetics of textbooks. When textbooks begin to resemble coffee-table books, we can say two things: the textbook will be extremely attractive and visually engaging and will (almost) always be spare of text. Clearly, books should be attractive and illustrations can be very helpful in extending the reader's understanding of an event or concept. But, this said, the place of illustrations and other instructional features in the design of a textbook must be secondary to content as represented by the written word. For it is through the text that the content and concepts of a discipline are conveyed. Illustrations can take up as much as 30 percent of the content pages of a textbook, and many of these illustrations may be of doubtful instructional value.[18] Over several decades it appears the intent of illustrations and other aesthetic features has changed from reinforcing learning to enticing selection committees, teachers, and students.

There are two important points to be made about the use of aesthetics as a criterion for selecting textbooks. First, many educators assume that textbooks must somehow mimic video.[19] In other words, textbooks try to match the tenor, excitement, and vibrancy of the visual media to entice students to open a textbook and read it. That the purpose of textbooks is fundamentally different from other media should be obvious.

The second point is related to the use of aesthetics to indicate textbook quality. A stunning cover, attractive layout, and colorful illustrations are frequently used as proxies for quality. Publishers and authors tell of the importance of cover design and the placement of color photographs at the edge of pages.[20] It is as if publishers assume that professional educators must be enticed to consider a particular text, as if it were a box of breakfast cereal. It is an unfortunate reality that educators must be lured to open textbooks by the prettiness of their covers, rather than by their content.

The textbook selection system has also resulted in a number of other market realities for publishers. First, adoption authorities are apt to buy an entire K–6 or K–8 series and then to readopt it in the next round of textbook adoptions. Therefore, it is profitable for publishers to give away free materials such as textbooks for the first level or two and so entice teachers and selectors into a long-term relationship with the company's product.

Second, publishers have found that adoption committees generally prefer a textbook written by a team rather than by an individual author, even if that author is a national authority. Committees favor author teams composed of college professors and teachers who have held office in national professional organizations. It is not unusual for an elementary textbook series to list four authors and twenty or more consultants. In all likelihood, however, development houses or in-house editors actually write the text. The aim of publishers seems to be to combine name appeal with regional diversity and minority/majority representation. It is assumed that authors with regional links (whether or not they have made any contribution to the book) can somehow ensure a textbook is congruent with the values and approach of that region. Individuals from the big adoption states are usually authors or consultants and are an added plus in helping textbooks receive a favorable adoption committee vote.

Third, administrators and teachers in decision-making roles can be encouraged to sway a textbook adoption toward a company's product line if they are invited to free dinners, offered an attractive freebie package, given small gifts, paid stipends for conducting a field test, employed as consultants, and sent to their national conventions at company expense.

The combined effects of the state adoption system—absence of national agreement about what should be taught, consolidation of state authority over curriculum and testing, use of textbooks and standardized achievement tests to demonstrate school success, and the assumption that teachers need extensive lesson plans and so forth make textbooks what they are. Given that the market for textbooks is determined by adoption agencies and the perceived preferences of teachers, it is not surprising that textbooks are not written for students or for learning.

There are, of course, well-designed textbooks available. These are usually written by single authors who have reasonable control over the editorial treatment of their manuscripts. Usually these books have small, specific markets and do not attempt to emulate the production quality of mass-market textbooks.[21] Few of these exceptional books are among the best-sellers because they generally fail to pass muster on the present set of formal and informal adoption criteria. There are also tradebooks that treat a subject in depth and off-beat offerings from small publishers who do not compete in the adoption state markets. But, few teachers have access to these alternative materials; in most cases they are either officially prohibited from buying them or lack the funds to do so.

TEXTBOOKS AND TEACHER PROFESSIONALISM

If one accepts that an important relationship exists between school improvement, teacher professionalism, and textbook quality, it follows that the present status quo must be changed. In our view teacher empowerment represents the most promising avenue to pursue in terms of changing market demand. This empowerment would not merely transfer power from one group of unknowing educators to another, but would build the knowledge base necessary to professionalize the selection of materials and force into being a wider variety of materials. These developments would help liberate teachers and their students from the stultifying effects of textbooks at present.

Suddenly giving teachers more authority over textbook selection would be a futile and probably counterproductive move. Many teachers —perhaps a majority if one judges by the market-sensitive behavior of publishers—prefer the kind of textbooks they currently have. Teachers have been conditioned both by their overseers and by the publishers to want glitz and the cookbook style of teaching encouraged by the teacher's manual. While many teachers observe that their students cannot or will not read their textbooks, few conclude that the fault lies with the texts themselves. Rather, television, broken homes, poverty, and the failures of prior teachers are more often cited as culprits. In fact, attitudes about the importance of television and so forth often influence textbook preferences. It is said that textbooks must be more attractive and colorful, the reading level easier, and the content more "relevant."[22]

Teachers, like their superiors, only dimly perceive the cause and effect relationship between state textbook bid specifications and trivial texts, stories not worth reading, or problems not worth solving. A minority of teachers and administrators understand the relationship between mandated readability formulas and monotonous, confusing prose. Both are apt to blame special interest groups and politicians for the curious bulges and snippets in textbooks, even though the two have no direct influence over textbook adoption.

True professionalization of teaching, the concomitant right of teachers to select books that inspire their students and the prerequisite knowledge will be a long time coming. As a first step, teachers, through their subject matter organizations, unions, and other groups, need to set up subject-specific training institutes that empower them to judge the learnability (as distinct from readability) of text materials, to share their experiences with existing books, and to learn to compensate for textbooks' evasions and weaknesses.

Teacher organizations and groups need to engender in their members a critical attitude toward the current textbook system. The profession's textbook reform agenda will have to be far more sophisticated, subject-based, and professional than it has been in the recent past. Teacher unions in many areas have successfully negotiated all-teacher-voting on textbooks, a scheme that has actually made textbook selection even more trivial than it was before. For when everyone is responsible, no one is responsible. The evidence suggests that this pseudodemocratic solution puts an even higher premium on textbook cosmetics and pedagogical faddism than the committee approach it replaced.

To encourage change, school boards should be urged to establish knowledge-based criteria for the selection of textbook adoption panels, provide for teacher participation in adoption criteria, organize substantive training for selectors, pay selectors for the time spent actually reading the books, and encourage open discussion among selectors about the merits of various offerings. If school boards are unwilling to pursue these initiatives, then unions should lobby for them.

Teacher organizations should create mechanisms for teachers to share information on books in use and to communicate with publishers about a textbook's strengths and weaknesses for various types of students. (We discount the market research conducted by publishers because it reinforces the status quo.) If there are no intellectually defensible, uncontaminated field trials being conducted to determine the worth of books under consideration, then the profession should lobby for the development of such field trials. At the same time, disciplinary organizations of college and public school teachers need to establish centers that disseminate reliable, candid, and fine-grained information about current mainstream textbooks, nonconforming textbooks, trade books, software, and equipment that might be useful to students' learning.

Finally, teacher organizations need to establish professional standards for textbook selection and a code of ethics concerning dealings with textbook publishers—even if their administrative and political superiors fail to do so.

CONCLUSION

In our view, school restructuring will require the dismantling of the state textbook adoption system. Even states that appear to be asking for more coherent, better focused, more practical textbooks (as California is now doing) are still acting on assumptions that are inherently incompatible with the ideals of the restructuring movement. Even at its best, statewide adoption is still a top-down process on the old, authoritarian, industrial model. It presumes a number of things: that teachers cannot be trusted to decide which books are best for their own classes; that a small number of people can generate appropriate textbook criteria for an endless variety of children, teachers, and teaching situations; that there will be money and time enough to ensure that statewide committees of selectors fully understand the textbook selection criteria and have the time to apply them thoughtfully; that the state will have the money to train teachers in the appropriate use of new approaches embedded in the books called forth by the state; and finally, it also presumes that an enlightened state process can insulate textbook adoption from political or commercial pressures.

One or more of these presumptions did not hold fast in California's three recent attempts to improve quality through revised curriculum frameworks and stern dealings with publishers: the life science adoption of 1986,[23] the mathematics adoption of 1987,[24] or the reading adoption of 1988.[25] The results have not lived up to the state's self-congratulatory press releases.[26] Even if California's process catches up with its vision over time, the fact remains that even the best state textbook adoption system summons books geared to the mythical average student, to determinations of aggregate reading abilities, to Carnegie units, to bell and bus schedules, and to the number of days in the legislated school year.

At its worst, the statewide adoption system has become a national embarrassment. The Texas State Textbook Depository—a for-profit company that distributed textbooks adopted by Texas to school districts—recently faced financial collapse because of misappropriated funds.[27] In North Carolina, state education agency officials are reported to have pressed textbook publishers to pay for some activities at the July 1988 leadership conference of school district administrators, including an ice cream bar, motor speedway rides and lunch for children of state and local administrators, and cocktail paties for the adults.[28] The concentration of economic power at the state level appears to tempt into being the very abuses the state adoption sytem was intended to eliminate at the turn of the century, when most state textbook adoption codes were enacted. Although these instances of major and minor corruption may not contaminate particular adoption decisions, they do create a climate that discourages institutional criticism of either the adoption system or the textbooks it produces.

In any statewide adoption system, officials far from the classroom must pretend they know the best sequence of learning tasks, when in fact nobody has more than hunches based on tradition and subjective experience. Officials must pretend to know what pedagogy is best, although the evidence suggests that we know very little about what is best, especially for those who are poor, minority, or recent immigrants, not to mention those with mechanical, political, musical, or artistic gifts. State adoption presumes that there is one best way and that each separate state knows what it is. The system will not work in an era that cries out for a confession of ignorance, for humble, organized experimentation at the school site by those who see the children day by day, and for sensitive choices by reflective teachers.

The quality of teachers' preparation, the standards for their admission to the profession, their power to define professional growth and to gain authority commensurate with their awesome responsibility are central factors in the realization of restructuring. Yet, if teachers are obliged to give their students books designed for another era, we will almost inevitably fail the very children on whom our civil and economic future depends.

NOTES

1. Educational Products Exchange (EPEI) Institute. *Report on a National Study of the Nature and the Quality of Instructional Materials Most Used by Teachers and Learners* Report 76 (New York: EPEI Institute, 1977).

2. William C. Bagley, "The Textbook and Methods of Instruction," in *The Textbook in American Education,* The Thirtieth Yearbook of the National Society for the Study of Education, ed. Guy M. Whipple (Bloomington, Ill.: Public School Publishing Company, 1931).

3. Allen H. Barton and David E. Wilder, "Research and Practice in the Teaching of Reading: A Progress Report," in *Innovation in Education,* ed. Matthew B. Miles (New York: Teachers College Press, 1966); Richard E. Gross,

"American History Teachers Look at the Book," *Phi Delta Kappan* 33 (January 1952): 290 – 291; Gail McCutcheon, "How Do Elementary School Teachers Plan?" *The Elementary School Journal* 81 (September 1980): 4–23.

4. National Commission on Excellence in Education, *A Nation at Risk* (Washington D.C.: U.S. G.P.O., 1983).

5. Ellwood P. Cubberly, *Public School Administration* (Boston: Houghton Mifflin, 1916), p. 338.

6. Task Force on Teaching as a Profession, *A Nation Prepared: Teachers for the 21st Century* (Washington D.C.: Carnegie Forum on Education and the Economy, 1986); see also David T. Kearns and Dennis P. Doyle, *Winning the Brain Race: A Bold Plan to Make Our Schools Competitive* (San Francisco: Institute for Contemporary Studies, 1988); Melissa A. Berman, ed., *Restructuring Education: Highlights of a Conference* (New York: The College Board, 1987); and Michael Cohen, *Restructuring the Education System: Agenda for the 1990s* (Washington D.C.: National Governors Association, 1988).

7. Association of American Publishers industry statistics, 1982, New York.

8. Robert Rothman, "California Panel Urges State Board to Pick Reading Textbooks with 'Real Literature'," *Education Week*, September 14, 1988, pp. 1, 12.

9. Arthur Woodward, "Taking Teaching out of Teaching and Reading out of Learning to Read: A Historical Study of Teacher's Guides, 1920 – 1980," *Book Research Quarterly* 2 (Spring 1986): 53 – 73; Arthur Woodward, "Overprogrammed Materials: Taking the Teacher out of Teaching," *American Educator* 10 (Spring 1986): 26–31.

10. Kathleen Carter Nagel and Arthur Woodward, "Overskilling Social Studies" (unpublished paper, University of Rochester, 1988).

11. Bonnie B. Armbruster, Jean H. Osborn, and Alice L. Davison, "Readability Formulas May Be Dangerous to Your Textbooks," *Educational Leadership* 42 (April 1985): 18 – 20; Alice L. Davison and Robert N. Kantor, "On the Failure of Readability Formulas to Define Readable Texts: A Case Study from Adaptations," *Reading Research Quarterly* 2 (Spring 1982): 187–209.

12. Arthur Woodward and Kathleen Carter Nagel, "Old Wine in New Bottles: An Analysis of Changes in Elementary Social Studies Textbooks from New to Old Edition," *Book Research Quarterly* 3 (Winter 1987–88): 22–33.

13. Arthur Woodward and David L. Elliott, "Textbooks: Issues of Content, Consensus, and Controversy," in *Textbooks and Schooling in the United States,* The Eighty-ninth Yearbook of the National Society for the Study of Education, ed. David L. Elliott and Arthur Woodward (Chicago: University of Chicago, in press).

14. Ronald B. Edgerton, "Odyssey of a Book: How a Social Studies Text Comes Into Being," *Social Education* 33 (March 1969): 279–286; Eric Broudy, "The Trouble with Textbooks," *Teachers College Record* 77 (September 1975): 13–14; Henry W. Bragdon, "Ninth Edition: Adventures with a Textbook," *Independent School* 37 (February 1978): 37–41.

15. Roger Farr, Michael A. Tulley, and Deborah A. Powell, "The Evaluation and Selection of Basal Readers," *The Elementary School Journal* 87 (January 1987): 267–281; Deborah A. Powell, "Selection of Reading Textbooks at the District Level: Is This a Rational Process?" *Book Research Quarterly* 1 (Fall 1985): 23–35.

16. Jesus Garcia and D. E. Tanner, "The Portrayal of Black Americans in U.S. History Books," *The Social Studies* 76 (September/October 1985): 200–204; Carol Hahn and G. Blankenship, "Women and Economics Textbooks," *Theory and Research in Social Education* 11 (Fall 1983): 67–76.

17. Arthur Woodward, "Stress on Visuals Weakens Texts," *Education Week,* March 9, 1988, pp. 19–20.

18. Arthur Woodward, "When More Means Less," (unpublished paper, University of Rochester, 1987); Mary Ann Evans, Catherine Watson, and Dale M. Willows, "A Naturalistic Inquiry into Illustrations in Instructional Textbooks," in *The Psychology of Illustration, Vol. 2 Instructional Issues,* ed. Harvey A. Houghton and Dale M. Willows (New York: Springer-Verlag, 1987).

19. Woodward, "Stress on Visuals Weakens Texts."

20. Mauck Brammer, "Textbook Publishing" in *What Happens in Textbook Publishing,* ed. C. C. Grannis, (New York: Columbia University Press, 1967), pp. 320–349; Michael Bowler, "The Making of a Textbook," *Learning* 6 (March 1978): 38–43.

21. Keith Henderson, "A Maverick Publishing House that Bucks the Big Business Trend," *The Christian Science Monitor,* October 25, 1985, p. B8.

22. Woodward, "Stress on Visuals Weakens Texts."

23. William Bennetta, "Meeting the Miracle Mongers, Part 2," *California Science Teacher's Journal* 16 (1988): 4.

24. M. Blouke Carus, "California and Textbook Reform: Too Little Too Late, Too Much Too Soon" (paper presented at the Annual Meeting of AERA, Washington D.C., April 1987); Arthur Woodward, "On Teaching and Textbook Publishing: Political Issues Obscure Questions of Pedagogy," *Education Week,* January 21, 1987, pp. 22, 28.

25. Jean Osborn, Testimony before the Curriculum Development and Supplemental Materials Commission, Sacramento, Calif., 21 July 1988.

26. ''No More Lo-Cal Literature for California,'' news release, California State Department of Education, August 1, 1988.

27. Robert Rothman, ''Publishers Probe Text Warehouses after Scandals,'' *Education Week,* October 12, 1988, pp. 1, 15.

28. William Graves, ''Publishers Curry Favor with North Carolina Education Officials,'' *The New Observer* (Raleigh, N.C.), June 19, 1988.

BILL HONIG

Chapter Seven

California's Experience with Textbook Improvement

The push for stronger curriculum standards and quality textbooks and instructional materials is one of the most critical challenges facing California's sweeping educational reform movement. Because too many textbooks are not well written and fall short of the quality we want for our students, our state has taken a strong stand on providing textbooks that reflect curriculum integrity.

Publishers will produce better books when their customers insist on higher standards. California is one of twenty-two states that adopt kindergarten through eighth grade textbooks on a statewide basis. Districts then select textbooks from the approved list that match their students' needs. As a result, California and other large adoption states, such as Texas and Florida, have considerable impact on textbooks nationally. We are using our 11 percent share of the market as a force for textbook reform.

Our leadership role has resulted in some giant steps forward in California to improve the content of instructional materials, and other states are following our lead. Yet much remains to be done in the fight for better instructional materials. This essay will describe the textbook market, California's textbook adoption process, the curriculum frameworks upon which we are basing our decisions about textbooks, and what lies ahead.

THE TEXTBOOK MARKET

Research indicates that as much as 90 percent of classroom instructional time is structured by instructional materials, especially textbooks.[1] Clearly, then, these books play an important role in developing the skills, knowledge, and understanding that will help students achieve both personal and professional success.

The textbook industry is faced with many competing forces, including school administrators, scholars, teachers, and interest groups, striving to influence textbook content. Unfortunately, many publishers, driven by their need to sell books to as many schools as possible, try to satisfy all the competing forces and offend none of them. By shunning controversy publishers have all too often created boring texts.

In addition, the writing in too many books is of poor quality, with vague, dull prose, and reading becomes onerous rather than rewarding. In fact, many textbooks are not written by professional writers but by editors who assemble collections written by groups of 20 to 200 people. The outcome is books that lack a coherent voice.

Textbook writers also rely too frequently on readability formulas—mathematical equations based on vocabulary and sentence length. Theoretically, these formulas make books easier for children to read. The actual result, however, is meaningless prose that often discourages students from reading.

Furthermore, many textbooks cover topics superficially. Not enough detail is provided to make the subjects interesting or understandable. The books do not look beneath the surface, nor do they explain such things as the motivation, consequences, and relevance of what is being presented. We have been trying to correct these weaknesses in instructional materials through our textbook reform efforts in California.

TEXTBOOK ADOPTION PROCESS

The textbook adoption process is the primary avenue for providing quality instructional materials to California students. The lengthy, complex process has three major levels of review: social content, educational content, and public comment.

Social Content Review

California's guidelines for textbook adoption, contained in *Standards for Evaluation of Instructional Materials with Respect to Social Content,* reflect the state's legal and policy requirements for a wide range of social concerns, including the appropriate depiction of male/female roles, ethnic and cultural groups, older persons, religion, and dangerous substances and the avoidance of brand names and corporate logos.[2] These standards are intended to help dispel erroneous stereotypes by emphasizing people in diverse and positive roles. The social content review panels are balanced in terms of age, gender, and ethnicity and an attempt is made to include disabled individuals.

Educational Content Review

The next level of review is an examination of the materials' educational content. The approved materials must contain quality, up-to-date curriculum. This content review is based on the best consensus among curriculum experts of what should be taught in the particular subject area.

The Instructional Materials Evaluation Panel (IMEP), which makes this content review, is comprised of teachers and other curriculum personnel who have particular subject matter expertise. The composition of the panels reflects the state's ethnic, gender, and geographic diversity.

Evaluation of instructional materials for factual and technical accuracy, educational value and quality is accomplished in accordance with the state's curriculum framework and evaluation instruments. The evaluation instruments are developed by the Curriculum Development and Supplemental Materials Commission and approved by the State Board of Education. The curriculum commission is comprised of teachers, administrators, college and university personnel, and curriculum experts.

The IMEP members receive extensive training to evaluate materials. Each IMEP member first reviews the materials independently; panel members then meet to review the materials together. Panels rate and either recommend or reject the materials. Before the IMEP members finalize their recommendations, publishers of the materials being evaluated can make presentations.

Public Participation

Woven throughout the review process are opportunities for the public to comment on the materials under consideration. These materials are available for review at thirty Instructional Materials Display Centers throughout California.

The IMEP findings are reported to the curriculum commission, which recommends materials to the State Board of Education for adoption. The commission conducts public hearings as part of the information-gathering process.

Using all the data collected, the commission makes recommendations to the State Board of Education. The state board also conducts a public hearing and then decides on materials that should be adopted for use in California schools.

District Selection

Selecting from the state board's approved materials, school districts conduct their own adoption process to choose the materials that match their needs. The state annually apportions Instructional Materials Funds (IMF) to districts to purchase instructional materials. IMF is allocated to districts for each student in kindergarten through grade eight, based on average daily attendance. In 1988, $27.63 per pupil average daily attendance — $88.5 million in total — was allocated for K–8 materials. IMF totaling $24 million is also apportioned to districts for students in grades 9–12, but there is no state textbook adoption at this level.

Districts have several options for obtaining instructional materials with IMF allocations for kindergarten through grade eight:

- At least 80 percent of IMF must be spent on state adopted materials. Because of this allocation of funds, textbook publishers recognize that it is extremely important for their books to appear on the list of adopted materials.
- Up to 15 percent of IMF may be spent on materials that have passed state social content review and on library/trade books.
- Up to 5 percent may be spent on any instructional materials, as well as tests and in-service training.
- Districts may petition the state board to spend more than 20 percent on basic materials that are not state adopted but have passed social content review.

CALIFORNIA'S CURRICULUM FRAMEWORKS

California issues its standards for publishers through curriculum frameworks, which represent a consensus of curriculum development and instructional leaders. Besides being a resource in the selection and evaluation of instructional materials, the frameworks guide the development of instructional programs, curriculum planning, and staff development.

In California, curriculum frameworks are produced on a seven-year cycle, with a framework completed two years before textbook adoption in that subject. The frameworks are produced by a committee under the direction of the Curriculum Development and Supplemental Materials Commission. The framework may take over a year to draft, followed by extensive field review and public comment before adoption by the State Board of Education.

Science

In the last several years, California's curriculum frameworks have served educators well by making a powerful statement on what should be taught. In 1984 the California Board of Education issued a *Science Framework Addendum,* which made the following assertions:

- Certain science concepts and skills are basic to scientific literacy —to a rational understanding of ourselves and our surroundings. These concepts and skills need to be addressed appropriately at several developmental stages. The development of attitudes and values, rational thinking processes, and manipulative and communicative skills should take place in close association with the development of concepts.
- Science processes (observing, communicating, comparing, organizing, relating, inferring, and applying) are woven through content and instruction, so that the teacher covers both the what and how of science.
- In covering the content and processes of science, teachers relate this information to technological applications and ethical issues that confront students.
- Science should be taught as an integrated subject; integrated among the science disciplines (earth, life, and physical sciences) and integrated with other subject areas, especially mathematics, the arts, and language skills.[3]

The forty-five evaluators who reviewed the science materials submitted for adoption in 1985 found that the seventh and eighth grade science textbooks fell short of the framework in three areas: the discussion of evolution, human reproduction, and ethical issues. The curriculum commission accepted the evaluators' findings and recommended that the State Board of Education ask the publishers to revise their books or they would not be adopted. Although controversial, California's message to publishers was clear: our guidelines have meaning, and we expect our textbooks to reflect these guidelines.

Mathematics

In September 1987, the State Board of Education rejected all fourteen K–8 mathematics textbooks series submitted for adoption. The *Mathematics Framework for California Public Schools: Kindergarten through Grade Twelve* stated that children should not just learn procedures by rote without also learning how to apply these procedures to new or perplexing problem-solving situations. Once again, the books did not meet the framework's guidelines. Textbook publishers were asked to revise their texts in three areas:

- *understanding* — The math program's focus should be on developing student understanding of concepts and skills, not on "apparent mastery."
- *problem solving* — The program should give students many opportunities to be actively involved in applying their mathematical knowledge, skills, and experience to problem-solving situations that are new or perplexing.
- *number sense* — Instead of emphasizing computational facility, with students spending most of their time practicing algorithms with paper and pencil, the program should incorporate various experiences to help students understand numbers.[4]

English-Language Arts

California's English-language arts curriculum has recently undergone similar scrutiny. Recent research, such as *Becoming a Nation of Readers* from the National Commission on Reading, has advocated changing the English-language arts curriculum.[5] The 1986 *English-Language Arts Framework for California Public Schools: Kindergarten through Grade Twelve* reflects the best of this research.[6]

California's English-language arts instructional philosophy is based on the idea that most children initially come to school with a remarkable ability to speak and understand their native tongue, despite the lack of formal schooling. Their school program should offer a similar learning environment, and opportunities for students to engage in listening and speaking should abound. Students should have meaningful language experiences before they learn phonics, word attack skills, vocabulary, and the conventions of language, important as these details may be. Furthermore, these details, when taught, should be in context and not in isolation.

Instead of reading pointless prose, students must have the opportunity to read great classics. Literature provides us with the best in human character and the most articulate in human speech.

According to Lynne Cheney, Chair of the National Endowment for the Humanities, "In the basal readers most widely used now, 10 percent or less of the content is classic children's literature. The emphasis in current readers is overwhelmingly on contemporary writing, generally by writers whose names are unknown outside the textbook industry. They produce a variety of materials, mostly aimed at developing skills, everything from how to recognize cause and effect to how to make grocery lists and use the telephone book."[7]

Schools have numerous options and tremendous flexibility in implementing a literature-based, integrated program. By using a blend of the best of technology, textbooks, and trade books, an effective English-language arts program can be available for all students. As we move away from the basal and skill-centered approach toward this literature-based approach, new vistas are opened for students.

California's *English-Language Arts Framework* calls for:

- a literature-based program that encourages reading and exposes all students, including those whose primary language is not English, to significant literary works. Students should read literature that encompasses the passion, drama, and emotions of life's richest experiences.
- instructional programs that emphasize integrating listening, speaking, reading, and writing and the teaching of language skills in meaningful contexts.
- a systematic kindergarten through grade twelve developmental language arts program articulated and implemented at all grade levels.
- a writing program that includes attention to the various stages of the writing process — from prewriting through postwriting and from fluency and content through form and correctness.
- an assessment program encompassing the English-language arts program's goals and providing alternative strategies and forms of testing.

Such a program will provide our students with (1) a solid body of knowledge derived from a common cultural heritage; (2) experience in confronting important human issues and conflicts; (3) a strong sense of personal, social, and aesthetic values; and (4) the necessary language and thinking skills.

Publishers made progress toward these goals during California's 1988 English-language arts textbook adoption. The State Board of Education adopted English-language arts materials that reflect some of the framework's criteria. The adopted series contain classical and contemporary works representing a range of literature, including well-known works, and authors such as Carl Sandburg, James Thurber, Aesop, John Steinbeck, Leo Tolstoy, and Isaac Asimov. The literature in some of the texts stresses ethics and values to provide students with moral and civic guidelines. Well-known Bible stories are included in the classic literature series.

However, the submitted materials still contain far too many adaptations and abridgments to literature. Hundreds of selections cover only fragments of language, reinforce ineffective past practices, and rob students of valuable time to engage in meaningful listening, speaking, reading, and writing activities. These books will have to carry "warning labels" indicating that adaptations are included. In addition, none of the spelling programs were adopted because they failed to teach spelling in a reading and writing context.

Nonetheless, when the new English-language arts materials begin appearing in classrooms in the fall of 1989, they will represent a significant improvement over previous textbooks.

History–Social Science

Another subject area going through extensive reform both nationally and in California is history–social science. After examining the results of the first national assessment of history and literature, Diane Ravitch and Chester Finn concluded in *What Do Our 17-Year-Olds Know?* that American seventeen-year-olds and future generations may be gravely handicapped by their ignorance of important knowledge as they enter adulthood, citizenship, and parenthood.[8] The authors' proposals for improving history instruction correlate with proposals in California's 1987 *History – Social Science Framework for California Public Schools: Kindergarten through Grade Twelve*. The framework presents a history-based curriculum that integrates geography, the humanities, and other social sciences at every level of instruction.

The twenty-three educators and professionals who developed this landmark framework provide an introduction to the document that captures its significance:

> As educators in the field of history–social science, we want our students to perceive the complexity of social, economic, and political problems . . . to have the ability to differentiate between what is important and what is unimportant . . . to know their rights and responsibilities as American citizens . . . to understand the meaning of the Constitution as a social contract defining our democratic government and guaranteeing our individual rights. We want them to respect the right of others to differ with them . . . to understand the value, the importance, and the fragility of democratic institutions . . . to realize that only a small fraction of the world's population (now or in the past) has been fortunate enough to live under a democratic form of government, and we want them to understand the conditions that encourage democracy to prosper. We want them to develop a keen sense of ethics and citizenship . . . to care deeply about the quality of life in their community, their nation, and their world.[9]

The framework's goals fall into three broad categories: "knowledge and cultural understanding," incorporating learnings from history and the other humanities, geography, and the social sciences; "democratic understanding and civic values," incorporating an understanding of our national identity, constitutional heritage, civic values, and rights and responsibilities; and "skills attainment and social participation," including basic study skills that are essential for effective citizenship. These goals are all related and interact within this curriculum.

The framework's singificant features that will alert publishers that we are looking for better quality textbooks include:

- a history-centered curriculum presented in its geographic setting that stresses the importance of time and place and when and where events occurred.
- an integrated approach covering the political, economic, and social aspects of a given society. The curriculum stresses the important role of literature; it connects with other subjects, such as language arts, science, and the visual and performing arts.
- an emphasis on history as a story well-told. Instruction provides vivid examples of the struggles and triumphs of men, women, boys, and girls. It provides a compelling narrative as a source of motivation for studying history.
- enrichment of curriculum at primary grades. The curriculum develops in children a repertoire of knowledge about significant individuals and events as they read, hear, and discuss biographies, myths, fairy tales, and historical events from different cultures and time periods.
- increased time for an in-depth study of American and world history.
- a multicultural perspective that reflects the experiences of men and women of various racial, religious, and ethnic groups. Students understand that the national identity, heritage, and creed of the United States is pluralistic.
- a major focus on ethical literacy. Students are encouraged to reflect on the individual responsibility and behavior that create a good society.
- civic and democratic values with basic concepts such as justice, equality, and liberty emphasized at each grade level. In addition, the fundamental principles embodied in the U.S. Constitution and Bill of Rights are emphasized.
- explanation of the major religions and ethical traditions throughout history. Religion's role in this country's founding is also explained.

What led to this dramatic change in the way history is to be presented was a consensus voiced around the nation by scholars such as Gilbert Sewall, co-director of the Educational Excellence Network, Teachers College, Columbia University. He found history textbooks lacking in what he called, "incandescent acts of charity and wisdom, triumphs of technology and political genius, the exploits of heroes and villains."

Sewall went on to note:

> The writing grows discursive, wandering from subject to subject, piling event upon event. As prose becomes flat and voiceless, the content of textbooks, becomes encyclopedic, serving mainly as reference material. Names and episodes dart past the reader as swiftly and memorably as telephone poles from the window of a fast moving train. Figure and event make the scene. But individuals in textbooks are curiously disembodied, without flair, personality, or real distinction. No one receives much credit for achievements. No controversy, no triumph, no debacle is explored in much depth. Heroes are absent, except when textbooks are trying to score points with advocacy groups.[10]

WHAT LIES AHEAD

Because of the impact California often makes across the nation, we are encouraging other states to examine the direction we propose for each content area. Through national symposiums and conferences, we are establishing an information exchange with other states. As more states reach a consensus on curriculum content, publishers will have a larger market for developing creative new materials.

Finally, exciting opportunities exist for furthering instructional goals in virtually all curriculum areas by using computer and video technologies. The microcomputer, video cassette recorder, and computer and video programs have technological advantages and the potential to make learning more fun. By engaging students and increasing their attentiveness, technology can serve as a powerful instructional tool.

However, to realize this potential fully, we must ensure that technology supports the regular curriculum and does not become an end in itself. Publishers can help by providing opportunities for using technology that is integral to their instructional materials and tailored to the curriculum frameworks.

Until now, if states had different requirements on content, publishers would concentrate on pleasing one state. With the latest technology, publishers in the future can easily revise materials to tailor them specifically to local and state needs. For example, each state's history books could emphasize that state's history, with publishers using computer technology to make the adaptations in their "designer texts." The new technologies also allow publishers to produce up-to-date textbooks, as they can easily replace outdated information.

CONCLUSION

In all subject areas, California has issued criteria for publishers that reflect the best advice of the nation's top experts. Our expectations are clear. We want content-driven books that are engaging; that tell stories; that make key points but also go into depth when necessary; that have a coherent point of view; and that open up a field of thought and encourage further, independent reading.

Change will not occur overnight. It takes four or five years, from conception through writing, editing, field testing, and publishing, to prepare a new textbook for market. Our task is not an easy one; yet it is one of the most crucial that we face as educators. We must not veer from our course. We have an exciting opportunity to guide the direction of classroom instruction into the twenty-first century. When textbook buyers talk, textbook publishers listen and the message they are hearing from California is focused on excellence.

NOTES

1. Arthur Woodward, "Beyond Textbooks in Elementary Social Studies," *Social Education* 50 (January 1986): 51.

2. *Standards for Evaluation of Instructional Materials with Respect to Social Content* (Sacramento: California State Department of Education, 1986).

3. *Science Framework Addendum for California Public Schools: Kindergarten and Grades One through Twelve* (Sacramento: California State Department of Education, 1984).

4. *Mathematics Framework for California Public Schools: Kindergarten through Grade Twelve* (Sacramento: California State Department of Education, 1985).

5. Richard Anderson et al., *Becoming a Nation of Readers: The Report of the Commission on Reading* (Champaign: University of Illinois, 1985).

6. *English-Language Arts Framework for California Public Schools: Kindergarten through Grade Twelve* (Sacramento: California State Department of Education, 1987).

7. Lynne V. Cheney, *American Memory: A Report on the Humanities in the Nation's Public Schools* (Washington, D.C.: National Endowment for the Humanities, 1987), p. 15.

8. Chester E. Finn, Jr., and Diane Ravitch, *What Do Our 17-Year-Olds Know? A Report on the First National Assessment of History and Literature* (New York: Harper and Row, 1987).

9. *History–Social Science Framework for California Public Schools: Kindergarten through Grade Twelve* (Sacramento: California State Department of Education, 1987), p. 2.

10. Gilbert Sewall, ''American History Textbooks: Where Do We Go from Here?'' *Phi Delta Kappan* 69 (April 1988): 553.

J. DAN MARSHALL

Chapter Eight

State-Level Textbook Selection Reform: Toward the Recognition of Fundamental Control

---

INTRODUCTION

"What knowledge is of most worth?" is the classic question of curriculum workers. If Finn is correct, this question is soon to be highlighted as national interest swings toward a concern for schooling's intellectual content.[1] Following "anxiety about student achievement" and "worry about the caliber of [the] educational workforce," concern about content will be the third swell in our nation's current educational reform movement.

Textbook quality is sure to be the bandwagon upon which reformers will leap should Finn's predicted "third wave" actually crest. This focus is predictable based upon the interest in and scholarly study of the textbook's role in American schooling that has enjoyed sustained growth throughout much of this century. The growing fervor within the school book protest movement[2] as well as recent critiques related to students' lack of general knowledge and cultural literacy[3] foreshadow the cresting of this third wave. We can also predict that, should the nation decide to engage in this "cultural war" on the intellectual content of school books,

---

An earlier version of this essay appeared in the *Capstone Journal of Education*, 8, no. 2 (1988).

its army of national reformers will soon find themselves confronting an ominous foe, which Tyson-Bernstein and Woodward aptly dub "The Great Textbook Machine."[4]

Tyson-Bernstein and Woodward provide would-be reformers with a historical overview of their prospective foe, describing this machine as "maddeningly complex" and "jerry-built," meshing the gears of publishing houses, elected state and local bodies, members of the public school establishment, and the scholarly community as it churns out textbooks for use in our schools. And, like so many others who have investigated the questions surrounding textbook quality, they recognize the process of textbook selection as the machine's centripetal force.

Importance of Adoption States

Most often in public schools, textbooks are chosen by committees of teachers and subject specialists. In recent years, these committees have also included administrators and community members. Textbook committees operate at the building and district levels on the premise that students' needs are best known and most likely to be accommodated by local/district textbook selectors. Although sound in theory, perhaps, this premise offers little hope for those who would improve the quality of textbooks, for textbooks are a commodity and their content is most directly affected by market forces. With all due respect to local/district textbook selectors, reformers would be advised to look instead at textbook selection and adoption practices within our large "adoption states"—where the real money is spent. As Apple explains:

> Publishers themselves, simply because of good business practice, must by necessity aim their text publishing practices toward those states with such state adoption policies. The simple fact of getting one's volume on such a list can make all the difference for a text's profitability. Thus, for instance, sales in California and Texas can account for over 20 percent of the total sales in any particular book—a considerable percentage in the highly competitive world of elementary and secondary school book publishing and selling. Because of this, the writing, editing, promotion, and general orientation and strategy of such production is quite often aimed toward guaranteeing a place on the list of state-approved material.[5]

Some twenty-two states screen and select textbooks for use in their schools. Although no two states conduct this process in a like fashion, their intentions are clear: choosing books at the state level provides curriculum uniformity, quality textbooks, and cost controls.[6] Publishers admit that such practices exert enormous influence over their wares, and they pay special heed to "super states" like California, Texas, North Carolina, and Florida.[7] As third wave reform draws near reformers must look directly at textbook selection as it occurs in these adoption states.

Importance of Texas

Texas represents "the largest instructional materials market in the United States with a school population exceeding 3 million students."[8] Should reformers earmark the Texas system as fertile ground for change, they would first do well to understand how the state's textbook selection and adoption system functions.

Briefly, the Texas system for procuring textbooks contains three distinct phases.[9] In the first phase, a group of fifteen active Texas educators, the majority of whom are classroom teachers, receives a one-time appointment to the State Textbook Committee (STC). This committee is charged with reviewing all books submitted by publishers in each of the subject areas under consideration. Since there is a large number of subject areas and dozens of books in each, STC members enlist the aid of advisers with competence in each subject area. These committee members and their advisory groups spend the summer meeting with publishers[10] and reviewing and evaluating books. In September (typically), the appointed committee meets for a formal hearing during which books are protested and defended. Members then choose the best books (no more than five) in each of the subject areas under consideration to formally recommend to the commissioner of education for eventual adoption.

During the second phase, books recommended by the STC are carefully screened by curriculum experts at the Texas Education Agency (TEA) and by the commissioner of education. Publishers of these texts may be asked to make certain content corrections, additions, and/or deletions. (Note: For many years, the commissioner could remove as many as three books from any list of five, but could not add books. This power was recently revoked, however.) Following this review, the commissioner formally presents the TEA's lists of books to the State Board of Education (SBOE) for adoption.

Books recommended by the commissioner/TEA are reviewed and discussed by the State Board of Education in the final phase of this textbook selection and adoption system. A round of protest hearings is scheduled for this group as well. This body may ask for content changes and may remove books from any list, so long as at least two remain in each subject area. It cannot add books to any list. A vote to adopt is taken on each book on each list. From the final adoption lists, districts and schools throughout the state select texts.

The importance of the original STC decisions in this process is evident: books which are not selected by this committee are not eligible for further consideration and eventual free use throughout the state. Thus, this *initial* phase would be a likely spot for reformers to converge and ask how educators who serve on this STC go about the business of selecting textbooks.

SELECTING TEXAS TEXTBOOKS

A recent study was conducted in order to provide a better understanding of several aspects of the Texas textbook selection and adoption system.[11] One purpose of this study was to determine the bases upon which members of the State Textbook Committee evaluate and select books.

Coded survey instruments were distributed to State Textbook Committee members who served during three different years (N = 45).[12] Respondents were assured that data from these questionnaires would be used in aggregate form and that they would not be individually identified in the final report. Cumulative survey response rates exceeded 73 percent (N = 33).

Individual survey data were transferred to aggregate form. STC members from each of the target years whose individual responses most closely reflected the modal aggregate responses of their group were then randomly selected for interviews. In all, ten former STC members (30+ percent of respondents) were interviewed. Each interview was tape recorded and lasted approximately thirty minutes.

Available Criteria

The survey question (used as the basis for elaboration during interviews) which directly pertains to selection criteria read as follows:

> Please *rank order* your use of the following criteria in evaluating books offered for adoption. (1 = most important, 2 = next most important, etc.)
>
> _____ Adherence to the proclamation
> _____ Organization and presentation of content
> _____ Pedagogical strength (the best "tool" for the job)
> _____ Professional reports, evaluations, journal reviews, etc.
> _____ Suitability to your specific students, location, etc.
> _____ Effectiveness (based on student achievement)
> _____ Other (Please specify)

Item one, the Texas textbook proclamation, represents the sole mandated evaluation criterion shared by all STC members. These proclamations, as they are called, are policy guidelines developed by curriculum experts within the Texas Education Agency for review and eventual adoption by the State Board of Education. The proclamations serve as carefully worded "instructions" to publishers concerning what the State of Texas wants and does not want in its textbooks.[13] The study assumed that these proclamations would be important to STC members—an assumption resulting from printed information which stated, in part, that "[State Textbook Committee members] have one ... primary checkpoint: the proclamation for each textbook series ... "[14] as well as instructions given to the STC during its orientation meeting in Austin.[15] These proclamations thus serve as the sole evaluative threads formally binding the multigroup decision-making process and, as such, are an important dimension to centralized state textbook adoptions.[16]

Despite the presence and anticipated importance of these proclamations the study assumed that initial textbook decisions rested upon additional criteria as well. The first of these, "organization and presentation of content," was intended to suggest a level of awareness beyond simplistically looking at a book's content (commonly referred to as a "flip test") and was presumed to require the judgment of a trained and practiced educator (or textbook publisher). The phrase was designed to be broad enough to include such aspects as "relevance to the curriculum," "accuracy and authenticity," "format," and/or "appearance" used in an earlier study done by the Institute for Educational Development (IED).[17] Strong findings from a more recent study by Courtland et al. suggesting the virtual absence of attention to state curricula in the selection of Indiana reading books prompted the expectation that respondents would understand this criterion more as a concern for format, appearance, function, "flow," etc. than relevance to the Texas curriculum frameworks.[18]

In his reflections on the importance of the textbook, Warren writes that "the textbook, as an educational tool, has survived many centuries despite changes in educational philosophy, methodology, and social obligations undertaken by the American society. As a tool of instruction, it has no equal in America today."[19] The importance of the professional tool seemed to warrant the inclusion of an evaluation criterion called "pedagogical strength (the best 'tool' for the job)." Since the early decades of this century, educators have recognized that "nearly all beginning teachers are textbook teachers."[20] Porter recently found that in the area of mathematics, more than half of the teachers surveyed by the National Advisory Committee on Mathematics Education followed their textbooks closely.[21] Of all the criteria used to describe how books are evaluated, this one representing "teachability" would seem to be the one most pertinent to classroom teachers, and certainly lends importance to and justification for their participation in state-level textbook decisions.[22]

Print information is apparently neither aggressively sought nor easily available when judging textbooks.[23] While some professional textbook assessments do exist (e.g., *EPIE Reports* and *Curriculum Review*), studies suggest that their use by those who select textbooks is nominal.[24] Instead, much of the print information used by members of textbook committees and school administrators comes from publishers themselves.[25] The inclusion of the criterion "professional reports, evaluations, journal reviews, etc." was thus included to determine the relative importance of such information to those who chose textbooks for Texas.

"Suitability to your specific students, location, etc." was selected as the fifth textbook evaluative criterion in an attempt to incorporate what the 1969 IED study had called "relevance to needs" and "flexibility."[26] Although centralized textbook adoption is designed to promote some degree of curricular uniformity,[27] educators believe in the need to indivi-dualize instruction. While this ideal is all but impossible when heavy reliance is placed on a single textbook,[28] "suitability to your specific students, location, etc." was included as a criterion because it may have been more broadly interpreted by Texas educators.

Since many books are either new or completely revised for the Texas adoption schedule, knowledge of their effectiveness is virtually impossible for textbook selectors to ascertain. Nevertheless, in recent years publishers have been expected to produce learner verification data on their textbooks — data intended to provide textbook producers and consumers with a quantitative assessment of the product's effectiveness in actual classrooms and believed by many to be more valuable than reports of "pilot projects." Including the criterion "effectiveness (based on student achievement)" allowed the study to assess the importance of such a notion in the minds of those selecting texts.

Finally, the category "other (please specify)" was included in the event that criteria such as appearance, authorship, or "readability" were important enough to note.

Important Criteria

According to data provided by STC members in Texas, their three most prominent textbook evaluation criteria were ranked as "organization and presentation of content," "adherence to the proclamation," and "pedagogical strength." State textbook committee members used textbook evaluation forms of one sort or another to guide their assessments — a method recommended to them (with sample forms provided) by the TEA during their orientation meeting. Many members, with the help of advisers or district supervisors, constructed their own forms or borrowed forms used during previous adoptions. In most cases, according to respondents, these generic forms were used to evaluate textbooks representing all subject areas.

During interviews conducted to learn how these textbook judges understood and interpreted each of the selection criteria listed above, former STC members had a great deal of difficulty describing what it was, exactly, that they were looking for when judging both "organization and presentation of content" and "pedagogical strength." Probed for detail regarding the first of these, one respondent, referring to elementary social studies texts, claimed that he nixed a certain series because it "created a false impression of Texas and Houston." A second interviewee, when asked to elaborate and give examples of how he used "organization and presentation of content" as an evaluation criterion noted: "There's not a whole lot to say about that, other than you look at the books and you listen to what the publishers say [and] you listen to what your advisors tell you." Remembering her evaluation of a basal reading series, a reading specialist provided one of the most articulate examples of this criterion: she investigated content organization and presentation by asking herself questions such as "Why these five consonants *first*?" or "Why short vowels before long vowels?"

In short, practically none of those interviewed was able to describe, discuss, or give pertinent examples of how the criterion "organization and presentation of content" was used to judge textbooks. At best, a few seemed to understand the notion—as evidenced in the following excerpt:

> I think one of the things that they say, in general, about textbooks is "Evaluate the organization." I felt that . . . we looked at it from the perspective of . . . the simplest concepts to the most difficult and were they presented in an interesting and appealing but sequential manner. . . . And then also the way that the concepts [themselves] were presented in the text . . . was the content correct and was it presented in a correct manner?

At worst, most, like the following committee member, spoke largely in the abstract:

> As far as I'm concerned . . . , [organization and presentation of content] should be and must be the first thing you look for in a textbook. Each of us has a specific type of student that we're working with. . . . We had to look [for] a textbook that would be able to fit the needs of every one of our students, not only at our major schools, but those other schools where the kids do not come up, or [do] not have a very high average in test taking. . . . I feel that we had a very good selection [of books] to pick from. . . . They were alike in the sense that they had all the content that was needed, but what more or less led me to choose what we did was . . . the presentation or, I guess, the sequence in which it was done.

When discussing "pedagogical strength (best 'tool' for the job)," another highly ranked criterion, former Texas textbook selectors provided a mixed bag of responses. Asked to elaborate and give examples of how they went about making judgments based upon pedagogical strength, one respondent asserted: "I think I've had enough experience . . . to come up with what I feel is the best technique for approaching [the teaching of my subject]." Another noted that he " . . . looked at the pedalogical [*sic*] . . . values that could very well be clarified in certain textbooks; that is, you look at a certain book and you see the technique or the content that is being used to clarify a certain concept . . . " A third woman, who had actually rated this criterion as the *most* important of those listed in the question, explained that " . . . to me, the first criteria [*sic*] is that [textbooks] have to be sound . . . material; that it's going to do the job. That's what I selected first."

Several teachers were able to discuss pedagogical strength more specifically. One, for example, had this to say when describing a good teaching tool:

> How well it fosters the goals I would have in teaching a certain concept. That is to say, if I wanted to teach a point of grammar, how well does the book present it and how [long pause] in case the teacher is absent or something, could the students look it over and really figure it out for themselves?

Another, a music teacher, also rated "pedagogical strength" as the most important criterion when selecting textbooks. She was quick to explain her response:

> Pedagogical strength—I certainly was looking for music skills that the students could learn from those books. . . . Appeal to students. Whether there was a variety of song material in the books. . . . Illustrations — whether they were attractive or appealing to students. Things along that nature . . . "

Overall, these data indicate that although the respondents each made use of some sort of evaluation form or check sheet, and although the majority of respondents ranked "organization and presentation of content" as the most important textbook evaluation criterion, educators making textbook decisions for the state of Texas were largely unable to verbalize their understanding of this criterion very well. More respondents, though fewer than half of those interviewed, were able to describe and give examples of their understanding of "pedagogical strength," which was selected as the third most important evaluation criterion by the three groups surveyed.

Not surprisingly, perhaps, *all* of the interviewees were able to discuss, with examples, their use of the textbook proclamations — the criterion cumulatively ranked as the second most important when selecting Texas textbooks. STC members used the proclamation (which includes both the general content guidelines and the specific subject-area content requirements) alone or in conjunction with their textbook evaluation forms as an initial screening device. Faced with the task of selecting the best books from a relatively large number of textbooks offered, members typically read the proclamations quite literally and removed those books which did not comply. How did this initial screening work? Committee members explain.

> Member 1: I, myself, eliminated quite a few series because they did not meet the proclamation. I was very . . . conservative, that is, in following the proclamation first of all. And then looking at that group of books, you know, six or seven, that really met the proclamation. You know, you set priorities. Some didn't have . . . , I mean . . . , I didn't know they were for America . . . that type of thing.

> Member 2: [The problem with one series was that] all the way through it, it required workbooks to go with the series. [The proclamation] definitely stated that the text had to stand alone; that you couldn't require anything else . . . That was an unacceptable series for that reason. It was a tremendous series, a great series. But that made it unacceptable to me because it directly contradicted the [proclamation].

> Member 3: We built evaluation forms based on the proclamations. . . . We judged the books in all the areas of the proclamation . . . on a one-to-five scale and came up with a total number and ranked them according to that total number.

> Member 4: On my advisory committees, one of the things that I asked each . . . to come to a consensus [on] was, on a scale of one-to-ten, with ten being the highest . . . their assessment of how well that book . . . met the letter of the proclamation. . . . I had some rankings down . . . as low as a 2. . . . Quite frequently, those with low proclamation rankings were generally ones that I would not support *unless* the committee could give me some telling reasons why they were going to select that as one that I should vote for.

With this task accomplished, committee members would then conduct a second evaluation in which the remaining books were compared according to other criteria (e.g., "organization and presentation of content" and "pedagogical strength"). In other words, STC members first determined which were the "good" books and then determined and rank-ordered which of those were the "best." According to respondents, not all books adhered to the proclamation, and of those which did, some were more closely aligned than others. Nevertheless, the proclamation was an important criterion for textbook selectors. The largely sociocultural mandates each contained were but slightly less influential to these decision makers than their own experiential professional concerns related to format and "teachability"—concerns which became critically important in the evaluation of those texts surviving the initial proclamation purge as the intentions of the STC shifted from elimination to selection.

Using "organization and presentation of content" and "pedagogical strength" as major selection criteria, these initial Texas decision makers *comparatively* reviewed those books which survived earlier elimination. As a collection of textbooks representing a specific subject and designed for a specific grade level, texts considered in this second level of STC evaluation were very similar in the way their content was organized and presented and in the ease with which they could be successfully utilized in the classroom. Therefore, textbook evaluators were left with making comparative judgments about very specific aspects of these books (e.g., name recognition of the author, end-of-chapter student activities, and visual appeal of the teacher's manual). The data leave little doubt that these comparative decisions were, in many cases, influenced by members of the textbook publishing industry who pitched their books to STC members in various public and private settings.[29]

After having made judgments based upon the differences between the "good" books, these educators then prepared rank-ordered lists of the "best" textbooks. Although their work was not yet complete (members still had to attend public hearings and vote on the books to be selected), the initial selection process—in which the proclamation had played a crucial role—had reached its end.

LOOKING AT RELATIVE DATA

How might this information aid in an effort to battle The Great Textbook Machine? What advantage might it give to warrior-reformers who are preparing to improve textbook selection procedures in one of the adoption states?

These findings can be placed in the context of other research in hopes of establishing a clearer picture of how textbooks are selected at the state level. Unfortunately, the body of related research is quite thin. Studies of state-level textbook selection and adoption are few—an unsurprising fact, given the complexity of these systems and the taken-for-granted nature of textbooks as a whole. However, several research endeavors, including the investigation of Indiana's basal reading adoption[30] and the IED study of educational materials selection, have produced findings that can be triangulated with the Texas data to tell us more about textbook selection.

Farr and Tulley summarize the findings of the Courtland study as follows:

1. The most frequently mentioned influence on textbook selection was the "personal teaching style" of the selector.
2. Theoretical viewpoints regarding instructional style or current research in the field were seldom mentioned as criteria by selectors.
3. Curriculum objectives developed by selectors' districts carried little weight, because reviewers "knew what they were looking for."
4. Reviewers typically used a "flip test" to gauge eye appeal.
5. Publishers' presentations were ranked high on reviewers' lists of decision factors.[31]

The Texas data reported earlier comfortably match these points.

Experiential Relevance

Several interviewees in the Texas study struggled with the fact that their individual decisions would have direct consequences for thousands of teachers in an unimaginable array of teaching/learning situations throughout the state. Without training for this global responsibility, Texas textbook decision makers at the state level were left with uncomfortable doubts about the adequacy of their personal teaching experiences as pedagogical bases for textbook decisions, yet they had little else to rely upon. For those STC members whose role was broader than that of classroom teacher (e.g., district curriculum coordinator), this concern was less apparent—a finding similar to that of the IED study which noted that "Similarities among respondents' perspectives on materials selection seemed to be related to their distance from the classroom."[32]

Furthermore, those selected for STC membership were seasoned veterans (respondents' average number of years of experience was eighteen-plus). Virtually all of them responded on the survey that they were selected for their "experience and performance as an educator as well as my professional activities." Given this remarkable pool of expertise, who would argue that making decisions based largely upon "personal teaching style" is inappropriate? As for whether or not these decisions would be similar to those made by others throughout the state, one respondent noted that "What [the state] really did was randomly select a group of teachers. So we have to assume that [our textbook decisions] would be about like [any other randomly selected group]." An unjustified conclusion based upon an incorrect premise, perhaps, but the logic would seem to be sound with respect to how any group might ultimately rely on the collective experience of its membership when selecting textbooks at the state level.

Sufficient Information

Few participants in the Texas study made mention of theoretical or research-based arguments underlying their textbook decisions. Of those who did, three were district content specialists (two in reading, one in science) and one was a classroom teacher. Less than 15 percent of the survey respondents listed "professional reports, evaluations, journal reviews, etc." as one of their three most important textbook evaluation criteria, suggesting that the group as a whole was neither using nor seeking theoretical or research-oriented bases for their textbook decisions. Respondents in the IED study, too, generally believed that the amounts and kinds of information they had about materials were sufficient, and "Respondents . . . who said they needed more information generally did not specify what kinds of additional information they would like to have had."[33]

Prior Knowledge

Members of the Texas State Textbook Committee, like their Indiana counterparts, most definitely "knew what they were looking for." This is evidenced in several ways. First, the state of Texas provides no training for the textbook selection task. Consequently, evaluators are left free to determine their own criteria, produce their own evaluation forms, and conduct their own styles of evaluation. Again, the IED findings coincide:

> Another interesting finding from the data on selection criteria . . . is that all categories of respondents tended to speak of criteria other than cost and durability and dependability in very general terms. This may imply that individual respondents interpret criteria such as "teachability" and "relevance to the curriculum" in highly subjective ways. Or it may be . . . that many educators, confronted with the variety of new equipment and materials incorporating new methods, are not certain what criteria should be used in selecting these products other than cost and durability, and therefore must rely on their own intuitive judgement.[34]

Second, STC members are free to select their own advisers (who, in fact, do an enormous amount of work for the STC member) and to select them in any manner they consider appropriate. The importance of this process of filling positions vis-à-vis "knowing what to look for" is noted in the IED study as an "indirect set of selection criteria."[35] And finally, the Texas interview data confirm that interviewees tended to be especially comfortable when discussing the evaluation criterion "pedagogical strength (best 'tool' for the job)"—certainly the most individualistic or idiosyncratic of the three they identified as most important. While their discussion about specific criteria was, overall, both general and vague (as it was in the case of the IED respondents), the comparative ease with which STC members talked of "teaching tools" suggests that their evaluative frameworks for such tools reflect their personal understandings of the relationships between curriculum and instruction, self as teacher, and what has worked for them in the past. One consequence of this position is that textbook selectors "tend to select and use materials about which they have most knowledge; conversely, they tend to have more knowledge of those products which their school systems already own."[36]

Publisher Information

Certainly, the Texas data support the Courtland et al. findings that publishers' presentations played an important part in reviewers' decisions. The way in which STC members apparently winnow a rather large collection of books down to a more manageable number of six or seven before comparatively scrutinizing the remaining texts provides those publishers with a welcome opportunity to influence textbook decisions.[37] Here findings from the IED research also agree. The authors discuss the importance of textbook representatives to textbook evaluators within the context of information sources. IED selection committee respondents indicated that personal sources of information were generally considered more important than nonpersonal sources (e.g., printed reports) and that textbook representatives were seen as important personal sources of information.

ACKNOWLEDGING IDIOSYNCRASY

What becomes apparent when viewing results from these studies is that textbook selection is fundamentally idiosyncratic, relying greatly on the knowledge and experiential wisdom of educators and their eventual ability to reach consensus. In Texas, however, the influence of state guidelines was pervasive and highly determinate.

Recent calls for reform provide any number of step-by-step procedures for improving textbook selection processes. Most include the need, first, for clear definition of criteria,[38] although several writers would begin by having selectors determine the *purpose* of the books to be chosen.[39] Others include a step to ensure that selected texts will be aligned with existing curriculum goals and related tests.[40] Many reform proposals underscore the importance of providing adequate training, compensation, and time for evaluators to carry out their task,[41] while some argue that textbook decision makers should be more aware of recent theory and research pertaining to curriculum and instruction.[42] In one of the more detailed and interesting proposals to improve textbook selection, Norby proposes two sets of questions for textbook committees to pose that will not only assure the selection of better books, but offend the fewest people in the process![43]

The problem with this direction of reform, however, is that it rests upon the following premise: *"It is when a textbook is in the hands of a reviewer that the most important phase of the textbook evaluation process takes place"* (emphasis added).[44] The author of this statement is correct in identifying this *phase* as most important; too many writers, however, when calling for the reform of the *reviewer,* neglect to acknowledge that, in the case of state-level textbook selection, the reviewer at this initial phase is frequently holding a textbook in one hand and a set of state-mandated textbook guidelines in the other.

RECOGNIZING FUNDAMENTAL CONTROL

The influence that adoption states have over the textbook publishing industry is both infamous and well noted, and "any attempt to influence the content of textbooks must be done with the cooperation of . . . large-market, centralized states."[45] The Texas data reported here tell us that textbook guidelines (proclamations) provided by the SBOE have a significant impact on those educators who use them and represent one of the many "underlying forces that shape instructional materials."[46] When we recall that Texas textbook proclamations are based upon the state's actual curriculum guidelines, we see that similar "outside" effects were found in the IED study:

> Aside from cost, the most frequently mentioned criterion was that substantive materials be selected to fit the curriculum. This fact would seem to make the curriculum a principal constraint for the selectors and users of materials as well as for materials producers. If

> materials are chosen to fit a predetermined curriculum, selectors are not entirely free to choose materials they consider "best" or most appropriate; teachers who use materials are similarly restricted in the materials available to them; and materials producers, who wish their products to be selected, are likely to design and produce substantive materials which correspond to the requirements of various curricula.[47]

The point is a simple one: better prepared and informed textbook selectors at the state level will do little good unless the policies, guidelines, and practices of state boards of education undergo similar improvements first.

Again, Texas provides a case in point. Since its inception, the state's selection and adoption system has undergone continuous adjustments and "fine tuning" in order to ensure the selection of the "best" textbooks.[48] The state system appears to both invite and respect the input of educators (STC), content experts (TEA), and the representative body politic (SBOE). It has a long history of citizen activisim[49] and was recently altered to include balanced commentary from the interested populace.[50] When asked whether or not the state's schools receive the "best" textbooks, *95 percent of the STC survey respondents answered yes*. As one might expect, the Texas system of procuring textbooks is seen, by Texans at least, as "close to perfection."[51]

Given the economic clout that Texas has with textbook publishers, its pivotal importance in the improvement of textbook selection is clear. Reformers who would look toward Texas as a battle front must look beyond the function of its initial decision makers: the pervasive impact of the Texas textbook proclamations on both the publishers who produce textbooks and the educators who initially judge them is the proper starting point. Created by curriculum experts at the Texas Education Agency to be refined and adopted by the State Board of Education, these proclamations act to delimit textbook choices from the outset. As indicated by the data presented above, members of the STC pay remarkably close attention to these documents yet have absolutely nothing to do with their creation. In virtually every case, interviewees acknowledged the taken-for-granted influence proclamations had on their best professional judgments and in most cases STC members embraced the proclamation guidelines wholeheartedly. Furthermore, when asked about the weaknesses of the Texas system, *only two* survey respondents noted the absence of training related to selecting textbooks and *none* mentioned any desire for additional information regarding current theory and practice. As for the issue of adequate time, more respondents suggested *reducing* the amount of time they spend than increasing it! It seems evident that the above-mentioned efforts to better prepare textbook selectors would have had limited impact on these former Texas STC members.

Data presented here suggest that reform should begin with those who set policy. In his discussion of science textbooks Moyer argues that professional societies must teach school board members (along with teachers and administrators) "not only *why* science is important but *how* it works and what its limits are."[52] As a former California state board president, Michael Kirst has also come to believe that board members must be better trained.[53] Although few in number, respondents in the Texas study made similar suggestions. When asked how the Texas system might be improved, several spoke to the need for tempering the board-mandated proclamations: "Seek professional input on the development of the proclamation," wrote one. "Proclamations need review by 'field' professionals before [being] approved by State Board," wrote another.

A deeper issue, and one which gets at the very nature of the system's basic structure, is the fact that members of the Texas SBOE can and do veto textbooks selected by educators at the initial selection stage. One Texas STC member, suggesting ways in which the system might be improved, noted that " . . . once the selections are made by the textbook committee, the State Board should exercise good judgement in their alterations of the choices." Another was more blunt: "Have the final decision of the [textbook] committee stand." Such SBOE textbook vetoes did not even require public justification or reasoning until recently.[54] Given the source and influence of the Texas textbook proclamations and the ultimate veto power of its state board, efforts to improve the skills of textbook evaluators would be misguided if not first directed toward state board members themselves.

CONCLUSION

According to Tyson-Bernstein and Woodward, "the best hope for reform [of The Great Textbook Machine] is a slowly evolving understanding of the effects of various components of the machine on the total effort. . . . Finding the proper levers to pull and switches to throw will take years."[55] The findings presented in this essay are offered for those who believe that the quality of textbook content is an issue waiting to be embraced on a large scale. These findings seem to indicate which levers *not* to pull and which switches *not* to throw—at least not initially. Those who would support the refinement of evaluation criteria used by state-level textbook committees[56] or their training in "skills tracing" or reviewing current research[57] miss the point. At best, a cadre of professionally adept textbook evaluators might be more capable of conducting sophisticated reviews and less susceptible to publisher influence. As we see from the Texas data, however, the specter of the state's textbook proclamations looms large. Where is the wisdom in providing a state-mandated set of guidelines to an englightened group of textbook decision makers who must then operate within a system which allows their decisions to be fundamentally directed then possibly vetoed by noneducators? Textbook reform efforts must be directed toward the lay persons at the state level who create textbook specifications and bear ultimate veto control.

If state-level textbook selection and adoption must continue (despite growing evidence that it should be abandoned[58]) several changes must occur. First, those who work most closely with textbooks must be welcomed into the process of developing state guidelines[59] as valued and respected partners. Second, those who select textbooks — particularly noneducators — must begin to push for funding to establish systematic ways to determine textbook effectiveness.[60] Such data would be invaluable not only in the development and refinement of selection guidelines but in subsequent selection and adoption efforts. They would also provide an important common knowledge base for educators and noneducators who determine selection guidelines.

Finally, if state textbook selection practices must continue, then state-level leaders and policymakers must end their use of the veto over texts selected by practitioners. In cases where state guidelines are created with the participation of practitioners and/or reflect data-based generalizations about effective textbooks such power is obviously not needed. In cases where such respect for and common ground with educators remains absent, vetoing teachers' textbook decisions will eventually "make teachers even more cynical than they already are about their role in textbook selection. It is good public policy to encourage teachers to take the task seriously and to live with their choices."[61]

Many would agree with English that "The adoption states are a major incubus on integrity, brilliance, originality, and variety [in textbooks]"[62] and yet little seems to change. Until and unless state board members see the need to educate themselves and reconstruct their state textbook selection and adoption systems in ways which share the power of textbook selection with practicing educators, efforts to reform how textbooks are selected aren't likely to reform much at all.

Appendix A

Books to Be Adopted in the 1980 Texas Adoption Cycle and General Content Guidelines Contained in the *Proclamation of the State Board of Education Advertising for Bids on Textbooks No. 56*

(Texas Education Agency, 1980, March, pp. 35–38)

Elementary Subjects (all multiple listings)*
Basal Readers Readiness through Grade 8
Basal Readers Readiness through Grade 3 Bilingual (Spanish)
Earth Science

High School Subjects (all multiple listings)*
Psychology
Sociology
Business Management & Ownership
Business Communication
Business Law
V.I.E. Drafting Trades
V.I.E. Graphic Arts Trades
V.I.E. Electrical Trades

---

*Note: These total twenty-six subject areas.

SPECIAL PROVISIONS

Textbook Content—General

- The content of all textbooks . . . shall be in accordance with *Description of Subject Content of Textbooks* attached as Exhibit A [see Appendix B] to the Proclamation . . .
- Textbook content and suggested readings which are in violation of these general content requirements and limitations shall be de-

leted from any adopted textbook and teacher guide prior to purchase of the textbook by the State.

- Textbooks that treat the theory of evolution should identify it as only one of several explanations of the origin of humankind and avoid limiting young people in their search for meanings of their human existence.

1. Textbooks presented for adoption which treat the subject of evolution substantively in explaining the historical origins of humankind shall be edited, if necessary, to clarify that the treatment is theoretical rather than factually verifiable. Furthermore, each textbook must carry a statement on an introductory page that any material on evolution included in the book is clearly presented as theory rather than fact.
2. Textbooks presented for adoption which do not treat evolution substantively as an instructional topic, but make reference to evolution, indirectly or by implication, must be modified, if necessary, to ensure that the reference is clearly to be a theory and not a verified fact. These books will not need to carry a statement on the introductory page.
3. The presentation of the theory of evolution should be done in a manner which is not detrimental to other theories of origin.

- Textbooks shall contain no material of a partisan or sectarian character.
- Textbook content shall promote citizenship and understanding of the free enterprise system, emphasize patriotism and respect for recognized authority, and promote respect for human rights. Textbooks adopted shall be objective in content, impartial in interpretations, and shall not include selections or works which encourage or condone civil disorder, social strife, or disregard for the law.

1. Textbooks shall present positive aspects of America and its heritage.
2. Textbooks shall not contain material which serves to undermind [*sic*] authority.
3. Textbooks shall present balanced and factual treatment to both positions when significant political and social movements in history generate contrasting points of view.

- Violence, if it appears in textbook content, shall be treated in context of cause and consequence; it shall not appear for reasons of unwholesome excitement, sensationalism, or as an excuse for relevance.

1. In the design of textbook content the amount of violence should be minimal.

- Textbooks offered for adoption shall not include blatantly offensive language or illustrations.
- Textbooks, whenever possible, shall present varying life styles, shall treat divergent groups fairly, without stereotyping, and shall reflect the positive contributions of all individuals and groups to the American way of life. Illustrations and written material will avoid bias toward any particular life style, group, or individual and should present a wide range of goal choices and life styles. Particular care should be taken in the treatment of workers, and respect for all productive work.

1. Textbooks shall provide an objective view of cultural confluence, with the information necessary for developing mutual understanding and respect among all elements of our population. Materials shall reflect an awareness that culture and language variation does exist and can be utilized to promote successful learning.
2. The books shall present examples of men and women participating in a variety of roles and activities and shall further present the economic, political, social and cultural contributions of both men and women, past and present.
3. Content which treats aspects of the world of work should reflect the positive contribution of all types of careers to the American economic system and way of life. People presented in the books should reflect varieties of work and should be treated without bias toward particular kinds of work.
4. Traditional roles of men and women, boys and girls shall be included as well as those changing roles in our society.
5. Textbook content shall not encourage life styles deviating from generally accepted standards of society.

- Authors of all textbooks offered for adoption . . . should have expertise and experience which provide authoritative credibility to their work.
- All textbooks offered for adoption should present up-to-date, factual information accurately and objectively without opinionated statements or biased editorial judgements by the authors.

Appendix B

Basal Reading Content Guidelines from ''Exhibit A'' of the 1980 Texas Textbook Proclamation Description of Content of Textbooks Basal Reading: Readiness, Pre-Primer, Primer, Grades 1–8

(Texas Education Agency, 1980, March, pp. 49–50)

Basal readers form the foundation for reading instruction and should provide a structured program consisting of a sequence of reading skills and appropriate selections or contexts in which these skills are introduced, taught, practiced, reinforced, and refined. They should exhibit the following:

- Basal readers should establish a scope and sequence of skills and concept development tasks compatible with [the state's existing curricular frameworks in elementary and secondary reading and language arts].
- The basal readers should be textbooks for reading instruction, not subject matter books or reference books. However, the books should include content from Grade 1–8 curriculum areas, such as literature, social studies, science, mathematics, and fine arts because reading comprehension of such content is emphasized in these grades.
- The readability, determined by factors such as vocabulary, structure, length of sentences, organization of material, and size of type, should be appropriately more difficult at each successive grade or level and should be designed for that grade.
- The books should be attractive and the content interesting and appropriate to students assigned to that grade level. Vocabulary words, sentence structures, or other generalizations that do not conform to the developmental scheme and that will cause the students problems in recognition should be treated in the supportive teaching materials.
- The books selected should be well written and carefully edited. Stories and poems included in the books should have literary

> merit; that is, they should have value in developing appreciation of literature for students in Grades 1 – 8. Other content should have value as examples of well-organized prose.

Each book and its accompanying teacher's manual should contain all the materials necessary for reading instruction at that level, i.e., it should not require additional materials to be complete.

Each book should be accompanied by a teacher's edition or manual giving information as to the book's purpose and design for reading instruction and suggesting instructional approaches.

NOTES

1. Chester E. Finn, Jr., "The Textbook, the Curriculum, and the Culture," in *A Policymaker's Guide to Textbook Selection,* ed. Caroline B. Cody (Alexandria, Va.: National Association of State Boards of Education, 1986), pp. 33–35.

2. Edward B. Jenkinson, *The Schoolbook Protest Movement* (Bloomington, Ind.: Phi Delta Kappa Educational Foundation, 1986).

3. See Alan Bloom, *The Closing of the American Mind* (New York: Simon and Schuster, 1987); E. D. Hirsch, Jr., *Cultural Literacy* (Boston: Houghton Mifflin, 1987); and Diane Ravitch and Chester E. Finn, *What Do Our 17-Year-Olds Know?* (New York: Harper and Row, 1987).

4. Harriet Tyson-Bernstein and Arthur Woodward, "The Great Textbook Machine," *Social Education* 50 (1986): 41–45.

5. Michael W. Apple, "Regulating the Text: The Socio-historical Roots of State Control," *Educational Policy* 3 (1989): 98.

6. Michael A. Tulley, "A Descriptive Study of the State-level Textbook Adoption Processes," *Educational Evaluation and Policy Analysis* 7 (1985): 289–308.

7. Raymond English, "The Politics of Textbook Adoption," *Phi Delta Kappan* 62 (1980): 275–278.

8. Sherry Keith, "Choosing Textbooks: A Study of Instructional Materials Selection Processes for Public Education," *Book Research Quarterly* 1 (1985): 26.

9. For a much more detailed presentation of how this system unfolds, see Laura Tynes, "Texas Textbook Adoption Process," in *How Can We Improve Both the Quality of Textbooks and the Process for Selecting Them?,* ed. Robert L. Brunelle et al., (ERIC Document Reproduction Service No. ED 247 000,

1983): 16–18; C. J. Seidenberger, "A Study of the Adoption, Purchase, and Distribution of Public School Textbooks in the Various States of the United States" (masters thesis, University of Texas at Austin, 1953); and "How Textbooks Are Adopted," *Texas Outlook* 56 (1972): C2, C3.

10. Whenever the state regulates textbooks, representatives of the textbook publishing industry become involved in state political processes. See John T. Thompson, *Policymaking in American Public Education* (Englewood Cliffs, N.J.: Prentice-Hall, 1976). It might seem unwarranted to mention this fact except that, in earlier years, there was some debate as to whether or not textbook decisions should be made by "secret committees" unknown to publishers' representatives. See J. B. Edmonson, "The Ethics of Marketing and Selecting Textbooks," in *The Textbook in American Education,* Thirtieth Yearbook of the National Society for the Study of Education, part 2, ed. Guy M. Whipple (Bloomington, Ill.: Public School Publishing, 1931), pp. 199–220; and Malcom E. Mellott, "A Study of Reactions Concerning Certain Practices in the Selling of Textbooks to Public Schools in the United States" (Ph.D. diss., Temple University, 1953). The proposal for secret adoptions stemmed from a concern held by many that textbooks were as likely to be *sold to* as *selected by* those responsible for such decisions. See W. B. Spalding, "The Selection and Distribution of Printed Materials," in *Text Materials in Modern Education,* ed. Lee J. Cronbach (Urbana: University of Illinois Press, 1955), pp. 16–187. While publishers participate in the Texas process, great care is taken to control their activities.

11. Findings reported in this essay are taken from the author's larger study. See John D. Marshall, *The Politics of Curriculum Decisions Manifested Through the Selection and Adoption of Textbooks for Texas* (ERIC Document Reproduction Service No. ED 270 900, 1986).

12. A complete rationale for case selection criteria as well as a thorough description of the research design and methodology are found in Marshall, *Politics of Curriculum Decisions*.

13. See Charles R. Duke, "A Look at Current State-wide Text Adoption Procedures" (Paper presented at the Fourth Annual Meeting of the National Council of Teachers of English Spring Conference, Houston, TX. ERIC Document Reproduction Service No. ED 254 864, March, 1985). It is important to note that some writers characterize the wording of these documents as vague. See, for example, Stephen Aarons, *Compelling Belief: The Culture of American Schooling* (Paper presented at the Annual Meeting of the American Educational Research Association, Montreal. ERIC Document Reproduction Service No. ED 231 712, April, 1983). The author, having discussed the composition of Texas proclamations with members of the TEA and SBOE who are responsible for their wording, understands that while they may appear vague, they are, nonetheless, meticulously worded.

14. "How Textbooks are Adopted," p. C3.

15. Texas Education Agency, *Report of the State Textbook Committee* (Austin: TEA, 1983).

16. In addition to the three decision-making groups (State Textbook Committee, Texas Education Agency/commissioner of education and the State Board of Education), textbook publishers and protesters are recognized participants in the selection and adoption procedures. See Sherry Keith, *Politics of Textbook Selection*. (Stanford: School of Education, Stanford University, Institute for Research on Educational Finance and Governance, Project Report No. 81 – A7, 1981).

17. Institute for Educational Development, *The Selection of Educational Materials in the United States* (New York: Institute for Educational Development. ERIC Document Reproduction Service No. ED 044 030, 1969).

18. M. C. Courtland et al., *A Case Study of the Indiana Reading Textbook Adoption Process* (Bloomington: Indiana University, 1983). See also John T. Guthrie, "Forms and Functions of Textbooks," *Journal of Reading* 24 (1981): 554–556.

19. Claude C. Warren, "Adopting Textbooks," in *The Textbook in American Society,* ed. John Y. Cole and Thomas G. Sticht (Washington, D.C.: Library of Congress, 1981), p. 45.

20. Elwood P. Cubberly, *The School Textbook Problem* (Boston: Houghton Mifflin, 1927), p. 4.

21. Andrew C. Porter, "Elementary Mathematics Textbooks" in Cole and Sticht, *The Textbook in American Society,* pp. 19–20.

22. Michael W. Kirst and Decker F. Walker, "An Analysis of Curriculum Policy-making," *Review of Educational Research* 41 (1971): 479–509.

23. Connie Muther, "Reviewing Research when Choosing Materials," *Educational Leadership* 42 (1985): 86–87.

24. Gail J. Saliterman, "The Politics of Decision-making in an Incompletely Bureaucratized Organization: A Study of Textbook Selection in Public School Systems" (Ph.D. diss., The American University, 1971).

25. See A. L. Hall-Quest, *The Textbook: How to Use and Judge It* (New York: Macmillan, 1918); John P. Dessauer, *Book Publishing* (New York: R. R. Bowker, 1974); and Thomas P. Ruff and Donald C. Orlich, "How Do Elementary School Principals Learn About Curriculum Innovation?" *Elementary School Journal* 74 (1974): 389–392.

26. Institute of Educational Development, *Selection of Educational Materials*.

27. Tulley, "A Descriptive Study."

28. See Robert L. Church and M. W. Sedlack, *Education and the United States* (New York: Free Press, 1976); and W. Schramm, "The Publishing Process," in Cronbach, *Text Materials in Modern Education,* pp. 129–165.

29. For a more complete discussion of publisher influence, see J. Dan Marshall, "With a Little Help from Some Friends: Publishers, Protesters, and Texas Textbook Decisions," in *The Politics of the Textbook,* ed. Michael W. Apple and Linda K. Christian-Smith (London: Routeledge and Chapman Hall, in press).

30. Courtland et al., *A Case Study.*

31. Roger Farr and Michael A. Tulley, "Do Adoption Committees Perpetuate Mediocre Textbooks?" *Phi Delta Kappan* 66 (1985): 467–471.

32. Institute for Educational Development, *Selection of Educational Materials,* p. 304.

33. Ibid., p. 292.

34. Ibid., p. 290.

35. Ibid., p. 288.

36. Ibid., p. 291.

37. See Marshall, "With a Little Help."

38. These include Phyllis Blaunstein, "An Overview of State Textbook Selection Procedures," in Brunelle, *How Can We Improve,* pp. 10–15; Roger Farr, "Do Our Textbook Selection Processes Work: Recommendations for Improving Textbook Adoption," in Cody, *A Policymaker's Guide,* pp. 31–32; Finn, "The Textbook"; and Bonnie B. Armbruster, "Do Textbooks Encourage Reading," in Cody, *A Policymaker's Guide,* p. 24.

39. These include Connie Muther, "What Every Textbook Evaluator Should Know," *Educational Leadership* 42 (1985): 4–8; and Farr and Tulley, "Do Adoption Committees Perpetuate?"

40. See, for example, Michael W. Kirst, "Choosing Textbooks: Reflections of a State Board President," *American Educator* 8 (1984): 18–23; and Blaunstein, "An Overview."

41. Farr, "Do Our Textbook Selection Processes Work"; Kirst, "Choosing Textbooks"; Blaunstein, "An Overview"; Farr and Tulley, "Do Adoption Committees"; and Connie Muther, "How to Evaluate a Basal Textbook: The Skills Trace," *Educational Leadership* 42 (1984–85): 79–80.

42. See Wayne A. Moyer, "How Texas Rewrote Your Textbooks," *Science Teacher* 52 (1985): 22–27; Muther, "Reviewing Research"; and Armbruster, "Do Textbooks."

43. Janet R. Norby, *What to Do Till the Book Salesmen Come, or Making Basal Reader Adoptions Work* (Paper presented at the Ninth Annual Meeting of the Far West Regional Conference of the International Reading Association. ERIC Document Reproduction Service No. ED 236 550, March, 1983).

44. Farr, "Do Our Textbook Selection Processes Work," p. 32.

45. Blaunstein, "An Overview," p. 11.

46. P. Goldstein, *Changing the American Schoolbook* (Lexington, Mass.: Lexington Books, 1978): p. 1.

47. Institute for Educational Development, *The Selection of Educational Materials,* pp. 305–306.

48. For a historical overview of the Texas textbook system and the reorganization that took place at midcentury, see Margaret E. Patrick, "The Selection and Adoption of Textbooks: Texas—A Case Study" (Ph.D. diss., Stanford University, 1949). For more recent accounts of selection procedure changes in Texas see Marshall. *Politics of Curriculum Decisions;* Moyer, "How Texas"; and Carl E. Schomburg, "Texas and Social Studies Texts," *Social Education* 50 (1986): 58–60.

49. See Frank E. Piasecki, "Norma and Mel Gabler: The Development and Causes of their Involvement Concerning the Curricular Appropriateness of School Textbook Content" (Ph.D. diss., North Texas State University, 1982).

50. People for the American Way, *As Texas Goes, So Goes the Nation: A Report on Textbook Selection in Texas* (Washington, D.C.: People for the American Way, 1983).

51. For an elaboration of this perception see Tynes, "Texas Textbook Adoption Process," pp. 16–18.

52. Moyer, "How Texas," p. 27.

53. Kirst, "Choosing Textbooks."

54. Moyer, "How Texas."

55. Tyson-Bernstein and Woodward, "The Great Textbook Machine," p. 44.

56. Denise A. Wenger, "How Do Professionals Use Textbook Selection Instruments" (1987, mimeographed).

57. See Muther, "How to Evaluate" and "Reviewing Research."

58. Farr and Tulley, "Do Adoption Committees Perpetuate?"

59. Roger Farr, Michael A. Tulley, and Deborah Powell, ''The Evaluation and Selection of Basal Readers,'' *The Elementary School Journal* 87 (1987): 267–281.

60. Jean Osborn and Marcy Stein, ''Textbook Adoptions: A Process for Change,'' in *Reading, Thinking, and Concept Development,* ed. T. L. Harris and E. J. Cooper (New York: College Entrace Examination Board, 1985), pp. 257–271; Michael A. Tulley and Roger Farr, ''Textbook Adoption: Insight, Impact, and Potential,'' *Book Research Quarterly* 1 (1985): 4–11.

61. Harriet Tyson-Bernstein, *A Conspiracy of Good Intentions* (Washington, D.C.: Council for Basic Education, 1988), p. 99.

62. English, ''The Politics of Textbook Adoption,'' p. 275.

HOWARD D. MEHLINGER

Chapter Nine

American Textbook Reform: What Can We Learn from the Soviet Experience

---

Efforts to improve school textbooks now occupy center stage in the drama of education reform in America. Whether American textbooks are as poor as some critics believe or whether they are worse today than they were in the past are interesting but not crucial questions. It is more important that people recognize the vital role that textbooks play in instruction, and that they understand that schooling is unlikely to achieve desired results until textbooks change.

The critics have identified flaws in the textbooks themselves, and they have pointed to problems in the ways textbooks are produced and sold in the United States. In general, the critics believe that the marketplace has failed to provide high-quality products at reasonable prices. They charge that consumers (teachers, school administrators, school boards, state and local adoption committees) pay inflated prices for ineffective products, as a consequence of slick salesmanship by publishers and a preference for style over substance by consumers. (Apparently, Americans select their textbooks in much the same way as they choose their clothing, automobiles, and other consumer goods.) The critics want consumers to become smarter textbook buyers, thereby encouraging publishers to produce better products.

Of course, it is easier to see what is wrong with the present system

---

*Reprinted, with permission, from *Phi Delta Kappan* (September, 1989).

than it is to propose convincing alternatives. This fact suggests that we might profitably spend some time investigating how other nations develop and market textbooks. Perhaps American publishers and educators could learn from the experiences of others. Moreover, if Americans were to examine practices employed in a system greatly different from their own—e.g., the Soviet system—this effort would provoke fresh thought about how textbooks might be improved.

In this essay I compare history and geography textbooks used in American and Soviet schools. My focus is not on the specific content of the textbooks—how each nation treats World War II, for example. Rather, I focus on the different assumptions that educators in the two nations make about what students should learn, who should decide what they learn, how students learn, how the history and geography curriculum should be organized, and how much choice should be left to teachers. The differences in assumptions lead to different types of textbooks and different processes for developing and distributing books. The data source for the comparison is a twelve-year investigation of American and Soviet history and geography textbooks conducted by teams of scholars and educators in the two nations.[1]

My analysis deals with a set of issues drawn from findings and recommendations contained in three recent critiques of American textbooks. One focused on world history textbooks; the second treated American history textbooks; the third was a more general report on the status of American textbooks and how they are produced.[2] I use these studies to identify the issues that disturb American textbook critics, but I ignore some issues that have bothered American reviewers (though these issues are reported in the three studies) because no useful comparison with Soviet practice exists. After identifying the issues, I try to suggest what lessons we might draw from Soviet experience.

APPROVED KNOWLEDGE

Textbooks have special status in both American and Soviet societies. Textbooks provide knowledge that adults in positions of authority believe children and youths should acquire. Only the innocent and naive believe that textbooks present all the knowledge in a given academic domain. Clearly, choices of what to include and what to exclude must be made, and someone or some group must make these decisions. Decision makers may exclude certain information because it is inappropriate for students of a certain age or grade; because it is too complex to explain thoroughly;

because it is too controversial, offends some group, threatens the stability of society, or undermines faith in the political leaders; because it detracts from the overall purpose of the course or the curriculum; or for a variety of other reasons. The point is that textbooks do not contain all that is known about a subject; someone decides what information they will contain. In short, textbook censorship exists in both the United States and the USSR.

Censorship is not a nice word; people do not like to be called censors. Yet someone must decide what is appropriate and inappropriate textbook content. Establishing criteria for appropriateness is one step in a process of censorship. Another step is deciding who is worthy of the level of trust and confidence required to serve as textbook censor for society.

The authority for censorship is more widely diffused in the United States than in the USSR. In America censors can be found in publishing houses; on state and local textbook adoption committees; in special interest groups representing racial, ethnic, religious, gender-related, or social causes; in the teaching profession; and in government. In the United States individuals and groups do battle with one another to make certain that their opinions or perspectives are represented in textbooks and that contrary views are excluded. Textbook critics have pointed out the difficulties that these battles create for history and geography textbooks. In order to ensure sales, publishers tend to avoid controversial issues whenever possible, to briefly mention hosts of people and scores of events that seem relatively insignificant in order to gain support from widely disparate groups, and to reduce the amount of coverage given to more significant people and events in order to keep the textbook to a manageable size.

By contrast, decisions about the choice of content are centralized in the USSR. Until recently, censorship was chiefly the responsibility of the Ministry of Education; today, under terms of the recent reorganization of Soviet education, censorship falls under the authority of the State Committee for Public Education.[3] Because the USSR produces only one textbook for each course (albeit in as many as fifty-three different languages), all who teach the same course use the same textbook, whether in Moscow, Tallinn, or Yerevan. Any changes in content deemed necessary to satisfy local and regional ethnic groups are determined at the national level and appear in textbooks throughout the nation.

Textbooks in the USSR must conform to ideological perspectives established by the Communist party and by Soviet political leadership. Teachers are fully informed of these perspectives. For example, the history syllabus for Soviet schools clearly states the purposes of teaching history:

> The teaching of history is given the task of forming in youth a Marxist-Leninist world-view, deep ideological convictions, a clear, class-oriented approach to phenomena of social life, Soviet patriotism, loyalty to proletarian internationalism, devotion to the Party's cause, the task of developing a Communist attitude toward work, a feeling of duty and discipline, and irreconcilability to bourgeois ideology.[4]

Although Soviet textbooks do change from time to time, the changes are preceded by changes in official points of view. For example, the treatment accorded Joseph Stalin in Russian history textbooks changed following Nikita Khrushchev's 1956 speech denouncing Stalin's leadership. At the same time, efforts by ethnic or religious minorities to gain greater attention in textbooks will be futile until they can attract sympathetic support from top leadership in the Communist party. No U.S. president or secretary of the Department of Education has such influence on American textbooks.

One critic of American textbooks has proposed that a national panel be established to review textbooks on American history. According to Gilbert Sewall, such a panel is needed because "no authoritative system exists to help historians and educators evaluate textbooks and distinguish the superior from the mediocre."[5] This suggestion, prompted by frustration with practices that permit interest groups to tear out objectionable pieces of textbooks or affix their own ideas like so many barnacles on a ship, is an effort to achieve in the United States the uniformity that the Soviet system allows.

However, given the decentralized system of textbook selection and purchase in the United States, it is difficult to imagine that a national textbook review panel could become much more than another interest group clamoring for attention. Unless the United States develops a national curriculum, establishes a national syllabus for each course, and increases the authority of the federal Department of Education, a national panel would probably have little or no influence. And there is little chance that such centralization will occur here. The Soviet model, vesting the authority for textbook censorship in a national organization, seems wholly inappropriate for the United States.

But there is another way to influence textbook publishers that could work in the United States. Authority over the general goals and content of courses could be left with the individual states, where it rests today. Meanwhile, the decision about what instructional materials can be used to satisfy the syllabus of each state could be delegated to individual teachers—or at least to individual schools. Individual teachers could be given textbook allocations equal to their appropriate share of the textbook budget. Neither the state nor the local school board would decide which books would be purchased. Teachers would choose, taking into account the particular populations they serve. Teachers would not be required to buy a particular textbook—or to buy any textbook at all. The wisdom of teachers' choices would ultimately be judged according to the performances of their students on state-mandated examinations or by other measures.

While this approach would not eliminate the influence of special interest groups on textbooks, it would force such groups to act at the local level rather than at the state level, where textbook content is now decided. From time to time, a particular teacher might be prevented from using a particular book because of the hostile reaction it attracted from a vocal and powerful local group. But such actions in a single community need not be magnified into a force that neuters textbooks for everyone, everywhere.

Let state authorities decide the overall goals and content of the curriculum. Let individual teachers decide how best to address those goals and teach that content to their own students.

THE COST OF TEXTBOOKS

Perhaps the most dramatic difference between U.S. and Soviet textbooks is price. The price of a Soviet textbook averages roughly one-tenth the price of an American textbook. While the Soviet government subsidizes textbooks, this fact alone cannot explain why one can buy ten Soviet textbooks for the price of one American textbook.

A variety of factors drives up the price of American textbooks. Many critics see the following factors as central to what is wrong with the way American books are brought to market.

Cost of Paper and Binding

Soviet textbooks are cheaper because, for a variety of reasons, they cost less to produce. Soviet textbooks are printed on cheap paper and use cheap cover stock and cheap bindings. Soviet textbooks are expected to last only two or three years, until the next printing. American textbooks, on the other hand, must conform to a specific set of manufacturing regulations that ensure that the books will stand use for five to seven years, a typical school adoption cycle. Moreover, American textbooks are attractively illustrated, usually with four colors; extra care and attention are devoted to cover and internal design, making the books approach the visual quality of coffee-table volumes.

One reason so much expense is lavished on visual qualities in American textbooks is that publishers believe that, in order to be adopted, their books must pass the "flip test"—a hypothetical test performed by teachers and school administrators who, lacking time to read each text presented for adoption, merely "flip" through the pages while trying to form an impression of the quality of the book. It is surely the case that publishers spend as many hours agonizing over color, layout, illustration, and design as they do over editorial style and content.

Soviet books also have fewer pages than American textbooks. Soviet texts are shorter because Soviet students spend fewer days each week attending a particular class (while enrolling in more subjects) and because the proportion of text to illustration and white space is far greater in a Soviet textbook than in its American counterpart.

Peripherals

A typical American textbook is accompanied by workbooks, ditto masters, tests, transparencies, computer software, games, simulations, video tapes, teacher's guides, and other ancillary materials. American publishers list these items in their catalogs and would like to sell them. However, they often are used as "freebies," gifts that teachers expect to receive when they purchase classroom sets of textbooks. Since a way must be found to cover the production costs of these items, the vast majority of such costs are built into the cost of the textbook and are written off as the cost of doing business. Publishers must compete for sales, and no publisher is willing to run the risk of losing a sale because it did not provide tests, workbooks, or a teacher's guide with its textbook. Few such items are provided for Soviet teachers, and so their costs are not included in the price of Soviet textbooks.

Sampling

American publishers are expected to provide free samples to teachers and members of adoption committees. In a large adoption state, such as Texas, a publisher may give away a thousand or more books before making the first sale. The cost of producing and distributing free books must be covered in the price of those that are eventually sold. The Soviet system does not require the use of free samples to generate sales.

Salaries and Training Costs for Salespeople

American publishers must sell their books in competition with other publishers. Therefore, they employ salespeople to represent the company and peddle the books from school to school. Sometimes a school will agree to purchase textbooks only if the publisher will provide in-service training without cost to the school corporation. The expense of such "free" training must also be absorbed in the price of textbooks. The Soviet Union has no need for textbook salespeople; what training costs exist are paid from other budgets.

Royalties for Authors

It may surprise American readers to learn that the authors of Soviet textbooks earn royalties. While the royalty rate is substantially less in the USSR than in the United States, the number of books sold is much greater. Therefore, a Soviet textbook author can derive significant income from textbook royalties, roughly equivalent to a professor's annual salary. Nevertheless, the proportion of the cost of a Soviet textbook that is devoted to royalties is about a one-third to one-half that of a comparable American textbook.

Recency of Copyright

American publishers are expected to make minor revisions in textbooks every two or three years, so that the books will show a recent copyright date. No state or school wants to adopt a textbook that is four or five years old when it can choose a book showing the current year as the date of copyright. Many of these "copyright revisions" are superficial; yet even the most trivial changes require the making of new plates and add to the cost of the books. Soviet textbooks are revised as frequently as American textbooks, but the textbooks do not last as long. Therefore, the production run for each revision is enormous — and thus much less expensive per unit.

Field Tests and Correlational Analysis

American publishers must conform to rules and regulations intended to satisfy state and local adoption committees. For example, Florida requires that a publisher's products be field tested and that the results of the field test be shared at the time of adoption. In some states publishers are also asked to show how their books are "correlated" with standardized tests, with state syllabi, and with other products used in teaching a particular course. These requirements are part of the cost of doing business. Soviet publishers have none of these costs. Soviet tests are designed to fit the textbooks, and the textbooks are designed to match the only approved syllabus for each course.

Rules, regulations, and unstated expectations that surround state and local adoption practices contribute to the high cost of textbooks in the United States. We could achieve substantial savings by eliminating many of these regulations and by delegating the responsibility for selecting textbooks to classroom teachers.

TREATMENT OF CONTENT

Americans can learn useful lessons from (1) examining the way Soviet curricula in history and geography are structured and (2) noting how Soviet textbooks respond to differences in course structure and organization. While American schools are unlikely to transport the content of Soviet history and geography textbooks directly into American textbooks, the Soviet approach to the treatment of content may be transportable. The way in which Soviet schools approach the organization of history and geography courses seems in line with some of the views expressed by critics of the American social studies curriculum and of American social studies textbooks. Some of these criticisms are as follows.

Too Little Attention to History and Geography

Many critics believe that the study of history and geography has been neglected in American schools. American students are typically required to study only one year of American history in high school; less than half of U.S. high school graduates have studied world history. While American history is often offered in grades 5 and 8, not all students are required to take these courses. Frequently, American history courses include content other than history. Many students study world geography in grade 7, but this course may be taught as "world cultures," with geography being only one of the themes addressed. Critics believe that even the officially designated history courses have been diluted by attention to social issues, which undermines more traditional academic presentations. In addition, the critics believe that history and geography, rather than social studies, should be taught in the elementary grades.

Superficial Treatment

Because each of the history and geography courses is taught as a yearlong or one-semester survey, it is necessary to cover a great deal of material rapidly. The tenth-grade world history course, for example, is expected to present the history of humankind from the Stone Age through the Atomic Age — in a single year. The yearlong eleventh-grade survey of American history must cover the period from the early explorers to the current day.

Pressures from various interest groups have led publishers to include the names of many people and references to many events that were not previously included in textbooks. However, while many people and events are now mentioned, there is little space to analyze them in depth.

Superficiality also arises from the need to teach such skills as reading, thinking, information gathering, and so on. To some extent educators encourage publishers to dilute the treatment of content in order to devote attention to the development of skills; many educators believe that it is more important for students to know how to learn than it is for them to acquire any specific amount of information.

Lack of Narrative

One result of superficial coverage is the absence of narrative. History textbooks no longer "tell a story" as they once did. Consequently, students have a difficult time making sense of the myriad events and people presented to them. Textbooks no longer weave people and events together into an easily understood narrative fabric. While students learn what happened, to whom, and when, they have less opportunity than in the past to know why things happened as they did. A major purpose for teaching history and the social sciences in public schools is to help students understand how the contemporary world came to be what it is and where it seems to be heading. Textbooks today have little time to deal with reasons why certain events occurred.

Lack of Congruence Across Courses

Social studies teachers cannot build confidently on what students have learned in previous classes. Moreover, they have no basis for judging what foundations they should be laying for future instruction, because the United States has no national consensus on the scope and sequence of social studies. The result is both gaps and redundancies in social studies education.

What the Soviet Union does is remarkably close to what many critics believe should happen to social studies education in America. First, Soviet youngsters begin their study of history in grade 5, and they continue to study history through grade 10, the last year of secondary school.[6] In grades 8 through 10 Soviet youngsters study two courses in history each year: history of the USSR and world history. Each year builds chronologically upon the preceding one, so that by grade 10 students have an entire year to study the last fifty years of both Soviet history and world history.

Soviet students study geography every year in grades 5 through 9. In grade 10 they take a course called "social sciences," which is essentially Marxism-Leninism. Except for a few special courses — such as a regional history of Lithuania taken only by students in that republic — there are no other requirements for history and geography. Social studies education as we know it in the United States is unknown in the USSR.

While Soviet history textbooks cover considerable ground and mention many people, dates, and events, they are built around a narrative of how and why things happened as they did. Marxism-Leninism is based on a teleological, materialist view of history, and Soviet textbooks do not miss opportunities to make that interpretation clear to students.

Skills are given much less prominence in Soviet textbooks. Students are expected mainly to master the content of the courses, and they are held accountable by examination.

Changing American textbooks in ways suggested by Soviet textbooks would require changing the social studies curriculum. As long as teachers must cover the history of the world or the history of America in a single year, it will be difficult to avoid superficiality. Two policies must change: social studies should be required every year, and the schools should abolish the Carnegie unit. If social studies were required every year, we would no longer need to cram every skill and every bit of knowledge into a one-year course. This would help us to reduce redundancy and eliminate gaps in content.

The Carnegie unit has been anathema to curriculum innovation. The Carnegie unit calls for 120 hours of instruction to be spread over approximately thirty-six weeks, with classes meeting four or five days a week for an average of about fifty minutes each. Adherence to the Carnegie unit limits the number of courses students can take each year; five courses are usually considered a full load. In Europe, students can take eight or nine different courses, because each class does not meet every day. The reason Soviet ninth-graders can take two courses in history and one in geography is that the total time devoted to the three courses is only slightly more than half the time an American student would spend in a class that carried equivalent credits.

If we abandoned the Carnegie unit, American high school students could study world history and American history each year in grades 8 through 11, leaving time to study geography, American government, economics, and other subjects in grade 12. Furthermore, no student would have to study all of American history or all of world history in any single grade. Rather, students could proceed chronologically through historical time as they moved from one grade to another. A tenth-grade world history textbook, for example, might cover only the period from World War I to the present. An American history textbook for grade 10 could cover a similar period, thus allowing the courses to be taught in parallel fashion on alternate days.

These simple steps—requiring more social studies and abolishing the Carnegie unit—would contribute greatly to resolving the criticisms directed at the content of today's history textbooks.

PEDAGOGICAL AIDS

Critics of American textbooks believe that publishers pay undue attention to the development of teacher aids and to prescriptions for teachers regarding how textbooks should be taught. As I pointed out above, one reason for such criticism is that providing peripheral materials and detailed teacher's guides drives up the cost of textbooks. Critics worry that such materials also have the secondary effect of "dumbing down" the teaching process. They are doubtful that good teaching can be carried on according to instructional recipes in teacher's guides. The effect of the proliferation of such guides may be that school administrators will be encouraged to assign people to teach history and geography who have had only minimal preparation in these fields.

In defense of publishers, I must point out that they know that adoptions and purchases of their textbooks are likely to depend on whether they provide materials to support teachers. They also know that teachers may be assigned to teach courses for which they are only marginally prepared. In such cases, the teacher's guides, tests, and workbooks may be all that stands between teachers and embarrassment before their classes.

A second reality is that even when teachers are qualified by virtue of college credits to teach a given course, they will find many of the supporting teacher materials useful because they provide shortcuts to classroom preparation. American teachers, as a group, carry a greater classroom load than teachers in nearly every other developed nation. American teachers teach more hours and typically have more preparations than Soviet teachers. They have less time to prepare for classes than their Soviet counterparts. Thus most American teachers welcome the assistance that publishers provide.

Soviet teachers rely almost exclusively on teacher-directed recitation, whereas the American public expects its teachers to vary the teaching methods they use. American teachers are supposed to look for new ways to capture students' attention, and they are expected to use a greater variety of instructional techniques. Yet they are given less time to prepare for classes than are Soviet teachers. It is not surprising that American publishers do more for American teachers than Soviet publishers do for Soviet teachers.

AUTHORSHIP

Critics of American textbooks complain loudly about the way in which textbooks are typically produced. In a few cases a single author may prepare a manuscript that is edited for style by a professional editor and then turned into a final product. Unfortunately, this approach, commonly used to produce trade books, is the exception rather than the rule in the publication of textbooks.

Textbooks are usually produced by a team of authors under contract with a publisher. At least one of the authors will probably be a recognized scholar in the field. This author will be joined by coauthors — perhaps a professor of education and one or more classroom teachers. The publishing firm will often provide an outline for the textbook. The firm will have determined what the largest adoption states specify as their criteria for textbook selection. The publisher may also select an author from one of the large adoption states in the hope of influencing the adoption process.

The authors then generate a manuscript and the editors at the publishing firm apply their skills. The editors will be especially concerned about the "readability" of the text; thus they will reduce complexity in sentences, seek shorter and more familiar words, and so on. A "good textbook" is one that meets the readability test for the designated grade level; style and reader interest are of secondary concern. Editorial assistants search for illustrations, design maps and charts, and provide much of the student "apparatus" for the book — study aids, end-of-chapter questions, index, supplementary reading lists, and so on. If these tasks cannot be done by the publisher's staff, these sections of the book may be prepared by a firm that specializes in such matters. The authors whose names appear on the cover may have contributed a little or a lot to the final product.

Authors in the USSR are selected through competition. The State Committee for National Education announces that it wishes to produce a textbook and invites scholars to compete to become authors. The syllabus for the course has already been determined, and the chosen author is expected to produce a textbook that matches that syllabus. The competition is limited to those who are judged to have an academic background sufficient to produce a sound textbook, and such a competition also serves to weed out those who lack the talent for writing a general textbook.

Because the final product will be routinely adopted by every school, it is not necessary to add additional authors for political reasons in order to satisfy specific constituencies. Nor is the task of developing ancillary materials a hugh one, because such materials are rarely provided. End-of-section and end-of-chapter questions are included in the text, but they are largely designed to help students recall what they have read.

Readability formulas play little or no role in the production of a Soviet textbook. The texts are first written and then edited to fit what adults believe children of the target age are able to read. If passages prove difficult, they are altered in subsequent editions.

The Soviet method for developing textbooks is so simple that we should find it easy to emulate. However, the USSR is not plagued by the complex hierarchical, highly politicized textbook adoption process that operates in the United States. It should be possible for U.S. publishers to hire talented authors and urge them to write interesting textbooks for students to read. But, until the present adoption system is changed, Americans can only envy the practices in the Soviet Union.

ACCOUNTING FOR STUDENT ACHIEVEMENT

American teachers are increasingly being held accountable for the performance of their students, and the teachers' concerns for accountability influence the kinds of textbooks they want to buy. First, teachers want textbooks to be at or below the reading level of every student in their classes. In the absence of other reliable measures, teachers have come to depend on readability formulas. Second, teachers want textbooks to provide the factual information that will be assessed on standardized tests. Since most such tests are multiple choice or require only short answers, teachers who want their students to look good on the tests make sure that all topics likely to be covered on the test are covered in the textbook. This concern for coverage contributes to the "mentioning" problem that textbook critics frequently cite.

In the USSR it is assumed that all students enrolled in a given class can and will learn the material. It is the teacher's job — in cooperation with the parents — to make certain that this happens. Soviet teachers do not have access to information from readability formulas to guide their selection of textbooks. In any case, they have no choice about the books that they use.

Students in the USSR are expected to pass examinations on the material covered in their courses, but American-style standardized tests are largely unknown. Soviet students take both teacher-made tests and tests that must be passed at the end of a school year or prior to entering college. The greater proportion of these are essay tests that require students to deal with materials in greater depth than is necessary in a short-answer test.

The current emphasis in the United States on measuring performance by nationally normed, standardized, short-answer examinations surely must have a direct negative impact on classroom teaching and an indirect negative impact on the kinds of textbooks that teachers prefer. Teachers are not likely to desire other kinds of textbooks — e.g., those that explore topics in depth rather than engage in superficial coverage—until the criteria by which teachers are held accountable are changed.

Although few Americans would choose to exchange the U.S. system of textbook production and selection for the Soviet system, some aspects of the Soviet system do seem desirable. Soviet educators can at least avoid some of the problems that beset textbooks and textbook publishing in the United States.

While complete federal control of the production and selection of textbooks in the United States seems unlikely, it is equally unlikely that greater regulation at the state and local levels will cure the problem. Having each state seek to solve the problem on its own will clearly lead to chaos. What might help, however, is more deregulation of the system. Let states retain the overall authority to determine the courses that must be taken to complete a high school education, let states provide general advice regarding the content of each course, double or triple the funding for each school to purchase instructional materials, and then delegate decisions about what to purchase to each school or even to each teacher within a school. Such changes would allow publishers who cannot currently afford to play the high-stakes game required by state adoption systems to enter the market with less expensive but highly attractive products that teachers would find useful. Let the market decide whether four-color illustrations and expensive ancillary materials are what teachers most need. Teachers who are given the choice of what to buy may be more attracted to $6 paperbacks than to $24 hardback, multicolored textbooks.

Finally, a word is in order about the reforms now under way in the USSR. The preceding descriptions have dealt with Soviet textbooks as they have been in the past, but major changes are being planned. During the first six months of 1988, considerable public attention was drawn to Soviet criticisms of the way history and geography were being taught in Soviet schools. The Academy of Pedagogical Sciences came under criticism for its "conservative" ways, and a new, comprehensive history curriculum adopted only as recently as 1986 was severely attacked. In May 1988 examinations were canceled for the stated reason that the textbooks were so bad that it was foolish to require students to be tested on their contents. Entirely new textbooks were promised.

In the spring of 1989 the examinations were reinstated, but teachers were given greater voice in how the exams were carried out. Teachers also began to use a combination of textbooks and reprints from the periodical press for instruction; this has encouraged more freewheeling discussion and classroom debate than before.

In June 1989 I was told by representatives of the Academy of Pedagogical Sciences that a new policy had been approved that would lead to the publication of alternative textbooks for each course and each grade level. It was unclear to me who would publish the alternative texts, when the policy would be fully implemented, and who would decide which textbooks would be selected among the alternatives — whether the choices would be made by individual teachers, by local school authorities, or by ministries of education in each of the fifteen republics. It was even suggested to me that American world history textbooks might be considered for use in Soviet classrooms.

Regardless of whether alternative textbooks become available, Soviet educators confront two important issues. One is a general reexamination of portions of Soviet history that have not been treated openly and frankly in Soviet textbooks. The second is the manner in which history and geography courses have been taught in the past. Soviet teachers have depended on recitation and have focused on helping students recall information contained in the textbooks. Today, greater emphasis is being placed on helping students think critically. What previously was discouraged is now being promoted, and existing textbooks were not designed to support such instruction. Ironically, Soviet educators are now interested in how American textbooks are designed because American schools are judged to be international leaders in promoting inquiry and critical thinking.

While it is unlikely that American and Soviet textbooks will come to resemble each other in the near future, it is time that American and Soviet educators look at each other's practices and borrow what they can to help solve the problems inherent in each nation's system.

NOTES

1. The U.S./USSR Textbook Study Project was established under the auspices of the Program of Exchanges Between the U.S.A. and the USSR for 1977–79. The project began in 1977, continued until the interruption of cultural and educational exchanges in December 1979, resumed in May 1986, and was recently brought to a close. The project was originally sponsored on the Soviet side by the USSR Ministry of Education and on the American side by four associations: The American Association for the Advancement of Slavic Studies, the Association of American Publishers, the Council of Chief State School Officers, and the National Council for the Social Studies. More than 100 American and Soviet historians, geographers, teachers, textbook writers, and educators have participated in the project. The purpose of the project was to examine history and geography

textbooks used in secondary schools in the two nations in order to determine what each nation teaches its youth about the other and about relationships between the two nations. In 1978 the two sides agreed on procedures for selecting and reviewing textbooks and for reporting their findings. Reviews of the textbooks were completed, exchanged, and discussed in 1979. Work on the final report was halted in December 1979 because of the political ramifications of the Soviet invasion of Afghanistan. In June 1981 the American side of the project produced an *Interim Report* on the work accomplished prior to December 1979. As a result of the Geneva Summit Conference between President Ronald Reagan and General Secretary Mikhail Gorbachev in November 1985, the project was restarted, along with many other educational and cutlural programs. In November 1987 representatives of the American and Soviet delegations met to renew their work on textbooks; in June 1989 American and Soviet textbook authors and editors met in Moscow to review the work they had accomplished. While contacts and efforts involving American and Soviet textbook authors and editors will continue under other auspices, the project has formally completed its work.

2. Paul Gagnon, *Democracy's Untold Story: What World History Textbooks Neglect* (Washington, D.C.: American Federation of Teachers, 1987); Gilbert T. Sewall, "American History Textbooks: Where Do We Go from Here?" *Phi Delta Kappan* (April 1988): 552–558; and Harriet Tyson-Bernstein, *A Conspiracy of Good Intentions: America's Textbook Fiasco* (Washington, D.C.: Council for Basic Education, 1988).

3. It should be noted that ministries of education exist in each of the fifteen republics as well. They exercise control over the content of certain textbooks that cover the history and literature of each republic. For example, the textbook on the history of the USSR is approved at the national level, while the textbook on the history of Estonia is approved by the Estonian Ministry of Education.

4. *Program for Eight-Year Schools and Secondary Schools: History* (Moscow: USSR Ministry of Education, 1976), p. 3.

5. Sewall, "American History Textbooks," p. 558.

6. The Soviet system of schooling has provided for both an "incomplete" secondary education through eight grades and a "complete" secondary education through ten grades. Today, an effort is under way to extend schooling through eleven grades. Such a reform cannot be achieved everywhere at once, but the target is now eleven years of schooling for everyone. The analysis in this essay is based on the more common ten-year curriculum.

Part 3

From the Trenches: Publishers and Authors

NAOMI SILVERMAN

Chapter Ten

From the Ivory Tower to the Bottom Line: An Editor's Perspective on College Textbook Publishing

---

Like breakfast cereals or automobiles or shoes, college textbooks are products that are manufactured and sold for the purpose of making a profit. Other (interrelated) factors play a significant role and cannot be dismissed: course curricula; pedagogical styles, trends, and fads; textbook selection criteria of instructors; interests and goals of authors; editorial management; the internal structure and operating procedures within individual publishing companies; external pressure groups and lobbies; the sources and distribution of funding for research within the various academic disciplines; social, political, economic, and cultural forces that shape ideas about what should be taught and why. But in any calculation of the weight these other factors carry in deciding what gets published and why, the bottom line remains constant: Will the book make a profit for the company?

Does this mean that college textbook publishing is a soulless enterprise coldly devoted to the bottom line? Or, is the profit-making function of college textbook publishing simply a reality of the world of business? Does pursuit of profit interfere with the role of textbook publishers as one of our society's institutional "gatekeepers of knowledge"? Can the *business* of producing textbooks also serve a socially useful function of disseminating knowledge, ideas, and information to students?

Like any other for-profit industry, commercial college textbook publishers are first of all in business to make money. From the corporate perspective, all other considerations are subordinated to this fact. At the same time, however, creation and distribution of the profit-making textbook product depends on specific author's and specific editorial, marketing, and sales personnel within the publishing company who bring goals, perceptions, ideas, and interests of their own to the task; these are sometimes, but not inherently or inevitably, in conflict with the financial goals of the corporation. Tensions — between the corporate profit motive, on the one hand, and the individuals who create, promote, and sell the profit-making product, on the other — shape the particular content and market destiny of each textbook that is put into the marketplace. The industry has been described as one that "remains perilously poised between the requirements and constraints of commerce and the responsibilities and obligations that it must bear as a prime guardian of the symbolic culture of the nation."[1] From my perspective, the interplay of these tensions, more than any other single factor, is what drives the complex process of college textbook publishing.

College textbook publishing is differentiated from other sectors of the publishing industry by a set of defining characteristics. First, the publisher targets specific markets, the size of which can be fairly accurately determined from available demographic and course enrollment data. Second, books produced to fit into the targeted market slots are promoted mainly through direct mail advertising, personal calls by sales representatives on professors who teach the course for which a given book is intended, and in some companies by telemarketers. Third, instructors select the books for their courses (they are major decision makers) and order the number of copies needed from a college bookstore (the bookstores are the major consumers of books directly from the publisher). Fourth, the publishing company sells the books to the bookstore at a base price, and students then purchase assigned books at a list price established by the individual bookstore, usually 20 to 25 percent higher (the difference between the base price and the list price is the bookstore's profit). A fifth factor in college textbook publishing is the used-book market, which operates outside the control of the publishing companies. Publishers are forced to hike up prices and to produce frequent revisions of texts to offset the loss of revenue that results from the existence of the used-book market.[2]

Now consider the fact that textbooks, along with lectures based on the content in them, are the major conveyors of knowledge, ideas, and information to students in college and university courses. Also consider these numbers: There are roughly 3400 postsecondary institutions in the

United States today, in which approximately 12,500,000 students are enrolled as undergraduate or graduate full-time or part-time students.[3] In almost every course, at least one textbook is assigned. The power of textbooks to shape the knowledge, ideas, values, and interpretive frameworks of the students who read them is clearly immense.

Given the influence textbooks have on students' minds, it is important to ask: Who decides what books will be published and what content they will contain? What actually guides these decisions and what constrains them? What are the effects and consequences of these decisions? What is the process by which an author's ideas become a printed book? More specifically, what role is played by the editor whose job it is to acquire and develop new books for publication?

The purpose of this essay is to pose some answers to these questions from my own perspective as an acquiring editor. In the next essay, Joel Spring presents an author's view of college textbook publishing. His essay and mine are intentionally related to each other; together they comprise a perspective on commercial college textbook publishing today.

FUNCTIONS AND REQUIREMENTS OF AN ACQUIRING EDITOR'S JOB

In a word, acquiring editors are product developers. We are the creative folks in the business, with responsibility for acquiring, dreaming up, or otherwise generating new products. To return to an earlier comparison, we are the counterparts of personnel in other industries who develop new automobile models, or cereal lines, or shoe styles.

Generally speaking, the job of an acquiring editor is to find authors to write textbooks that fit into the company's publishing plan and will make a profit; to oversee (but not with total authority) the development and production of these books; and to transmit accurate information about new products to the company's marketing department for use in sales and promotion efforts. But to describe the job in these terms is like saying, for instance, that a professor's job is to teach students and to be a scholar. Neither of these "job descriptions" spells out the complexities of the actual work or the specialized skills and knowledge that are required to do it. I'll first describe the sequential steps that comprise the process of acquiring and developing a book, and then lay on top of that picture the constraints and pressures within which the job is done — although, of course, in reality, these two aspects of the job cannot be separated.

Fulfilling the Company Publishing Plan

My work as an acquiring editor is governed by a publishing plan—developed by the corporation's top executives—that defines the company's long- and short-term goals. More specifically, the publishing plan designates the targeted markets for the company's products, outlines the type and range of products that will be offered, and specifies how the company wants to position its products within the textbook market as a whole and within each specific targeted market sector. The publishing plan determines, in an overall way, what books the editor is charged with acquiring, and it provides the economic logic for these decisions.

Individual college textbook companies concentrate on publishing specific lists of books. Decisions about which lists to publish are rooted in the company's historical identity and prior publishing experience and also based on information about current and projected market conditions (such as the existence of weak or open slots in the market, curricular trends pointing to the emergence of a new market, and demographic changes affecting market size). The plan for each list is structured as closely as possible to match the typical course structure of its corresponding academic discipline.

In "The Lid on the Garbage Can: Institutional Constraints on Decision Making in the Technical Core of College Textbook Publishing," Barbara Levitt and Clifford Nass make the point that:

> college-text publishing is inextricably interstructured with higher education, and this interdependence leads to higher education exerting coercive pressures on college-text publishers to achieve "structural equivalence," that is, a match between the hierarchical or functional divisions of the organizations. For example, college-text publishers create positions such as physics and sociology editors to match structural subdivision of higher education into academic disciplines. Thus, coercive institutional forces lead to the structure of academe being reproduced in the structure of college-text publishers, thereby shaping the organizational field such that publishing houses come to resemble each other structurally.[4]

An acquiring editor is assigned to one list, to a section of a list, or sometimes to several related lists. The goal is to "fill in" the list—that is, to publish at least one textbook for each course that constitutes a market (enrolls enough students to make publishing a book for the course profitable) within the given discipline. More than one book will be published for a course if there is reasonable evidence that a particular course market is segmented (in other words, that instructors vary significantly in their methodology for teaching their course, in their interpretation of the general course content, or in their selection of content to be covered). In addition, some companies publish textbooks for use as supplementary or recommended readings in specific courses; these texts do not provide comprehensive coverage of the course content but, rather, deal in depth with a piece of the course content or a related topic, or offer a particular point of view.

Essentially, the publishing plan is market driven. Or, more precisely, it is driven by the publisher's *perception* of the market, formed through its past publishing experience, market research findings, and other market information gathered from various sources—including editorial, marketing, and sales personnel. The publishing plan is not written in stone; it evolves over time and is constantly revised and adjusted in response to changing market conditions. In the end, the publishing plan represents the company's best efforts to assess its markets, to define its position in those markets, and to develop products for them. But development of the publishing plan is more the process of making educated guesses than it is the methodology of an exact science. An anecdote in *Books: The Culture and Commerce of Publishing,* Lewis Coser, Charles Kadushin, and Walter Powell's insightful study of the publishing industry, captures this perfectly:

> Given the built-in uncertainties of the market, the book trade, like the fashion business or the movie industry, often operates on the shotgun principle. As one Hollywood mogul is said to have told an inquisitive reporter, "One of the films on this list of ten will be a big success"; but when the reporter queried, "Which one?" the producer answered, "I have no idea." Publishers attempt to reduce such uncertainly. . . . [But ultimately the market research and the sales estimates they rely on]. . . . may be as unrealiable as weather forecasts in Maine.[5]

On one level, the business of college textbook publishing is simply a matter of matching books to markets so as to best maximize profits. Each publishing house works toward this same goal, but the end results differ, sometimes markedly, from publisher to publisher. For instance, two textbook publishers carry financially successful education lists, but company A is known for its serious, scholarly, "no-fluff" textbooks, whereas company B has a reputation for putting out glitzy, glossy, "dumbed down," superficial books.

Within the limits set by the publishing plan (this is important), acquiring editors have a relative degree of autonomy to set specific goals, to prioritize the projects they will pursue, and to make editorial decisions about numerous matters relevant to the books they acquire (including content, style, organization, level of difficulty, pedagogical orientation, interior design, and packaging). This contributes to the distinct shape or cast of an individual editor's list of books; one education editor's list, for example, may be quite different from the list a different editor in the same job would build, even though both lists would conform to the company's overall publishing plan. But, in the end, an acquiring editor cannot publish a book that does not conform to goals and requirements established at the highest levels of the company.

In sum, authority for defining the overall goals and market position of the publishing house belongs to its highest-level executives, but implementation of the publishing plan depends on decisions made by individual editors and marketing managers who together share responsibility on a case-by-case basis, but do not have ultimate decision-making authority for selecting the books to be published.

Finding Authors

College textbook authors emerge through a complex process of scouting and networking that is fundamentally the same for each editor but, at the same time, uniquely mediated by the particular combination of knowledge, skills, talents, interests, and personality traits the individual editor brings to the job.

Essential to my work as an acquiring editor is access to the pool of faculty members from which authors are eventually drawn. Authors can be actively sought or they can come unbidden via a phone call, a letter addressed "To the Editor," or through other unplanned encounters. Although a large number of unsolicited ("over the transom") proposals and manuscripts arrive in the mail, most of these either do not fit the publishing plan or do not meet the requirements and standards of the company (or the particular editor). Thus, most book proposals that are eventually accepted for publication (my totally unscientific guess is approximately 70 to 80 percent) are written by authors with whom the editor has had prior contact. As Coser, Kadushin, and Powell point out,

> Were editors to rely solely on formal means of manuscript submission . . . publishers would soon go out of business for there would be no efficient, low-cost way of separating the good from the bad. Prior screening by friends, by friends of friends . . . by professors who intercede for their proteges, and by a host of other informal "brokers" is the only flexible, trustworthy, and manageable way editors can cope with the avalanche of ideas or outlines for books . . . and actual full-blown manuscripts that routinely swamp editors. . . . To get a book published, recommendation through an informal circle or network is close to being an absolute necessity.[6]

Part of every college textbook acquiring editor's job is to visit college campuses (in my company we are required, during the academic year, to spend five days every month on the road). Before I visit a campus, I set up appointments with faculty members, including authors, prospective authors, and reviewers with whom I am already working, as well as other people whom I know for some reason—people who have been recommended to me as potential authors, whom I know to be "rising stars" or "risen stars," or whose work interests me. If I am going to a campus for the first time and don't know anyone on the faculty, I ask my assistant to make "blind" appointments with at least one person who teaches course A, one who teaches course B, and so on.

A typical author-scouting meeting usually takes an hour or less. My purpose in these meeting is to make contact with prospective authors, to learn about their writing plans and interests, and to gather various types of market information. There are "standard interview" questions—the bread-and-butter scouting work of campus visits. But, as in any other encounter between two individuals, chemistry (or call it what you will) affects what happens. Each meeting is different. At one extreme, I sometimes feel like one of the two proverbial ships passing in the night. Nothing happens; no real communication takes place. At the other extreme, something "clicks." The standard interview turns into a lively and enjoyable conversation, ideas start to flow, book ideas begin to take shape (and, sometimes, a genuine friendship is sparked).

Campus visits are one method I use to find new authors. Like every other college textbook editor, I also attend academic conferences and conventions. As most readers of this essay already know, the book exhibit area, hallways, eating and drinking places, and other public spaces outside the formal meeting rooms turn into a bazaar of academic and editorial discourse, power brokering, and wheeling and dealing. I set up appointments at conventions, as I do when I visit campuses, to meet with contracted and prospective authors (in a typical day I meet with six to twelve people). Also, I attend selected sessions, if the presenter is someone whose work interests me or if the topic is one I want to learn more about. This is a way of meeting people, but, more important, it provides an opportunity to keep abreast of what is happening in the discipline. Following the field—understanding its general content as well as debates, issues, and emerging trends within it—is an important part of my job. Perhaps the most important editorial work that takes place at conventions is the networking that occurs informally, in unplanned meetings and chance encounters. Editors have widely divergent opinions about the value of attending conventions, but, in my own experience, the "unquantifiable" outcomes are significant.

Other avenues into the halls of academe and the ranks of future authors include phone calls or ''scouting letters'' to people who have come to my attention as potential authors; tips from editors at other companies (most of us will refer a prospective author to another company, if his or her project doesn't fit into our own list); and leads from our sales staff in the field, who are required to file a certain number of author/reviewer scouting reports each year. Finally, the reputation of the company, a specific list, or a particular editor can attract potential authors.

Out of all these scouting missions and referrals, a network takes shape and continually branches out in new directions. This ever-expanding network constitutes the ''invisible college'' each editor relies on as a source of authors, reviewers, informal advisers, and book adopters. In a chapter titled ''Networks, Connections, and Circles,'' Coser, Kadushin, and Powell make the important point that ''how an editor is plugged into various networks is the paramount factor in the flow of projects, ideas, and manuscripts.''[7]

The Decision-Making Process

Getting and reading reviews. Assuming an editor has successfully set up channels for finding authors and that book proposals and manuscripts are flowing in at an acceptable rate, the next step is to weed out the best author candidates from those who already have projects under way and, among those who do not, to decide whom I do and do not want to encourage to write a book.

An informal decision-making process begins as soon as I meet an author candidate and form a first impression about his or her potential as an author. (Prospective author's reasons for electing to write a textbook range from the most intellectually sincere to the most commercially or politically self-serving.) The formal review process begins when an author candidate submits a book prospectus outlining the book he or she wants to write or is writing, provides a rationale for it, describes the market, and compares the proposed book to competing books put out by other publishers. I supply a formal set of guidelines for preparing a prospectus and will rarely accept a proposal that does not include all the information requested. I have learned to insist in almost every case on sample chapters—experience has taught me that just because somebody has a good *idea* for a book does not mean they are able to actually write one.

I read every prospectus I receive. First, I weed out all projects that are obviously not appropriate, for one or more of these reasons: the content does not match or fit into a course in my assigned markets; the book ''fits'' but the market is too small; the content and/or the writing is unacceptable in some way. I reject these projects outright (about one-third to one-half of those I receive), trying in each case to give the author the reason(s) for my decision as well as suggestions for other publishers who might be interested in the book.

Other proposals (perhaps one-fourth to one-third of those I receive) fall into a category I call "almost but not quite" — these projects have potential but are not precisely on the mark. In these cases, I try to work with the author (assuming he or she is amenable) to resolve whatever the problem happens to be (for example, content, market fit, writing style). The original concept may be modified, embellished, expanded, slimmed down, or otherwise reshaped through collaboration with the editor, who contributes his or her own ideas and tries to guide the author toward an acceptable proposal. Or, it may be reshaped by the author, who may guide the editor to view the project in a different way. Perhaps half of these "almost but not quite" proposals are eventually revised and resubmitted for reconsideration.

A third category of book proposals (about one-fourth to one-third of all I receive) are acceptable as is: the prospectus is well written, the book fits squarely into the market, and the author has provided all information necessary to get the review process under way.

When a project is ready for external review, I make a series of decisions about how many and which reviewers to commission. As with everything else about acquisitions work, there is no automatic formula for selecting reviewers. Usually, I want reviewers who teach a course in which the proposed book could be used as a primary or supplementary text. Beyond this, however, my choice of reviewers depends on what kind of information I hope to get from the reviews; different criteria for selecting reviewers apply for different projects.

What weight do reviewers carry in the decision-making process? They play a significant role in helping editors make publishing decisions, but they do not *determine* the decision. Basically, reviewers provide two kinds of feedback: first, as potential adopters of the proposed text, they reflect (in a not-very-scientific way) what the market does and does not want; second, as academics with specialized knowledge, they contribute their subject-area expertise to identifying both problems and strengths to be developed in the content of a proposed book.

Part of the decision-making process involves interpreting the reviews and relaying my interpretation to the prospective author(s). When the reviews come in I send the author (or all coauthors) blind copies. Usually, we discuss the reviews in a phone conversation or in person. What happens next varies greatly from case to case. Some book proposals receive unanimously "rave" reviews. At the other extreme, the reviews are uniformly negative. Most often the reviews are mixed. First I decide if I want to encourage the author to revise and resubmit the proposal. If not, this is the end of the road. If so, I offer my suggestions, the author offers his or hers, and together we work out what changes will be made. For all projects that I decide to propose for publication, the author submits a written reply to the reviews; this becomes part of the formal publishing proposal that is routed through the approval process I describe below.

My own reading of reviews weighs heavily in a publishing decision. I rarely rush to offer a contract solely on the basis of a set of good reviews, nor do I necessarily or automatically reject a project some or all of the reviewers do not like for one reason or another. Acquiring editors learn early on to read between the lines, to extract what is relevant and useful from what is not. Reviewers sometimes have idiosyncracies, hidden agendas, or professional and personal motives that color their reactions to a book proposal. For example, one reviewer may be planning to write a similar book in the future, a second reviewer may have an ideological disagreement with the author(s) of the book he or she is critiquing, a third reviewer may suggest turning the proposed book into something altogether different from what the author wants it to be and totally inappropriate for my list. So reviews cannot be taken at face value. I need to sort out useful criticisms and suggestions from those that are idiosyncratic, irrelevant, misleading, hostile, or useless for whatever reason.

As Levitt and Nass point out, ''Reviewers sometimes reduce uncertainty, but they often disagree with one another.'' They go on to quote one editor in their study, who commented:

> It's easy to weed out the books you know you don't want to do, as well as the others you know you are definitely going to publish, no matter what. It's the ones that are in the middle that are hard. For example, the manuscript sitting on my desk right now. I wasn't sure what to do with it, so I got five reviewers. Two said great, two said terrible, one said don't know. So I'm back where I started.[8]

An important factor in the decision-making process is the author's response to the reviews, which run the gamut from angry/defensive to receptive/cooperative. Each author is different; each book proposal presents a different set of concerns. So in the end, what actually determines an editor's publishing decision? Levitt and Nass report, ''In performing structured, open-ended interviews with editors of the ten best-selling introductory textbooks in physics and sociology, we were struck by the way editors consistently described their work in gambling terms, such as 'a lottery with bad odds,' 'an attempt to hedge one's bets,' or 'a crapshoot'.'' I would concur with their assessment that ''the procedures for decision making are best described as 'guesswork, intuition, and opinion.' ''[9]

Up to this point in the decision-making process, I operate with a fair degree of independence. Formal approval from persons above me in the organization is not required for what I do in the course of finding authors and reviewing book proposals, as long as my work stays within the general guidelines established by the publishing plan and within the operating budgets that govern my activities. However, if I decide at the end of the precontract review process that I want to sign a particular book, I cannot proceed to make a binding contract offer until my proposal to publish the book has been approved by a committee of executives above me in the organization.

Each step along the way to a final publishing decision draws more people, at respectively higher levels of authority in the company, into an increasingly more formal decision-making process. A contract represents not only a publishing decision but also a legal commitment to make a financial investment in a project. The acquiring editor is entrusted with the job of finding and recommending books for publication, but does not have final authority over this kind of investment decision.

Routing the publishing proposal for approval. At this point in the decision-making process, several things are happening more or less at the same time: I conduct a profitability analysis to determine whether or not the bottom line is acceptable; I begin preliminary contract negotiations with the author; I start routing the publishing proposal for approval. These activities are not necessarily sequential; they can occur in any order, or simultaneously. Disagreements that arise at this point in the decision-making process often involve differing perceptions of what the market wants or varying degrees of willingness to take a chance on a project that has promise but could potentially pose a financial risk.

Let's say I do have an acceptable bottom line, that the author and I have agreed on contract terms (which must be factored into the financial analysis before I can calculate the bottom line), and that the marketing manager and my supervisor have both approved the project. Next I submit a formal publishing proposal to the committee of executives whose approval is necessary before I can release a contract. By the time the project reaches this stage, it has been thoroughly reviewed, screened, analyzed, questioned, and debated—by me, by the external reviewers, by the marketing manager, by my supervisor, and, finally, by the vice-president of the editorial division—in terms of its content, its market position, and its anticipated profitability. Our collective evaluation of the publishing proposals that make it to the last rung in the ladder of authority is not usually questioned. The primary concern of the executive committee is the bottom line. If it is acceptable, the project usually glides smoothly through this final step of the approval process.

Developing the Content of A Book

My primary functions after the contract has been signed and during the time the book is being written are threefold: working with the author to develop the content of the book, keeping the project on schedule, and keeping it on budget.

Each contract decision involves specific agreements between the author and the editor on the intended course market for the book, on the position in that market this particular book will occupy, and on how the author will develop the book to be most competitive in the targeted market slot. One of my responsibilities is to ensure that the content of the book stays "on course" — that it conforms to the original plan for the book in terms of content coverage, organization, level of writing, pedagogical features, and the like.

Almost every manuscript-in-progress is reviewed by external reviewers one or more times during the course of its development; *every* manuscript is reviewed when it is completed in draft form. This process is similar to the precontract review process described earlier, except that this time the purpose is not to make a contract decision, but to get feedback that will be helpful to the authors and to me in improving the content and the marketability of the book.

In addition, an in-house developmental editor also routinely reviews each partial manuscript and each complete manuscript. Many manuscripts do not require any exceptional developmental work, but some authors need a little (or a lot) of assistance. The developmental editor is concerned with writing, organization, and other technical and stylistic aspects of the book.

After the external reviewers and the developmental editor have reported to me, decisions about what kind of work is required and who will do it are made collaboratively by me and the author, referring to the external reviews and in consultation with the developmental editor as needed. The author and I agree on what changes will be made before the manuscript is turned over to the production department, where a production editor is assigned to shepherd the manuscript through the process that eventually results in a bound book.

The style, or influence, of an individual editor comes into play here. Different books require different kinds of developmental work; each relationship between myself and an author is different; different editors make different kinds of editorial decisions and provide varying degrees and types of guidance for authors. These decisions represent the individual editor's judgment, exercised within the existing market and organizational constraints. The dilemma that can be posed by such constraints is not a new one, as illustrated by this passage from a chapter on "Textbooks" in *Are American Teachers Free?* written in 1936:

> The position of the honest publisher is difficult. One of the most experienced and best known men in the textbook business, former head of a most reputable firm, concluded, after describing the publisher's dilemma: "He wants to tell the truth, and have his authors do the same. Yet he must sell books." Therefore, even the most honest publishers must modify books to remove "objectionable" features that will hurt sales, yet at the same time save their own and their author's consciences, and withal rationalize their business reasons into scholarly ones and never admit to the public that they change texts for the sake of sales.[10]

The Editor's Role in the Production Process

When all developmental work has been completed, the manuscript is turned over to the production department. My job, during the production process, is to oversee the smooth passage of the project from manuscript to bound book (the actual work is done by the persons described below). The simplest way to describe my role in the production process is to list the players involved and to describe the nature of my working relationship with these individuals.

The *managing editor* supervises a group of *production editors*. The production editor carries the major responsibility for trafficking the project through all the stages from manuscript to bound book (this usually takes about nine months). The *director of manufacturing* is the person responsible for providing estimated and actual manufacturing costs, and for selecting the suppliers (typesetters, printers, and other manufacturing services) to be used for each project. Several *manufacturing supervisors* report to the director of manufacturing. The manufacturing supervisor assigned to a given project is the liaison between the publishing house and the suppliers, and is responsible for keeping the manufacturing of the book on schedule. An *art director* also reports to the director of manufacturing. This person is in charge of interior book design and cover design, and assigns in-house or freelance staff to projects.

All of these people have clearly defined functions and responsibilities which they carry out with a large degree of autonomy as long as no problems arise that require decisions beyond the scope of their authority. Any problems or issues involving matters within the acquiring editor's domain are brought to his or her attention; the acquiring editor, within the limits explained throughout this essay, is the person most immediately in charge. If the problem involves major expenditures beyond those budgeted for the book or a serious delay in the publication date, the acquiring editor must consult with his or her immediate supervisor, and, as needed, with persons higher up in the organization.

The Editor's Role in Marketing a Book

I am first involved at the precontract stage, where, working with the author and the marketing manager, and using feedback from external reviewers, we identify where and how the book will fit into the market and what we expect its market share and projected revenue to be. After the book is in production and its publication date is set, I meet with the marketing manager to select the mailing lists we will use to promote the book and to make other marketing decisions as needed. As the book travels through the stages of production, I begin to feed information to the marketing and promotion departments as they request it for use in sales and promotional acitivities. The editor's most important role in maketing a book is to transmit clear and accurate information about the content of the book, its distinguishing features, and its targeted market. Commercial success depends to a great extent on how well this information is conveyed to the sales and marketing staff.

Requirements of the Job

So far, I have been describing the functions of an acquiring editor and the sequential steps that lead from finding authors to putting bound books into the marketplace. These functions have various requirements attached to them concerning travel, reports, quotas, budgets, schedules, and deadlines, which impose restrictions on my work insofar as they limit and control my day-to-day activities and decisions. These restrictions, however, are extensions of an interrelated set of constraining forces that operate on a larger scale, as I discuss below.

CONSTRAINING FORCES

The most powerful force, without question, is the tyranny of the bottom line. It wields at once the most far-reaching and also the most immediate and concrete impact. A second force, really a byproduct of the first, consists of two interlinked trends in ownership and management of college textbook publishing that have accelerated since the mid-1970s and, as a consequence, are significantly altering the industry: consolidation through takeovers, mergers, and acquisitions, combined with increasing foreign ownership of publishing companies in the United States.

To chronicle the history of changes in ownership and to analyze the economic forces that set them into motion is beyond the scope of this essay. What is important for my purposes here is, first, the simple fact that these changes are a direct consequence of, and inextricably linked to, the quest for profits that rules the world of corporate enterprise. Beyond this, repercussions of these changing patterns of ownership and management are rippling through every level of the college textbook industry, affecting the goals, management policies, and internal operation of publishing houses and the daily work lives of the people who work within them.

Stated in the briefest terms, what is occurring is concentration of the industry in fewer and fewer hands; installation of rationalized, bureaucratic management practices borrowed from other industries;[11] pressure to make conservative publishing decisions as a way of avoiding economic risk taking; and a focus on short-term profits. Growth, expansion, and cost-effectiveness are the goals that rule the day. The pace of work is speeded up accordingly; quality and craftsmanship are weighed against their costs. Books are mass-produced according to standard procedures and designs and within tight budgetary constraints. More specifically, in terms of my work as an editor, there is less time for the "personal touch" all the way around; less time to read manuscripts carefully; less time for in-depth, time-consuming development work on book proposals and manuscripts in progress.

But these are *trends,* not (at least not yet) monolithic realities; the publishing industry has not turned suddenly, dramatically, in a new direction. As Coser, Kadushin, and Powell put it, "The tensions between the claims of commerce and culture seem to us to always have been with book publishing." It is certainly true, as they point out, that "these tensions . . . have become more acute and salient in the last twenty years."[12] However, they go on to say:

> The myth is widespread that book publishing in the nineteenth and early twentieth centuries was a gentlemanly trade in which an editor catered to an author's every whim, whereas commercialism and hucksterism have taken over in our day. It is a useful myth, to be sure, for it permits authors to point to a golden past and allows publishers to fashion for themselves a fine pedigree going back to a time when their profession was not sullied by the crass requirements of the marketplace. . . . [But] in publishing, as in many other spheres of social life, there is little that is new. . . . book publishing in the past as in the present has operated under the pressures of the marketplace, the countinghouse, and the literary and intellectual currents of the day. The quest for profit and the demands of excellence have all too often refused to go hand in hand. One should not be surprised that these same tensions, albeit in somewhat different form, are still here today.[13]

In an article titled "A Publisher's Perspective on Textbook Publishing," Arthur M. Rittenberg takes a different point of view. For him, the bygone golden days of publishing are now long vanished. He is sharply critical of the changes that are taking place in the industry today. Rittenberg describes how "college textbook publishing in its beginnings was made up of relatively small, owner-managed, privately held, family-controlled companies" and laments the disappearance of the "owner-managers of that era [who] were men of significant accomplishment and erudition with a sense of dedication to publishing for education."[14] The industry today, he claims, is one that has shed its time-honored image of a "gentleman's profession" to become a modern business enterprise in which the controlling factors are:

> the combined onslaught of the conglomerate, foreign owners, and financial investors with their overriding concern for short-term profits and return on investment; . . . the endless reports and strategic planning demanded of creative editors and marketers by financial managers who dominate most publishing houses today; [and] the absence of people at the top of the chain of command with educational background, values, and concerns who can set professional standards for enhancing the quality of published materials.

He goes on to say, "It would be unreasonable to condemn publishers for a lack of concern for quality but there is a not so subtle distinction between concern for the bottom line and concern for the best educational materials."[15]

Rittenberg is discussing here what he views as the erosion of ideals and standards in the textbook publishing industry of today. But, Rittenberg idealizes the past; he fails to recognize that many people in the college textbook industry today—as in the past—are, in his words, people of "significant accomplishment and erudition, with a sense of dedication to publishing for education."

There is really no disagreement between Rittenberg, on the one hand, and Coser, Kadushin, and Powell, on the other, that what they respectively call "concern for the bottom line" and the "claims of commerce" shape the processes within and the products of the publishing industry; what they would argue is the extent to which this concern *dominates* the business. I would argue that it is dominant, in the sense that it guides the overall policies and decisions of the corporation. But, at the same time, it does not exclude the existence within the corporation of individuals who bring to their work concerns that transcend the bottom line. These people "find themselves often torn between the requirements of commerce and their sense of cultural responsibility."[16]

Publishing by its very nature tends to attract into its ranks book lovers, intellectuals, creative souls, people with a sense of social mission, and others as well, who genuinely enjoy being in the business of making books (rather than, say, breakfast cereals or automobiles or shoes). These people choose to work in the industry because they want to be involved with ideas, words, print, the art and craft of turning concepts for books into manuscripts and then into bound books. They could earn higher salaries as product developers, for example, or as marketing managers, in a different kind of business. But such people, myself included, make a choice. We *prefer* to work in the publishing industry for reasons such as these. The point is this: For editors such as myself, and for numerous others who work in the industry, the "claims of commerce" do impose limits on how free we are to pursue the "claims of culture"—particular visions in our minds of what textbooks *could be;* but within these constraints and limits, individuals can and do bring out textbooks that are scholarly, interesting, challenging, innovative. I know from my own experience that it is possible for a profitable textbook to also be a good textbook, for intellectually substantive, high-quality textbooks to enter the market — despite pressures placed on their creators by the *business* of publishing.

TRENDS FOR THE FUTURE: TWO SCENARIOS

Scenario One: The Postmodern Textbook

Here is one vision of what a textbook *could be:*

First, the goal of the text is not only to disseminate objective data and information, but also to stimulate the student to think critically and analytically; to lead the student to recognize that all knowledge is mediated by the "knower"; to engage the student in a dialogue with the text. The meaning of the text is in the interaction (dialogue) between the reader and the text, not specifically in the author's mind or in the words on the page.

Second, the author does not claim that the content of the textbook is comprehensive or all-inclusive, or that he/she is presenting a body of knowledge that is universally accepted or the unchallenged truth. The idea of a *canon*—a standard, official body of knowledge—and the concept of the textbook as an authoritative, neutral, objective, unchanging source of knowledge, not to be questioned, is reexamined.

Third, the text is conceived as a work of *original scholarship,* not as an encyclopedic compendium of objective information. It is acknowledged to be the author's own synthesis, interpretation, or configuration of the material and is presented as a subjective — not an objective — account. (The underlying assumption is that objectivity is a false construct.)

Fourth, the author *contextualizes* the content of the text, in two ways: (a) The author speaks in his/her own voice (which is clearly identified as such), and may describe his/her own relationship to the material in the book (how and why he/she got involved in the subject, what it means to him/her, and the like). (b) The text refers to the history of ideas, to intellectual traditions and schools of thought that inform current thinking on its subject; the author puts the material in a social/historical/political context, acknowledging the impact of these larger forces on the subject matter of the text, and recognizing that knowledge, ideas, and interpretative frameworks in any subject continually change over the course of time.

Fifth, the author weaves voices other than his or her own into the text, including anecdotal and narrative material (to illustrate and enliven abstract concepts and also to present a range of views on a given topic, e.g., the views of a teacher, a parent, and a student on the topic of grades), and other scholars' interpretations or approaches (which serve as "lenses" through which to view the content in the book and provide a framework for thinking about it). The text thus tells a story, it does not claim to tell the "truth."

This concept of what a textbook can be reflects thinking that is currently at the forefront of intellectual and creative life around the world. *Postmodern* is a term that is used today across the academic disciplines and the creative and performing arts to refer to works that reach beyond modernity and conventionality for the essence of a new mode of communication.

Is there a market for books such as these? Will they make a profit? I have worked with several authors over the past few years to develop textbooks premised on ideas that have germinated in the hotbed of postmodern thinking; these books embody the spirit and the defining characteristics of what I am calling the postmodern textbook. Textbooks like these appeal to a segment of the market that generally does not like and does not use "textbooks" in the traditional sense. My discussions with faculty members across the country leave no doubt in my mind that many are looking for alternatives to traditional textbooks. Sales figures for the books of this type on my list have exceeded expectations. I don't expect the postmodern textbook to push conventional textbooks out of the market; but I do envision a marketplace in which real alternatives are available.

Scenario Two: Computerized Textbooks

A November 15, 1989 article in the *Chronicle of Higher Education* is headlined: "With the Aid of Computers, New Publishing Ventures Allow Professors to Create Customized Textbooks." The subtitle reads, "Some observers foresee a revolution in the way information is delivered to students, faculty members." The article goes on to detail the characteristics of McGraw-Hill's "Custom Publishing System," which will enter the market in 1990. Essentially, "The McGraw-Hill system lets professors choose the information in the textbooks they use — specific chapters, worksheets, journal articles, and original material prepared by individual professors themselves." Professors will be able to select information from a huge computerized data base offering:

> both text and formats for textbooks, journals, magazines, and supplementary materials published by McGraw-Hill. . . . New computer and printing technologies allow the company to search the data base for the exact information needed in the customized text, organize it, paginate it, reproduce it, bind it, and deliver it to students in less than a week, often for less than the cost of a conventional textbook.[17]

McGraw-Hill's first customized text will be the ninth edition of *Accounting: The Basis for Business Decisions,* along with the seventy supplements for this text that have been written over the years by its father-and-son author team, Walter B. Meigs and Robert F. Meigs, both accounting professors at large universities. Some of the benefits of "print-on-demand" textbooks are obvious: it will be possible to update textbooks easily; neither publishers nor bookstores will have to store large inventories of books; books will be readily available on demand and will not go out of print because printing will become "a relatively trivial part of the process."[18] Using advanced, high-speed computers and laster printers, college bookstores will eventually be able to do on-the-spot printing of customized texts from digitalized information sent over computer networks.

Other companies are also developing a range of textbook-like products based on computer technology. For example, Xiamax is pioneering what it calls "the successor to the book — a tiny, lightweight computer that can store thousands of pages of text, find any word or phrase in those pages in a fraction of a second, and save it in electronic form. This 'Electronic Book' could bridge the gap between massive computerized data bases, and the eminently portable book."[19]

Several recent articles, in addition to the one in the *Chronicle* cited here, discuss the technology, economics, and market potential of electonic publishing products that would have been unimaginable before the technological advances of the Information Age.[20]

What will be the implications of these developments for the college textbook industry and, beyond that, for the teaching and learning processes that take place in college and university classrooms? "This is the transformation of print," says Kenneth C. Green, a senior research associate at the Center for Scholarly Technology at the University of Southern California. Robert D. Lynch, executive editor of the college division at McGraw-Hill and manager of the new Custom Publishing System, goes even further, stating, "Many of us have known for a while that we are not in the business of producing bound textbooks, but of delivering information." Electronically customized textbooks, he states, herald "the transformation from static to dynamic information . . . We are all heading toward electronic access to information."[21]

John R. Garret, manager of business development at the Copyright Clearance Center, observes that "in many ways the textbook is a great solace. . . . Somebody else has done the job of organizing and ordering core ideas. Do people really want to do that work themselves?" His comments hint at the potential of technology to revolutionize the way professors organize and teach their courses. Robert Meigs, one of the authors of the first customized textbook, is more explicit: "Professors had a relatively safe and secure environment in the past. They adopted a text, and had to follow the pattern. Now there will be an unlimited number of decisions to be made."[22]

The gap between the postmodern textbook and electronically produced, cutomized textbook products is really not as wide as it appears at first glance to be. Gary Shapiro's comments in "A Look Into the Future: What Will Happen to the College Textbook? (In Which the Author Describes Several Interesting Scenarios Which May Occur Between Now And the Year 2015)," speak to this point:

> The college textbook, as we know it today, is being transformed from a *passive* instructional tool to an *interactive* one as a result of the technological components being added to it. . . . The last of the postwar faculty are retiring. In their place are younger instructors . . . used to getting and reading academic journals on CD Rom and seeing them abstracted on computerized databases. . . . They read magazines rather than books, and fight to keep up with the tremendous volume of information being published about their specialties. . . . [These instructors] want their teaching materials customized, and *they don't like being forced to teach courses or use textbooks which follow other people's agendas*. [Emphasis added throughout.][23]

The question for the future is this: What will happen as technological advances continue to "drive the development of innovative ways to deliver textbooks and other material to students"[24] and as a new generation of instructors increasingly demand genuine alternatives to the old-fashioned, traditional text?

NOTES

1. Lewis A. Coser, Charles Kadushin, and Walter W. Powell, eds., *Books: The Culture and Commerce of Publishing* (Chicago: University of Chicago Press/ Basic Books, 1982), p. 7.

2. See Coser et al., *Books,* chap. 2, for a detailed discussion of "Publishing Worlds: Secotrs within the Industry."

3. *U.S. News and World Report, 1989: American's Best Colleges* (Washington, D.C.: *U.S. News and World Report,* 1988).

4. Barbara Levitt and Clifford Nass, "The Lid on the Garbage Can: Institutional Constraints on Decision Making in the Technical Core of College-Text Publishing," *Administrative Science Quarterly* 34 (1989): 198; see also John W. Meyer and Barbara Rowan, "Institutionalized Organizations: Formal Structure as Myth and Ceremony." *American Journal of Sociology* 83 (1977): 340–363.

5. Coser et al., *Books,* pp. 7–8.

6. Ibid., p. 73.

7. Ibid., p. 75.

8. Levitt and Nass, "The Lid on the Garbage Can," p. 196.

9. Ibid., pp. 191–192.

10. Beale, *Are American Teachers Free?* (New York: Scribner's, 1936), pp. 317–318.

11. This point is made in Coser et al., *Books,* p. 8.

12. Ibid., p. 7.

13. Ibid., p. 35.

14. Arthur M. Rittenberg, "A Publisher's Perspective on Textbook Publishing," *Educational Policy* 3, no. 2 (June 1989): 154.

15. Ibid., p. 161.

16. Coser et al., *Books,* p. 15.

17. Judith Axler Turner, ''With the Aid of Computers, New Publishing Ventures Allow Professors to Create Customized Textbooks,'' *Chronicle of Higher Education,* November 15, 1989, p. A19.

18. Ibid., p. A19.

19. Ibid., p. A25.

20. See, for example, Edwin McDowell, ''Facts to Fit Every Fancy: Custom Textbooks Are Here,'' *New York Times,* October 23, 1989, pp. D1, D11; Edwin McDowell, ''Publishing Turmoil: Running a Successful House Will Involve Knowledge of Numbers as Well as Letters,'' *New York Times,* November 21, 1989, pp. D1, D22; Gary Shapiro, ''A Look Into the Future: What Will Happen to the College Textbook? (In Which the Author Describes Several Interesting Scenarios Which May Occur Between Now and the Year 2015),'' *NACS College Bookstore Journal* (May/June 1989): 29–39.

21. Turner, ''Customized Textbooks,'' pp. A19, A25.

22. Ibid., p. A25.

23. Shapiro, ''A Look Into the Future,'' p. 36.

24. Ibid., p. 38.

JOEL SPRING

Chapter Eleven

Textbook Writing and Ideological Management: A Postmodern Approach

---

My experience as a textbook author involves an interesting interplay between learning to write a textbook and studying political and economic influences on the content of textbooks. I first considered writing a textbook in 1976, when I accepted a position at the University of Cincinnati involving the teaching of a large undergraduate introductory course on American education. Like many professors, I was not very happy with the quality of textbooks available for undergraduate instruction, which I found to be lacking in intellectual substance and critical perspectives. This was particularly true of textbooks for education courses, which are often filled with endless lists of platitudes about the role of schooling in American society and are designed to help students memorize rather than think critically about content. I decided to write my own textbook.

During my journey through the world of textbook writing I learned to distinguish between the modern textbook of the twentieth century and what I call the "postmodern textbook." The modern textbook is presented to the student as an authoritative statement of knowledge about a particular field. Often, the modern text presents knowledge as free of scholarly disputes and politically neutral. The impression is conveyed to readers that there is agreement among all scholars about the correctness or truth of a given body of knowledge. Often this impression is reinforced by the use of standardized tests that assume agreement on correct answers and on the importance of each question. Also, the modern textbook presents knowledge outside of its political context. What is considered important knowledge in a particular field of study is determined by the political attitudes of scholars. Even in the sciences and mathematics, knowledge has evolved as the result of political decisions about research funding. The domination of money for defense research after World War II shaped the development of these fields. Interpretations of knowledge in the social sciences and humanities are directly connected to the political orientations of scholars. For instance, there are conservative and liberal interpretations in history, sociology, economics, and political science.

Besides presenting knowledge as standard and neutral, the modern textbook is organized as a compendium of facts. These facts are presented in a language that does not make reading pleasurable and, in fact, often puts readers to sleep. Instructional aids in modern textbooks are primarily designed to help students memorize information as opposed to helping them think critically about the material. In addition, textbook writers do not attempt to make their texts a scholarly contribution to a field of study.

On the other hand, the postmodern textbook, as I conceive of it, retains the modern textbook writer's concern with pedagogical methods but attempts to develop critical thinking, to present material in an interesting literary style, and to make a scholarly contribution. What I think can be learned from the modern textbook is that textbook writers must be consciously pedagogical. They must develop strategies for teaching the reader while avoiding the worst features of modern textbooks. The postmodern textbook should not present knowledge in an authoritative fashion but should recognize scholarly debates over knowledge and the political influences that shape the knowledge of a field. The postmodern textbook should be organized so that students will think critically about the content and will interact about the content with the text and other readers. Writers of postmodern textbooks should try to achieve a writing style that makes the material intellectually interesting to the reader. Finally, they should attempt to make scholarly contributions by offering an important synthesis or interpretation of a field of study in the textbook.

I make the distinction between modern and postmodern textbooks after more than a decade of textbook writing. The following is an account of my experiences and the evolution of my thinking regarding textbooks. This account includes a description of the political and economic forces shaping textbooks, and the role of textbooks in what I call "ideological management."

LEARNING TO WRITE A TEXTBOOK

I gave little thought to the above issues when I entered the world of textbook writing in 1976. At the time, my editor was a person who several years earlier approached me in a hotel hallway at the annual meeting of the American Educational Research Association to ask if I would be interested in writing a book. Interestingly, the editor never mentioned what type of book. As I would learn in later years, editors frequently build networks of authors through casual contacts at academic meetings. I immediately expressed interest in writing a history of educational policy since World War II. "Fine," he said, "send me a book prospectus and we will work it out from there." After my history was published, the college list of the company was purchased by Longman Inc. and, consequently, both my book and editor found a new home.

When I telephoned my editor about writing an introductory textbook, he enthusiastically responded with a request for a prospectus. In a procedure that I would later learn was highly unusual in the publishing industry, the editor approved the prospectus and issued a contract without any reviews from other academics in the field. Typically, most proposals for textbooks are sent out for review to instructors who might use the book in their courses. In this manner, textbooks are more closely tied to the needs of the market. Not only was the prospectus not reviewed, but I did not intend to follow the plan outlined within it. I knew nothing about writing a textbook and the prospectus was made up one brief afternoon at a tyepwriter. My personal plan was to write the book while teaching the course.

So in the fall of 1976, I got up every morning at 5:30 and wrote material to serve as both lectures for my course and chapters for the textbook. This was all done without guidance from my editor or external reviewers. Writing the material in this manner closely tied it to the structure of an academic course. This solved a problem that I never gave much thought to in making my original proposal. Obviously, a textbook needs to be organized to fit the actual length of a course and chapters need to be organized to fit what might be a week or two weeks of instruction. In other words, the actual structure of a textbook must parallel the structure of college courses. By combining the writing of lectures with textbook chapters, I unconsciously included the rhythm of college instruction in the structure of the textbook.

While writing the textbook, I found myself wondering about the politics of textbooks. Like many university professors I had heard horror stories about pressures placed by publishing companies on authors of college texts. A close friend told me about a publishing company pressuring him to delete several pages on the John Birch Society from a college textbook on the history of American education because the editors worried that a negative discussion of this radical right organization might hurt sales to colleges in the South. My friend refused to comply, and the company informed him that the publishing contract gave them ownership of the book, and that they would lock it up and not release it until the objectionable material was removed. Faced with the possibility of having several years work sitting idle in the file cabinet of the publisher, my friend agreed to remove the disputed material. This was only one of many tales circulated through academe about publishers demanding the removal of controversial material they feared would hurt sales.

Contrary to the publishing industry's fear of including controversial and politically radical material in college textbooks, I came to the conclusion based on my experience that it is precisely this type of material that many, but not all, college professors and students enjoy finding in texts. But history taught the publishing industry a different lesson, particularly the history of publishing for elementary and secondary schools. This lesson is one of fear, fear that some group or individual will start a campaign against a textbook because of material they find objectionable and that the resulting controversy will cause schools to refuse to use the book.

I thought about the role of political pressure in shaping the content of textbooks while completing my own textbook on American education. Certainly, textbooks play a major role in American public schools and issues of censorship and freedom of thought are a recurring theme in the history of the schools. In a later book on the politics of education, I coined the term the "knowledge industry," which includes publishers of textbooks and tests, and writers and researchers. Within this framework, a study of textbook publishing is one part of the study of the politics of knowledge.

While considering the issue of political pressure on textbook publishers and writers, I completed my first textbook without concern for either the effect of the political content of my textbook on sales or about the marketplace in which the book would be sold. No editor told me that for a textbook to sell it should match the content of actual courses taught in colleges around the country. In fact, I never gave this issue much thought. I just wrote a book that matched the content of the course I taught without worrying about the material other people included in similar courses.

The poor sales of the first edition of my textbook reflected this lack of attention to the market. But this situation quickly changed when my editor left the company to start a small publishing firm.

My next series of editors taught me how to match a textbook with the needs of the market. But I quickly realized that strict adherence to the process would result in fundamental changes in content. Since no one really knows what is taught in all the college courses in the country, publishers often rely on the knowledge they gain by visiting college campuses, talking to professors, and collecting course syllabi. In addition, editors maintain their own stable of reviewers. These contacts form the "invisible college" of the publishing world. In addition, editors advise authors to study competing textbooks.

The combination of the invisible college and comparison with competing texts results in a pressure on authors to produce textbooks that are like all the others in the field. The impression editors develop about the market from campus visits and syllabi tends to support existing types of textbooks. What the editor can determine from course syllabi is only the most popularly used textbooks. The brief conversations with faculty often do not provide enough substance for the editor to put together a vision of a new type of textbook for a given field. Indeed, it is hard to imagine an editor knowing enough about each discipline to synthesize and plan an innovative textbook. For instance, in the field of education textbooks range from special education to methods of teaching science. Also, since an editor's job depends on the sales of books they acquire, they are often not willing to take chances with innovative approaches to publishing. The editor's stable of reviewers can also act as a conservative brake on innovation. Often, reviewers are asked to guage whether a book will do well in a textbook market and to compare it to other successful textbooks in the field.

In preparing a second edition of my textbook, I decided to both accommodate these conservative forces and, at the same time, try to develop a different type of textbook. For one thing, I concluded that I wanted my textbook to be an original piece of scholarship that contributed to the interpretation of the role of education in American society. I believed my interpretation of educational events would engage the student in a debate with the text and with other students. In part, I accomplished this with the interpretative lectures that I composed for the first edition. Second, I wanted my book to be a piece of literature that students would find interesting to read. I wanted to avoid disconnected chapters and facts presented outside of any meaningful intellectual context. And third, I wanted the book to be used, which meant I should pay attention to the content of the course as it was normally taught. To achieve the last objective, I looked at standard textbooks in the field. The following is a brief example of my method in achieving these goals.

Most introductory textbooks in education have sections devoted to curriculum, methods of instruction, and theories of learning. Given that these textbooks cover material ranging from history and philosophy to the organization of schools, chapters on curriculum, instruction, and learning theories are not usually directly related to other chapters in the text. Indeed, most chapters in such texts provide information about a specific aspect of education without reference to other chapters. In keeping with the theme of my book, I decided to add this material by placing it in the context of the political interpretation that runs through the book. Rather than just explaining these areas, I primarily wanted to demonstrate that the types of curriculum, methods of instruction, and theories of learning used in public schools are determined by political forces and reflect particular political ideologies. By doing this I was able to review different curricula, instructional methodologies, and theories of learning by linking them to particular political ideologies and political forces. In this manner, I connected the chapter to the rest of the book and maintained my general interpretative framework. In addition, I made the material into something controversial.

The success of the second and later editions of the textbook resulted in my editor asking me to write another textbook on the history of education. This again put me in the situation of writing a textbook and at the same time studying the role of textbooks in American education. As a result of writing this textbook, I began to think of textbooks as one aspect of what I would later call "ideological management."

Unlike my first textbook, I wrote the history text with a great deal of concern about pedagogical methods. Again, I wanted to achieve a contribution to historical literature by providing a general interpretation of American educational history. My intent was to cause the reader to question basic assumptions about the role of schooling in society and to engage in a debate with the text. To achieve these goals, I decided to discuss differing interpretations of each historical period and to link each interpretation with a particular political perspective.

I thought this approach would accomplish several things. First, I wanted the reader to understand that history is written from the perspective of historians who are influenced in their writing by the events and problems in their world. Second, by providing different interpretations I could turn a historical event into a debatable topic. For instance, consider the question raised by two of many interpretations of the development of common schools in the early nineteenth century. Was the common school the result of capitalists desiring a trained work force or of a desire to protect a dominant Protestant culture? Obviously, a discussion of this question raises issues regarding the role of schools in the modern world in protecting cultures and in economic development. In addition, I wanted readers to understand that how one views the past can influence future choices.

POLITICS AND TEXTBOOKS

After completing the second edition of the history textbook, I decided to explore the history of ideological management in the twentieth century in the United States. In addition to studying schools, movies, radio, and television, this project involves exploring the political pressures on the textbook industry. In general, the political battles of the twentieth century caused publishers to avoid textbooks for elementary and secondary schools that might be considered radical or might offend any major social group. In the publishing industry this pattern clearly emerged after World War I and is highlighted by the battle in the early 1940s over one of the most popular and progressive social studies series used in public schools. The pattern continues after World War II in the climate of the anticommunist hysteria brought on by the Cold War. Today, it is evidenced by continuing battles over the portrayal of evolution and creationism in science textbooks.

For example, in the 1930s, historian Howard Beale recorded these feelings of an author of American history texts: ''In trying to guard against criticism and opposition, authors are driven to sins of omission and commission.'' After describing how he adds material of little importance to his history texts and deletes other material because of pressure from outside interest groups, the textbook author told Beale, ''And, if any author tells you he is not influenced by such pressure, that he tells 'the truth, the whole truth and nothing but the truth' as far as he knows it, don't you believe him. He is a conscious or unconscious liar.''[1]

Beale's study of the textbook industry was part of a larger work on freedom of teaching in public schools for the Commission on Social Studies in the Schools, which was established in the 1930s by the American Historical Association. Beale's study focused on the effect of state legislation and outside interest groups on textbook publishing in the 1920s and 1930s. As part of the study, he interviewed authors and publishers. One head of a publishing firm described the publisher's dilemma as, ''He wants to tell the truth, and have his authors do the same. Yet he must sell books.'' Beale followed this quote with the summary statement, ''Therefore even the most honest publishers must modify books to remove 'objectionable' features that will hurt sales, yet at the same time save their own and the author's consciences, and withal rationalize their business reasons into scholarly ones and never admit to the public that they change texts for the sake of sales.''[2]

Beale catalogued the major pressure groups influencing textbooks following World War I. One important issue in the 1920s was the portrayal of the British in textbooks. In keeping with our alliance with Great Britain during World War I, textbooks were changed to present a more favorable portrait of the British. It should be noted that many Americans did not support U.S. entry into the war on the side of the British. After all, in this war to make the world safe for democracy, it seemed strange to be fighting on the side of a country with a monarchy and a large colonial empire. Following the war, the Hearst newspapers, Irish-American organizations, and the Catholic organization, Knights of Columbus, began a national campaign against what they felt was a pro-British slant to public school textbooks. Of particular concern was the treatment of the Revolutionary War. During World War I, publishers tried to tone down the nature of the antagonism between the colonists and the English. After the war, the above-named groups campaigned to have textbooks portray a more basic conflict between the two antagonists. For instance, American publisher George Putnam told a British audience in 1918, "Textbooks are now being prepared which will present a juster account of the events of 1775–1783, 1812–1815 and 1861–1865." In response to the postwar criticism of these changes, Beale quotes a statement made in 1922 by a New York school superintendent: "The publishers of all the books under criticism . . . have promised to bring out revised versions, correct passages found to be erroneous in fact, inadequate, or in bad taste." Or in the words of Professor William Bagley in 1934, "There was a tendency to change textbooks during the War to soft-pedal the American Revolutionary War."[3]

The Women's Christian Temperance Union besieged publishers in the 1920s to ensure that hygiene and physiology texts contained sections on the evils of alcohol. Religious groups protested references to evolution in science texts. And public utility companies tried to fight off attacks on their industry by influencing the content of texts. In 1928, it was reported that the utility interests negotiated with Ginn and Company to eliminate a sentence from a social studies text that stated, "As late as 1926 a man then serving as president of a number of electric light companies in the Middle West gave a single primary election over $200,000 to the campaign funds of both parties." At a public hearing in 1928 before the Federal Trade Commission, leaders of the utility industry complained that they were unable to eliminate all references in textbooks "to watered-stock and power ring political activities."[4]

The "patriotic" organizations were the best-organized and most relentless groups monitoring the content of textbooks in the 1920s. Leading the pack was the American Legion, which was formed by American army officers in Europe following the end of World War I. A major goal of the American Legion was to stop the spread of Bolshevik ideas in public schools. At the national level in the early 1920s, the American Legion formed an alliance with the National Education Association to sponsor

American Education Week. The relationship between the two organizations was strengthened in the 1930s when they formed a joint committee, after the American Legion pledged its support of the National Education Association's demand for federal aid to education. At the local level, the American Legion established legion posts with one member acting as an "Americanism" officer to assure the teaching of "100 percent Americanism" in local schools. The American Legion was joined in its efforts to rid schools and textbooks of radical ideas by the Daughters of the American Revolution, the United States Chamber of Commerce, and the Ku Klux Klan.[5]

The American Legion played an active role in forcing Harold Rugg's social studies texts out of public schools in the early 1940s. The attacks on the Rugg books caused a dramatic decline in sales and sent a warning to the textbook industry. At the peak of their popularity in 1938, annual sales were 289,000 copies. Six years later the annual sales plummeted to 21,000 copies.[6] The series was based on the idea that children should be educated to assume intelligent control of their institutions and environment. The books did not advocate communism or socialism, but they did argue that intelligence should be applied to planning the economy and operating public institutions.

The first major attacks against the Rugg textbooks came from the Hearst newspapers and B. C. Forbes, financial writer and founder of *Forbes* magazine. Forbes conducted his campaign against the books at both the national and local levels. As a member of the school board of Englewood, New Jersey, Forbes unsuccessfully tried to have the books removed from the community's schools. At the national level, Forbes conducted his attack through articles in *Forbes* magazine and in columns for the Hearst newspapers. His opening salvo in *Forbes* magazine came in August of 1939, with an article that called Rugg's books "viciously un-American . . . he [Rugg] distorts facts to convince the oncoming generation that America's private-enterprise system is wholly inferior and nefarious." In words that must have made the textbook industry tremble, Forbes wrote, "I plan to insist that this anti-American educator's textbooks be cast out . . . I would not want my own children contaminated by conversion to Communism."[7] In his column for the Hearst newspaper chain in 1940, Forbes asked this question every week: "Are too many educators poisoning the minds of the young generation with prejudiced, distorted, unfair teachings regarding the American system of economy and dazzling them with overly-rosy pictures of conditions in totalitarian countries?"[8]

The Advertising Federation of American joined the battle in early 1940 with a pamphlet titled "Facts You Should Know about Anti-Advertising Propaganda in School Textbooks." The pamphlet was specifically directed at the Rugg books, which contained lessons about why consumers should look out for false advertising claims. As an example of what the federation believed was an attempt to turn students against advertising, the pamphlet cited the opening section of a chapter on advertising in one of Rugg's books, which begins:

> Two men were discussing the merits of a nationally advertised brand of oil. "I know it must be good," said one. "A million dollars' worth of it is sold each year. You see advertisements of that oil everywhere." The other shook his head. "I don't care how much of it is sold," he said. "I left a drop of it on a copper plate overnight and the drop turned green. It is corrosive and I don't dare to use it on my machine."

The pamphlet issued by the Advertising Federation objected to this anecdote because it was hypothetical and bred distrust among students of widely advertised products.[9]

In April, 1940, the president of the Advertising Federation issued a letter to large advertisers that opened: "Advertised products are untrustworthy! That is the lesson taught to the children in 4,200 school systems by a social science textbook of Professor Harold Rugg of Teachers College, Columbia University."[10]

The American Legion quickly joined the battle in September 1940 with an article in the *American Legion Magazine* by O. K. Armstrong, which was later distributed as a pamphlet titled, "Treason in the Textbooks." The cartoon for the article depicts Rugg as a devil putting colored glasses over children's eyes. The caption on the picture states, "The 'Frontier Thinkers' are trying to sell our youth the idea that the American way of life has failed." The term "Frontier Thinkers" referred to the progressive educators primarily teaching at Teachers College, Columbia University. The legion article and pamphlet also listed several other books and *Scholastic* magazine as being subversive.[11]

Another "patriotic" organization, the Sons of the American Revolution, joined the legion in calling Rugg's books un-American. The chairman of the Educational Committee of the New York Chapter of the Sons of the American Revolution and member of the American Legion, A. G. Rudd, wrote an article against the books for the April, 1940, issue of *Nation's Business*. Rudd's attacks against the series extended into the late 1950s with the publication of his book *Bending the Twig: The Revolution in Education and Its Effect on Our Children*. Rudd placed the textbook series and Harold Rugg at the center of an attempt to overthrow American institutions. Rudd wrote, "He [Rugg] was one of the principal architects of the ideological structure known as the 'new social order'." Rudd states that, from his faculty position at Teachers College, "[Rugg's] propaganda and doctrines were spread throughout the United States. He also exercises influence . . . through his teachers guides, which interpreted his economic, political and social philosophies to thousands of classroom teachers using his social science courses."[12]

The combined attack of Hearst newspapers, *Forbes* magazine, the Advertising Federation, and patriotic organizations resulted in dramatic actions by school boards. In September, 1940, *Time* magazine reported that the members of the Binghamton, New York, school board called for a public burning of Rugg's textbooks. Also, *Time* reported, "last fortnight Rugg book burnings began to blaze afresh in the small-town, American Legion belt. In rapid succession the school boards of Mountain Lakes and Wayne Township, N.J. banished Rugg texts that had been used by their pupils nearly ten years. Explained Wayne Township's Board Member Ronald Gall: 'In my opinion, the books are un-American but not anti-American. . . .' "[13]

Particularly dramatic were the events in Bradner, Ohio, where the community was divided over the issue of teaching communism in the schools. According to a Cleveland newspaper account of the events, "The rural Red hunt . . . has resulted in: explosion of a dynamite charge and the burning of a fiery cross in front of the home of . . . [the] school board president." The explosions and cross burning were accompanied by the spectacle of school board members shoving books into the school furnace.[14]

Rugg's publisher, Ginn and Company, did not take lightly this attack against a highly profitable series of books. They financed Rugg's travel to communities where the series was under attack. But, as Rugg reported, most of these visits proved unsuccessful. From his perspective, communities were whipped up to such a high level of hysteria that little could be done to stop school systems from rejecting the books. When Rugg appeared in Philadelphia at a public hearing, a participant, pointing his finger at Rugg, exclaimed, "There sits the ringmaster of the fifth columnists in America financed by the Russian government. I want you people to look at him."[15]

According to Rugg's description, a typical pattern at public hearings was for a representative of a patriotic organization, usually the American Legion or Daughters of the American Revolution, to charge Rugg's books with poisoning children's minds with pro-communist propaganda. Typically at these hearings, someone would wave a copy of Elizabeth Dilling's *The Red Network* as proof of Rugg's communist leanings. Dilling's book contained nine lines referring to a five-page speech Rugg gave in 1933 on world youth movements, in which he made a favorable reference to the Communist Youth Association. After responding to this charge, Rugg reported, he would then be charged with writing for the Communist newspaper the *Daily Worker*. Rugg would respond, "I have never written one line for *The Daily Worker* in my life or authorized anyone else to do so in my name."[16]

At many of the meetings the attacks degenerated into a combination of flag waving and religious revivalism. At one hearing, Rugg wrote, a hugh middle-aged woman shrieked, "I am here, not thinking that I was going to be at all, but I am and I want to say just a few words. Righteousness, good government, good homes and God—most of all—Christ is on trial today." After admitting that, even though she had not read any of the Rugg books, she knew they were bad, she said, "You can't take the youth of our land and give them this awful stuff and have them come out safe and sound for God and Righteousness." At another meeting, according to Rugg, a youth of twenty leaped into the air waving his arms and shouting, "If you let these books go in and if what I've heard is true, it'll damn the souls of the men, women and children of our state."[17]

For Rugg, a frustrating part of the meetings was the open admission by many critics that they had never read any of his books. Person after person at these hearings, Rugg wrote, would begin their statements with the phrase: "I haven't read the books, but— " The phrase would be followed with comments such as, "he's from Columbia, and that's enough"; "I have heard of the author, and no good about him"; and "my brother says the schools and colleges are filled with Communists."[18]

The anticommunist hysteria typified by the crusade against Rugg's books continued into the post–World War II period. Not only textbooks, but school administrators and teachers were targeted by the religious and political right. The censorship of textbooks and books in school libraries remained a favorite method for ensuring that a particular ideology would be disseminated by the schools. By the 1980s, the religious and political right listed environmentalist and profeminist statements as forbidden items in public school textbooks.[19]

There are common threads in the history of attacks against public school textbooks in the twentieth century. Throughout the century, the religious Right fought the presentation of the theory of evolution in science textbooks. In recent years, the religious Right lobbied to place the doctrine of creationism alongside theories of evolution. The removal of any hints of political and economic radicalism from school books topped the list of efforts of so-called "patriotic" organizations. Of course, special interest groups such as the utilities industry in the 1920s and the Advertising Federation in the 1940s attempted to have favorable messages included in school textbooks.

In addition, other organizations tried to counteract the activities of the religious and political Right. For many years the American Civil Liberties Union fought efforts to censor textbooks. In the 1980s, People for the American Way was specifically organized to counter the influence of the religious Right on the public schools. A 1989 letter soliciting funds for the organization opened, "You probably thought this was in America's past . . . But well-funded, well-organized Far Right groups are demanding that our *public schools teach their religious beliefs as scientific fact.* In 1989!"[20]

THE POSTMODERN TEXTBOOK

The interplay between my role as a textbook writer and as a historian of education continues in my present work on ideological management in the United States during the twentieth century. I consider both activities as evolving projects without any final conclusions or solutions. But based on my experience, I reached several conclusions regarding the development of postmodern textbooks. At the college level, authors should resist the conservative tendencies of textbook editors. We do not need more textbooks that are clones of existing books. By the presentation of an original synthesis or interpretation, the postmodern textbook can make a contribution to the literature of a particular scholarly field. In addition, college textbooks should integrate a pedagogical strategy with their original synthesis or interpretation. On the other hand, the changes in public school textbooks depend on reform of the political structure of schooling. What editors and authors do will make little difference if interest groups are constantly pressuring public school authorities to censor content. Some type of political change is required if the schools are to be protected against these influences.

With regard to the college level, the postmodern textbook should avoid the presentation of information in a neutral language. Knowledge is not neutral. Knowledge is surrounded by scholarly debates and political issues. By presenting the reader with a compendium of information, the modern textbook, in contrast to the postmodern textbook, conveys the impression that scholars agree on a particular body of knowledge and that knowledge does not serve a political function. The postmodern textbook, I believe, should combine the pedagogical concerns of the modern textbook with a conviction that textbooks should be scholarly works that present the reader with a multiplicity of views of a given field of knowledge. The postmodern textbook should not give the appearance of neutrality but should engage the student in a debate about a particular body of knowledge.

NOTES

1. Howard K. Beale, *Are American Teachers Free?* (New York: Scribner's, 1936), p. 317.

2. Ibid., pp. 317–318.

3. Ibid., p. 295.

4. Ibid., pp. 298–299.

5. Ibid., p. 298.

6. Frances FitzGerald, *America Revised: History Schoolbooks in the Twentieth Century* (Boston: Little, Brown, 1979), p. 37.

7. Harold Rugg, *That Men May Understand: An American in the Long Armistice* (New York: Doubleday, Doran, 1941), p. 25.

8. Ibid., pp. 29–30.

9. Augustin G. Rudd, *Bending the Twig: The Revolution in Education and Its Effect on Our Children* (New York: New York Chapter Sons of the American Revolution, 1957), p. 85.

10. "Advertising Groups Pursuing Professor Rugg's Books," *Publishers Weekly* 138 (September 28, 1940): 1322–1323.

11. Ibid., p. 1323.

12. Rudd, *Bending the Twig*, p. 65.

13. "Book Burnings: Rugg Texts," *Time*, September 9, 1940, pp. 64–65.

14. Rugg, *That Men May Understand*, p. 3.

15. Ibid., p. 4.

16. Ibid., p. 8.

17. Ibid., pp. 10–11.

18. Ibid., p. 12.

19. I provide examples in my chapter on "The Knowledge Industry" in Joel Spring, *Conflict of Interests: The Politics of American Education* (White Plains, N.Y.: Longman, 1988), pp. 125–149.

20. I received this updated form letter with the signature of Arthur Kropp, president of People for the American Way. The organization's address is 2000 M Street, N.W., Suite 400, Washington, D.C. 20036.

Part 4

Literacy and Reading: Case Studies

ALLAN LUKE

Chapter Twelve

Basal Reading Textbooks and the Teaching of Literacy

A key decision facing educational policymakers is the selection of textbooks for the teaching of literacy in elementary schools. From a political and bureaucratic standpoint, such decisions are admittedly complex: state departments, regional jurisdictions and local school boards, university and state-based consultants and subject-area specialists, and school-level administrators and staffs all may be implicated in the selection of texts and methods through which children will be introduced to the culture of literacy. For administrators and teachers alike, increased demand for public accountability in the delivery of literacy to all students makes such decisions crucial for the credibility of the educational system as a whole. This essay sets out to show that it would be misguided to construe such decisions as purely technical ones about which (corporate) curricular package is most "efficient" at the transmission of literacy.

That early literacy is a contested terrain for educators is not a new historical phenomenon: attacks on the school system for failing to provide the "basics," however defined, have been near continual since the late nineteenth century. Since the advent of "scientific" approaches to curriculum and instruction in the United States, educational psychology

---

The author wishes to thank William Corcoran for his comments on an earlier draft of this text, Carole Edelsky for debate on issues covered here, and Edith Hoshino for her editorial suggestions.

has generally taken a dominant position in prescribing for publishers and educators what counts as literacy.[1] And, as others have noted in this volume, educational psychologists and linguists have come up with valuable technical criteria for assessing text accessibility.[2] Yet, such studies and the current policy debate often fail to consider adequately the vast and increasing body of cross-disciplinary research on literacy. My intent here is to draw attention to current research on basal reading textbooks—their history, economy, ideologies, and classroom uses — and to outline key considerations in the adoption and use of elementary school textbooks for the teaching of literacy.

The question of which reading series to adopt is indeed significant, but it is connected to a broader array of issues regarding institutional conditions of textbook use. The relationship between ideological content and semantic form of the narratives in beginning reading textbooks has been examined in considerable depth.[3] Here I want to focus instead on how the "technical form"[4] of literacy instruction fostered by basal series may work against the acquisition of literacy. For I suspect that the preoccupation of many administrators and consultants with finding the "right" basal and pedagogical approach to early literacy is premised on the assumption—dating back to the foundations of applied psychology and fostered by the marketing efforts of publishers—that there is a magic bullet for literacy training and that researchers and publishers *can* come up with a virtually foolproof and universal approach to teaching competence with text. This search, in turn, is based on at least three distinct but related fictions: first, that literacy is a neutral, ahistorical set of psychological skills divorced from larger societal contexts and issues; second, that educational science can ascertain the optimal way of transmitting that competence; and, third, that "new" educational commodities provided by (multinational) publishers, reflecting the best of that science, will ensure the teaching of literacy in an equitable and effective manner. If we understand literacy and literacy instruction as, respectively, cultural and ideological practices, then these beliefs become suspect and, more importantly, may impede the teaching of the kinds of social literacy and critical competence required for active and full participation in postindustrial society.

Significant mediating factors emerge in recent research: how teachers see the use of such textbook series; how well they are versed in *contending* theories of language development and acquisition; and the degree of flexibility they are granted by regional and school-level administrators to use texts. Beginning from this perspective, state and regional policy alternatives to a narrowly defined quest for the "state of the art" reading textbook series are possible. Here I want to highlight the potentially constructive role of in-service teacher education in the development of school- and community-based literacy programs, with reference to recent innovations in the United Kingdom, Canada, Australia, as well as the United States. To address such matters, however, we must first understand the historical character of literacy and the role of textbooks in the transmission of culture and ideology.

READING TEXTBOOKS AND IDEOLOGIES OF LITERACY: A HISTORICAL PERSPECTIVE

The first textbooks ''purpose built'' for the teaching of literacy were those prepared in the late fifteenth century by Luther and Melanchthon for the German state system. These texts included passages of scripture, psalms, hymns, and abridged exceprts from the literature of antiquity.[5] From their fifteenth century literacy campaign and those subsequently undertaken in Protestant European states like Sweden over the three centuries thereafter, we can see graphically that the selection and use of textbooks was not a matter of neutral skill transmission. School reformers during the Reformation understood perhaps better than many modern educators the intimate connection between how one learned to read—what one learned of the appropriate sites, norms of interpretation, relative power of genres of text, responses to text—and what one would ultimately do with text. For Luther and colleagues, literacy was not a matter of providing unbridled access to the word, but rather a way of providing a controlled access to texts which embodied a distinct Lutheran ideology.[6] In contrast to this, the later eighteenth century Swedish literacy campaign legally required the entire populace to become literate. Local parishes were charged with providing literacy to all genders and classes, although only reading was to be taught and not writing.[7]

From the social history of literacy we can surmise that in the short time that secular and nonsecular institutions have been charged with the transmission of literacy, they have deliberately molded and shaped the kind of selective tradition conveyed. This has been achieved by setting the ideological content of texts, by controlling the kinds of literate practices disbursed to the populace, and by developing centralized administrative mandates and instructions to monitor teaching and learning. In the case of Lutheran Germany, these were not innocent mechanisms of implementation but quite deliberate attempts to preclude theological and ideological deviation.

This legacy continued intact into the nineteenth century, when Protestant states like the United States, Canada, and Australia used literacy textbooks and teaching not as a way of teaching basic skills, but rather as a means of indoctrination and domestication. The content of McGuffey-style readers in the United States and the colonial readers used in Canada and Australia stressed allegiance to government and a learned resignation to the social and economic status quo. Such textbooks enshrined what Lee Soltow and Edgar Stevens call an "ideology of literacy,"[8] and there was a close match between the ideational content of such texts and the kinds of literate behaviors taught. Rote memorization, recitation, and imitation were the central methods used with text; these in turn matched the perceived need of the secular school to promote Protestant morality, the work ethic, compliance with law, and allegiance to the nation-state.[9]

Yet the matter of ideological content was rendered moot, theoretically at least, by the advent of instructional psychology, corporate commoditization of learning materials, and educational progressivism. The shift away from the literary textbook toward highly specialized pedagogical texts began in the early twentieth century when educational psychologists based at Teachers College, University of Chicago, and other locales began to produce textbooks, designed first and foremost to teach the "skills" of reading (e.g., word recognition, phonics) and only secondarily for moral inculcation.[10] Framing this scientific approach to reading instruction, William S. Gray, the author of the Dick and Jane series and the first president of the International Reading Association, later commented that: "As psychologists pointed out long ago, it is not what is presented to a child that promotes growth, but rather his reactions to the ideas acquired."[11] Two other contributing factors played into the diminution of traditional literary content: first, publishers began to compete increasingly for a lucrative national and international market; and second, with increasing religious and ethnic diversification of the American school populace, the demand for noncontroversial, secular textbooks emerged. The net result was a standardization and commoditization of literary instruction under the auspices of scientific design.

In the design of textbooks of the inter- and postwar Dick-and-Jane-style, prototypes for today's basal reader, matters of the ideological content of literary texts and of the ideological intent of literacy instruction were subordinated. Or, to put it more precisely, they were driven below the surface in the discourses of educational research and policy.

Yet to purport that there are no values or messages operant in the kind of "fat cat bat" text of the typical phonics program or even the simplified narratives used in modern series is at once both accurate and inaccurate. It is accurate in the sense that there is little that is culturally significant or intellectually challenging in such texts. They are very much the sanitized, safe multinational product; so the opportunity to teach someone to learn or analyze or critique *a* specific culture is missing.

It is inaccurate in the sense that the values conveyed constitute and prescribe a synthetic and inauthentic culture. Analyses of these texts have linked their ideological content to the complex relationships entailed in the production of educational products for both nationwide and multinational markets.[12] In order to capture a transnational audience, textbook design must be, to a certain extent, culture-neutral or "generic." The reader must be structured for the lowest (cultural) common denominator in its audience. This in turn allows editorial adoption with a minimal expense at both regional and national levels. The processes by which American reading series are "Canadianized" and "Australianized" are simple: in the United States *Reading 360* series later adopted for the Canadian and Australian markets, generic narratives about childhood, foreign cultures, and so forth were retained, while a certain amount of distinctive Australian or Canadian illustrations and literature was inserted by branch-plant editors. Additionally, there is further evidence that this genre of textbooks has lent itself historically to the editorial insertion of religious content for Catholic schools.[13] Hence, there are very simple economic and marketing reasons for the omission of distinctive local content and the absence of any texts that address problematic national, regional, or community issues: at once, the market is expanded and potential local objections to text adoption are precluded.

These efforts notwithstanding, the generic or "safe" versions of culture(s) *as text* used for the teaching of literacy cannot be without ideological messages and effects.[14] And it should be noted that despite the decade-long objections to biased portrayal of ethnic diversity, community life, social, economic, and gender relations, most basal series tend to remain one dimensional, effectively portraying a conflict-free, nonproblematic version of North American culture. While administrators may argue that such texts preclude objections from parents, special interest groups, and others, the very cultural insignificance of such texts in fact delimits the learning of a critical literacy.

Shirley Heath commented recently that "textbooks — or books of texts — no longer invite students to compare their own or others' life experiences or to offer multiple reflections on how and what literary writing can mean."[15] In terms of textbook semantic form and ideational content, several crucial factors come into play in acquisition of literacy: first, the possible world of childhood, language, and learning constructed in literature does indeed help define children's literate, cultural, and political sensibilities.[16] From this we could infer that the kinds of "interpretive possibilities" enabled by many basal texts are limited,[17] that such texts do not portray a diversity of "possible worlds" and invite readers to juxtapose, critique, analyze, and project these and other possible worlds.[18] If indeed the capacity to take language apart and to pattern it critically;

the establishment of a visible connection between classroom-based literacy learning and the actual uses of literacy in the community; and the development of a metalanguage for interrogating texts *are* crucial prerequisites to the development of literacy as critical social practice[19]—then it would appear that many of the mundane texts through which children learn the "skills" of literacy may stand as active deterrants.

So, which textbooks are adopted is an important policy decision, and to argue that cultural values, world views, and political ideologies are not significant considerations in such decisions is fallacious. But administrators and curriculum workers as well must confront the second variable in the selective tradition of literacy instruction: how teachers actually teach the text and convey to children what counts as reading. According to a range of contending theories of reading—cognitive, psycholinguistic, semiotic, reader-response — in literacy instruction, children are developing a broad knowledge of texts to be called upon to "read" and interpret further texts (i.e., "intertextuality"), and they are developing a sense of what will count as appropriate sites and texts for particular social functions and uses of literacy.

THE TEXT IN USE: CLASSROOM LITERACY EVENTS

Students are also learning the norms of what Heath has called "literacy events," occasions in which a piece of writing is integral to the nature of the participants' interactions and their interpretive processes.[20] How might we describe the classroom conditions by and through which basal reading textbooks are taught? Robert Calfee, in a recent *Educational Policy* article, observed that the teaching of reading in the United States is typified by:

> the teacher with . . . the basal reading manual spread across her [sic] lap, directing the youngsters through a routine typical of virtually every series on the market. The other students in the classroom will be at their seats completing worksheets.[21]

Calfee's observation is corroborated in recent reports on the status of reading in the United States: the National Institute of Education Commission on Reading notes of overreliance on this identifiable instructional format of streamed ability groups, each working with different levels of basal texts, and each devoting a good deal of teaching/learning time to filling in standardized activity worksheets.[22] There is a good deal problematic about this approach, which has stood virtually unchanged since interwar developments in reading psychology.[23] In case studies of elementary classrooms, Donna Eder has indicated that small-group teaching can lead to a selective distribution of kinds and levels of communicative competence and that, moreover, reading groups often are constructed for management purposes on fairly arbitrary grounds.[24] Similarly, the commission further comments that "there are qualitative differences in the experience of children in high and low reading groups that could be expected to place children in low groups at a disadvantage."[25]

With so many teacher educators and researchers involved in reading education and with many preservice college textbooks cautioning against abuse of this kind of routine and providing instructional alternatives,[26] it would appear that at least part of the responsibility lies in the scripts provided by publishers with packaged reading programs. Another major study, the Reading Commission of the National Council of Teachers of English's *Report Card on Basals,* notes the dominance of this mechanized approach and an overreliance on teachers' manuals, prepackaged worksheets and tests, and other "user-friendly" adjunct materials provided by publishers.[27]

The artificial narrative text, then, is only part of the technical form of the curricular package: teacher's manuals provide standardized scripts for the deskilling of students and teachers. Yet, they are at the heart of the appeal of series to administrators. In her survey of Midwestern administrators' and teachers attitudes toward and use of social studies textbooks, Avon Crismore found that administrators saw workbooks and manuals as key means for the maintenance of quality control. One administrator commented that "A textbook helps you keep direction, and it can give explicit answers. . . . A few years ago, we used in-service for new materials, but because of financial reasons, now we must have it all in the manual."[28] For many school- and state-level administrators, the purchase of textbooks thus amounts to buying into a set of control devices over classroom interaction. The result is a standardization of the classroom literacy event and normalization of the aspiring literate. The nationwide sales and distribution of such teacher's manuals is particularly dubious in light of sociolinguistic and ethnographic research that indicates that literacy is optimally taught and learned in contexts sensitive to children's particular cultural and subcultural patterns of language use and background knowledge.[29]

The exact routines of daily classroom interaction with reading textbooks bear closer inspection: in an ethnomethodological analysis of transcripts of elementary school reading lessons in Australian primary schools, Carolyn Baker and Peter Freebody describe how what counts in the reading is constituted through a series of identifiable conventional games[30] — many of which, I would argue, could be ascribed directly or indirectly to the instructional routines laid out in teacher's manuals. They detail teacher/student oral exchange patterns such as "imagine and consult" and "wait and see." Instead of teaching competence with text, in fact such routines function to teach competent participation in the reading lesson: the child might learn how to second guess what is a "correct" personal opinion in the estimation of the teacher, "how to do a reading of an illustration," "what to 'wonder' about," and so forth. Baker and Freebody conclude that the outcomes of such instruction "bear no apparent relevance to the children's acquisition of . . . reading" but in fact construct and maintain "teacher and textual authority."[31]

Once in use then, the text is reconstituted by teacher interpretation: teachers lead students to appropriate reading practices within the ritual of reading instruction. This has significant educational implications. It suggests that the possibilities for teaching children to criticize and for developing a metalanguage for talking about text remain *despite* the paucity of literary and cultural significance of the text itself. All texts can be criticized, even the "closed text" of standardized reading series.[32] However, where teachers follow the scripted guidelines prescribed in teacher's manuals, mimed by student teachers on practice teaching assignments, and preferred by many school-level administrators, where they continue to deploy acritical, standardized approaches, children might quite effectively learn the rules for the classroom literacy event—how to play a classroom game—but may not learn a literacy of any social or intellectual consequence.

Baker also notes a central characteristic of small-group work with basal readers—namely that teachers are interrogating children, children are not interrogating texts.[33] Where this is the case, authentic criticism of and educationally valuable talk about texts goes by the wayside: children instead learn "procedural displays" of correct school "reading."[34] Ironically, the interaction patterns that count as literacy in the school often have little real relation to either the critical requirements of citizenship or the vocational requirements of the community.

Nonetheless, many teachers and administrators we interviewed in a recent Australian study of literacy-related curricular implementation welcomed the introduction of teacher's manuals, even as part of the latest generation of "whole language" basal series and large-format print books.[35] What occurs from an overreliance on the instructional scripts provided in teacher's manuals is a variation on what Linda McNeil has termed "participatory deskilling": in settings with increased demands for accountability, principals may begin to value "procedure over quality instruction."[36] In the case of early literacy instruction, many principals come to see evidence of basal units completed, test score results, weekly spelling results, and so forth as more important than the identifiable signs of a literacy in use (e.g., student-generated sustained texts, acutal time spent reading and using text to get information, class time devoted to group composition or text analysis). In such settings, the results appear to resemble those described by McNeil in some Midwestern high schools, where the demand for standardized procedures and texts supplants quality of instruction.

I have argued thus far that the remaking of instruction to improve the quality and critical characteristics of student literacy requires a reconsideration both of textbook content and of the kinds of competent teaching that enable a critical interrogation of texts. In practice this will no doubt trouble many school-level administrators, particularly those who might read it as a call for more teacher freedom and, relatedly, less centralized control. But I have here outlined how such control advanced by and through the use of basal materials and attendant instructional regimes can be quite counterproductive to the development of literacy. In the United Kingdom, Canada, and Australia, moreover, various alternative courses of policy and curriculum development have emerged.

POLICY ALTERNATIVES TO BASALS

I review these alternatives as an interlocking agenda involving local/regional publishing, in-service work to verse teachers in text criteria and literacy acquisition, and administrative leadership. As described by Keith Kimberley, community production and use of student-authored texts as instructional materials have proliferated in the United Kingdom for many years. There the diversity of social class and cultural content of such texts, precisely what is lacking in multinational texts, has proven particularly valuable in instruction.[37] Following initial success in London schools, writers' cooperatives and presses have been developed across the United Kingdom. Moreover, desktop publishing technology should make local, school, and district-level text production increasingly time efficient and economical. A larger scale regional effort has occured in Alberta, Canada where the Can $8.3 million Heritage Fund publishing project led to the development of regional learning materials.[38] There local teachers, ministry consultants, and university-level researchers developed regional texts.

Most recently, in Australia entire regions and schools have begun the long-range task of breaking the reliance on packaged basal instruction through expanded use of children's literature, student-authored texts, and found print materials. In elementary schools in one capital city surveyed, basal series are being retired from daily classroom use — to be used as literature resources and support materials — and the cost of upgrading and expanding school and class libraries is to be offset by the avoidance of further major capital expenditure on reading series.[39]

Yet, if such policies and programs are to be successful in promoting literacy, teachers *and* principals require heightened expertise in the selection and use of such alternative materials. As noted, the basal series format tends to deskill teachers, providing them with a paint-by-numbers approach to early literacy instruction. In order for teachers and administrators to make informed decisions about which other conventional, locally developed or student-authored texts are most appropriate and about what kinds of literacy events will most benefit their children, they need to develop a critical eye for both cultural content and contending theories of language acquisition and literacy development.

Problems that have arisen in the reform of elementary literacy teaching in Australia underline the need for critical criteria. For example, some Australian teachers who have adopted "process writing" programs and have begun to use student generated texts for teaching reading, have not developed sufficient sensitivity to the gender, ethnic, and class issues related to text adaptation and use.[40] Others involved in the development of "literature-based" reading programs have made bulk orders from publishers of library and large-print books with little concern for linguistic structure, cultural, and political content. These are signs that many of those teachers who have adopted a "whole language" approach remain susceptible to the overstated marketing promises of publishers, which have quickly made the shift into the now lucrative fields of children's literature and large-print books. We can surmise from this that in order to prepare teachers to make conscientious decisions regarding materials, in-service courses should entail not only an introduction to sociolinguistic, ethnographic, and psychological perspectives on reading and writing development, but should also include a substantial component in the sociology of the curriculum that addresses the matter of discourse structures and cultural content.[41] Note here that I am not advocating local text development and use independent of the exercise of articulated and debated criteria. What is essential is increased flexibility in text production, adoption, and use to accommodate culture- and language-sensitive curricular and instructional innovation.[42]

A major in-service program has been undertaken, with varying degrees of success, in New Zealand and Australia. Between 1985 and 1988 the Australian government invested an estimated sum of Aus $8 million in literacy-related in-service for some 30,000 teachers nationwide. While we cannot at this stage fully assess the effectiveness of the Early Literacy In-Service Course, one positive effect has been a reduction in reliance on basal reading series and associated ability group/worksheet routines. Many teachers have quite successfully developed literature-based and community-focused programs. Others, we have found, have engaged in a kind of pro forma compliance—that is, they have adopted the surface features of a "whole language" pedagogy but lack sufficient understanding of literate development, linguistic diversity, and cultural and community characteristics to develop and implement effective classroom literacy programs.[43] In light of this, it seems imperative that pre- and in-service teacher development programs blend theory and practice critically so as not to deskill teachers again by reversion to overly simplistic teaching formulae, slogans, and cliches.

A final prerequisite for an effective literacy program is sufficient administrative support for teachers to select, augment, and analyze texts with children. For this, the kind of lock-step instruction prescribed in basal series, however attractive to principals and regional officers concerned with accountability and test score results, will not suffice. In literacy programs in Australian schools, principals' and regional administrators' completion and support of literacy-related in-service programs has greatly enhanced the development of school-level comprehensive literacy strategies. Additionally, administrative systems bear the additional responsibility of providing a context for change to take place: in this case, sufficient financial and career incentives for teachers to pursue upgrading through further post-secondary study and in-service work.

Provided with the proper kinds of collaborative professional and expert support, teachers can achieve significantly improved results in literacy teaching. Two examples are described in separate studies by Carole Edelsky and colleagues and Shirley Heath.[44] In these U.S. settings, with Hispanic and small-town Southern children, approaches to literacy teaching that were extremely sensitive to children's background knowledges, linguistic competences, and community contexts increased achievement markedly. There children *and* teachers were actively learning about, examining, and studying language and literacy use in the community; they were interrogating and generating texts. These approaches did not sanction pedagogical laissez faire as an alternative to the basal routine, but encouraged deliberate scaffolding by teachers sensitive to aspects of reading and language development and to the larger cultural and community contexts in which they worked.

BUILDING TEXTS AND CONTEXTS FOR LITERACY

I have tried in this brief discussion to shift the focus of debate in this volume from the question of "which textbook?" The actual ideological content of early literacy textbooks *is* important: the sterile, irrelevant content of most basal series is at least in part responsible for the boredom and failure of many learners, particularly those from minority and working-class backgrounds. But if indeed teachers remake texts through patterns of interaction in the classroom, then what is most detrimental about packaged reading programs is the manner in which they are used to routinize instruction, deskilling teachers and learners. Many of the conventional literacy events that occur in the classroom bear no direct connection to a literacy in use. And as long as teachers feel obligated to run a daily routine of fill-in-the-blanks worksheets, mechanized round-robin reading lessons, and so forth, literacy achievement is unlikely to decline, but it is also unlikely to rise either in quality or quantity.

Given the increasing recognition that children and adults alike need to develop the kinds of literate competence that will enable active and critical social participation, to go back to the "basics" of basal readers may not be a defensible policy response. In a related appraisal, Walter MacGinitie and Ruth MacGinitie argue that the problems many children have at critical comprehension in the upper-primary and secondary grades may in fact be the result of an overemphasis on basic skills and decoding in the early grades, achieved via packaged approaches and tests.[45] They suggest that it is a classic case of an educational axiom at work: what the curriculum emphasizes children learn. And all basals—even the recent generation of "whole language" and "literature-based" series—have serious deficiencies in this regard.

For educational policymakers and administrators it is not a simple matter of choosing a particular textbook series, the better to control teachers or to normalize students. It is a matter of teachers and students interrogating texts and criticizing them forcefully, and of administrators laying out the conditions and incentives for teachers to become truly competent teachers of literacy, not mere actors following scripts and leading children through standardized texts. To do so requires a redefinition of what we consider basic, both for critical social participation *and* for rudimentary textual competence. Children must be encouraged to do what packaged curricula often preclude, to hold texts up to the light of critical scrutiny, scrutiny based not only on their life experiences but on a learned intertextuality. The kind of educational policy needed is one that enables and encourages teachers to learn to challenge texts and thereby challenge students.

NOTES

1. For a description of the influence of psychological paradigms on educational conceptions of reading see Peter H. Johnston, "Assessment in Reading," in *Handbook of Reading Research,* ed. P. David Pearson (New York: Longman, 1984), pp. 147–182.

2. A comprehensive overview of text adoption criteria is provided in Avon Crismore, "Rhetorical Form, Selection and Use of Textbooks," in *Language, Authority and Criticism: Readings on the School Textbook,* ed. Suzanne de Castell, Allan Luke, and Carmen Luke (London/Philadelphia: Falmer Press, 1988), pp. 133–152.

3. Allan Luke, *Literacy, Textbooks and Ideology: Postwar Literacy Instruction and the Mythology of Dick and Jane* (London/Philadelphia: Falmer Press, 1988), chap. 4; Carolyn D. Baker and Peter Freebody, *Children's First Schoolbooks: Introduction to the Culture of Literacy* (Oxford: Basil Blackwell, 1989). For a contrasting analysis of Swedish and Danish textbooks, see Jacob L. Mey, *Whose Language? A Study in Linguistic Pragmatics* (Amsterdam: John Benjamins, 1985).

4. For a discussion of "technical form" of curricula, see Michael W. Apple, *Education and Power* (London/Boston: Routledge and Kegan Paul, 1982).

5. Carmen Luke, *Pedagogy, Printing, Protestantism: The Discourse on Childhood* (Albany: State University of New York Press, 1989), chap. 5.

6. Ibid.

7. Egil Johansson, "Literacy Campaigns in Sweden," in *National Literacy Campaigns: Historical and Comparative Perspectives,* ed. Robert Arnove and Harvey J. Graff (New York: Plenum Press, 1987), pp. 65–98.

8. Lee Soltow and Edgar Stevens, *The Rise of Literacy and the Common School in the United States* (Chicago: University of Chicago Press, 1981), p. 59.

9. Harvey J. Graff, *The Literacy Myth: Literacy and Social Structure in the Nineteenth Century City* (New York: Academic Press, 1979); Harvey J. Graff, "Literacy, Jobs, and Industrialization: The Nineteenth Century," in *Literacy and Social Development in the West,* ed. Harvey J. Graff (Cambridge: Cambridge University Press, 1981), pp. 232–260, pp. 258–259.

10. Luke, *Literacy, Textbooks and Ideology,* chap. 4.

11. William S. Gray, "Reading as Experiencing, Thinking and Learning," *California Journal of Elementary Education* 27 (1959): pp. 135–149, p. 137.

12. See Rowland Lorimer, "The Business of Literacy: The Making of the Educational Textbook," in *Literacy, Society and Schooling,* ed. S. de Castell, A. Luke, and K. Egan (Cambridge: Cambridge University Press, 1986), pp. 132–

145; Suzanne de Castell and Allan Luke, "Literacy Instruction: Technology and Technique," *American Journal of Education* 95 (1987): pp. 413–440; cf. Michael W. Apple, "The Culture and Commerce of the Textbook," *Journal of Curriculum Studies* 17 (1985): pp. 119–146. For commentary on aspects of multinational textbook production in the Third World, see Philip G. Altbach, *The Knowledge Context: Comparative Perspectives on the Distribution of Knowledge* (Albany: State University of New York Press, 1987), chap. 7.

13. Allan Luke, "The Secular Word: Religious Editions of the Dick and Jane Readers," in *The Politics of the Textbook,* ed. Linda K. Christian-Smith and Michael W. Apple (London: Routledge and Kegan Paul, in preparation).

14. Luke, *Literacy, Textbooks and Ideology,* chap. 4.

15. Shirley B. Heath, "Talking the Text in Teaching Composition," in *Language, Authority and Criticism,* pp. 109–121, p. 109.

16. Carolyn D. Baker and Peter Freebody, " 'Constituting the Child' in Beginning School Reading Books," *British Journal of Sociology of Education* 8 (1987): pp. 55–76; Baker and Freebody, *Children's First Schoolbooks;* Luke, *Literacy, Textbooks and Ideology,* chap. 4.

17. Carolyn D. Baker and Peter Freebody, "Possible Worlds and Possible People: Interpretive Challenges in Beginning School Reading Books," *Australian Journal of Reading* 11 (1988): pp. 95–104.

18. The role of "possible worlds" in the acquisition of literacy is discussed in David R. Olson, "Learning to Mean What You Say: Toward a Psychology of Literacy," in *Literacy, Society and Schooling,* pp. 145–158; how this features in the structure of narrative texts is examined in Allan Luke, "Open and Closed Texts: The Semantic/Ideological Analysis of Curricular Narratives," *Journal of Pragmatics* 13 (1989): pp. 55–80.

19. See, respectively, Shirley B. Heath, "Critical Factors in Literacy Development," in *Literacy, Society and Schooling,* pp. 209–229; Shirley B. Heath, *Ways with Words: Language, Life and Work in Classrooms and Communities* (Cambridge: Cambridge University Press, 1983); Nancy Torrance and David R. Olson, "Development of the Metalanguage of Literacy," *Interchange* 18 (1987): pp. 136–146.

20. Shirley B. Heath, "Protean Shapes in Literacy Events: Ever-Shifting Oral and Literate Traditions," in *Spoken and Written Language: Exploring Orality and Literacy,* ed. Deborah Tannen (Norwood, N.J.: Ablex, 1982), pp. 91–118, p. 93.

21. Robert Calfee, "Those Who Can Explain, Teach . . . ," *Educational Policy* 1 (1987), pp. 9–27, p. 11.

22. Richard C. Anderson et al., *Becoming a Nation of Readers: The Report of the Commission on Reading* (Washington, D.C.: National Institute of Educa-

tion, 1985); for a critical overview on basal use, see Patrick Shannon, "The Use of Commercial Reading Materials in American Elementary Schools," *Reading Research Quarterly* 19 (1983): pp. 68–85.

23. Luke, *Literacy, Textbooks and Ideology,* chap. 6.

24. See Donna Eder, "Differences in Communicative Styles Across Ability Groups," in *Communicating in the Classroom,* ed. Louise C. Wilkinson (New York: Academic Press, 1982), pp. 245–264; Donna Eder, "Organizational Constraints on Reading Group Ability," in *The Social Construction of Literacy,* ed. Jenny Cook-Gumperz (Cambridge: Cambridge University Press, 1986), pp. 138–155.

25. Anderson et al., *Becoming a Nation of Readers,* p. 85.

26. See, for example, Dolores Durkin, *Teaching Them to Read* (Boston: Allyn and Bacon, 1983), pp. 6–7, 368.

27. Kenneth S. Goodman, Patrick Shannon, Yvonne Freeman, and Sharon Murphy, *Report Card on Basals* (Katonah, N.Y.: Richard C. Owen, 1988), chap. 6.

28. Crismore, "Rhetorical Form," p. 134.

29. See, for example, Heath, *Ways with Words,* part 2; Carole Edelsky, Kelly Draper, and Karen Smith, "Hookin' 'em in at the Start of School in a 'Whole Language' Classroom," *Anthropology and Education Quarterly* 14 (1983): pp. 257–281.

30. Carolyn D. Baker and Peter Freebody, "Talk Around Text: Constructions of Textual and Teacher Authority in Classroom Discourse," in *Language, Authority and Criticism,* pp. 263–283.

31. Ibid., pp. 281–282.

32. Luke, "Open and Closed Texts."

33. Carolyn D. Baker, "The Social Context of Literacy Instruction," in *Towards a Critical Sociology of Reading Pedagogy,* ed. Allan Luke and Carolyn D. Baker (Amsterdam: John Benjamins, 1989).

34. For discussion of the role of "procedural display" in elementary instruction, see Len Unsworth, "Whole Language or Procedural Display? The Social Context of Popular Whole Language Activities," *Australian Journal of Reading* 11 (1988): pp. 127–137.

35. For a discussion of these and other Australian teachers' responses to reform in literacy teaching, see Allan Luke et al., *An Evaluation of the Implementation of Literacy Strategies at Two Australian Sites* (Canberra: Curriculum Development Centre, 1989).

36. Linda M. McNeil, ''Exit, Voice and Community: Magnet Teachers' Responses to Standardization,'' *Educational Policy* 1 (1987): pp. 93 – 114, pp. 104–105.

37. Keith Kimberley, ''Community Publishing,'' in *Language, Authority and Criticism,* pp. 184–194.

38. Rowland Lorimer and Patrick Keeney, ''Defining the Curriculum: The Role of the Multinational Textbook in Canada,'' in *Language, Authority and Criticism,* pp. 170–183, p. 171.

39. Luke et al., *Evaluation.*

40. Pam Gilbert, ''Student Text as Pedagogical Text,'' in *Language, Authority and Criticism,* pp. 195–202.

41. For an excellent introduction to salient issues in the critical sociology of the curriculum, see Joel Taxel, ''Children's Literature: A Research Proposal from the Perspective of the Sociology of School Knowledge,'' in *Language, Authority and Criticism,* pp. 32–45.

42. Heath, *Ways with Words;* for an Australian example, see Brian Gray, ''Natural Language Learning in Aboriginal Classrooms: Reflections on Teaching and Learning Style for Empowerment in English'' (Paper presented at the Eighth World Congress of Applied Linguistics, pre-congress conference, Darwin, August, 1987).

43. Luke, et al., *Evaluation.*

44. Edelsky et al., ''Hookin' 'em in''; *Ways with Words,* part 2.

45. Walter H. MacGinitie and Ruth K. MacGinitie, ''Teaching Students Not to Read,'' in *Literacy, Society and Schooling,* pp. 256–269.

PATRICK SHANNON

Chapter Thirteen

Basal Readers and the Illusion of Legitimacy

Basal reading series are different from textbooks intended for other disciplines. Not only are they more expensive, more colorful, and more plentiful, basal readers are also different in essence—not just in appearance. Although most textbooks attempt to standardize curricula among users, basal readers also determine the methods by which that content is transmitted from teacher's guidebook, to teacher, and then to students. Publishers promise to supply a complete system that will teach all children to read if the materials are implemented according to the detailed guidelines that accompany each series. In sum, basal readers eliminate the guesswork for teachers in the classroom. Because of this difference and this promise, basal readers give the illusion that they alone are the tools through which school districts, schools, and teachers can legitimize their reading programs in the eyes of the taxpaying public by raising students' test scores. This essay looks at how basals came to be different, the ways in which they are used to establish legitimacy for reading programs, and why their promise and powers are illusions.[1]

READING INSTRUCTION BEFORE BASAL READERS

Although legislation concerning formal reading instruction in America predates the U.S. Constitution by nearly 140 years, the textbooks and instructional methods before 1900 were remarkably simple and straightforward.[2] At first, teachers used the alphabetic method and religious themes of *The New England Primer* (or a close facsimile) to direct their work. *The Primer* was considered the prototype schoolbook for nearly 100 years until it was displaced by Webster's *American Spelling Book,* which substituted seventy-four pages of word lists and moral tales to instill proper patriotic character in place of the Protestant content of *The Primer.* This "Ol' Blue-Backed Speller" sold over 24,000,000 copies before McGuffey's *Eclectic Readers* with their phonic method and celebration of the principles of industrialization became a publishing success (selling over 120 million sets between 1836 and 1920).[3]

Most teachers used these textbooks in one of two ways: they either gave students assignments and then monitored students' independent learning through recitation, or they arranged choral drills to help students memorize text information. "The evidence [from over 1,000 diaries, journals, and observational reports from the 1800s] suggest that whether teachers taught in urban or rural schools in the North, South, East, or West; whether they instructed students according to the literal, syllabic, or word systems, they typically defined reading as reading aloud—an activity which required teachers to do little more than assign selections to be read, and if he chose to correct the pronunciation of his students."[4]

Although taxpayers, politicians, and educators expressed concern for particular reading programs from time to time during the first 250 years of American reading instruction, the first major crisis in confidence came in 1893, when Joseph Mayer Rice reported his survey of elementary schools from thirty-six cities in *The Public School System of the United States.*[5] Rice discovered that reading instruction in the schools of 90 percent of these cities was unscientific, mechanical, and totally ineffective. "I found the results in reading and writing language almost universally poor in schools where reading matter, at least during the first two years consisted of nothing but empty words, silly sentences, and baby trash, and where the time spent writing was devoted to copying such words and sentences from the blackboard or reading book."[6]

In contrast, teachers from Minneapolis, St. Paul, Indianapolis, and the Cook County Normal School provided "progressive" instruction. They attempted to put into practice the educational philosophies of Rousseau, Pestalozzi, Froebels, and Herbart in their primary programs, which unified the curriculum and successfully taught literacy "incidentally while students were acquiring and expressing ideas."[7] Rice attributed the imbalance concerning effective reading instruction to corrupt politicians who appointed cronies to school boards, to parents unfamiliar with school life, to uninformed and overworked supervisors, and to poorly educated teachers who were not well-versed in either content or pedagogical knowledge.

Combining the moral indignation against partisan politics, the public's fascination with science, and optimism about the future, Rice's survey was generally accepted as fact.[8] Despite teachers' protests to the contrary, most citizens felt that the public schools were unprepared and unable to help America adapt to the changes of rapid industrialization, urbanization, and immigration, leaving local superintendents of schools, whose jobs depended on public support, with a problem: should schools be completely overhauled abandoning the traditional emphases on teachers and textbooks in order to adopt the progressive emphasis on unified curriculum, or should the traditional programs be altered to make them more acceptable and effective?[9]

THE DEVELOPMENT OF BASAL READERS

In order to understand why the technical fine-tuning of traditional reading instruction won out over the unified curriculum of progressivism and led to the development of basals, it is necessary to consider the spirit of the times in which this literacy crisis took place. During the latter part of the nineteenth and the early twentieth centuries, many Americans became enamored with business—and the men, values, and practices of the business world—because they believed them responsible for the rapid industrial and material progress America enjoyed. Public attention turned to how the principles of business could be applied to social institutions and to private life. Schools did not escape this scrutiny, which came in a standard form—unfavorable comparison between schools and business using economy and efficiency as the criteria, followed by suggestions that schools should be more businesslike in their organization and instructional methods.[10]

Science was also influential in the development of American institutions at this time. First, science provided rational explanations for several apparent problems of industrialization, by relying on physical rather than metaphysical theories and providing emotionless arguments concerning the inequality of living standards among citizens based on survival of the fittest arguments of social Darwinism. Second, science understood as technology seemed to drive the material progress of American society, leading the public to look for technological solutions to social concerns. Third, science promised an explanation for any thing or phenomenon through the discovery of its compliance with the laws of nature, compelling social scientists into "one long orgy of tabulation" to provide mathematical equations to explain how the universe and all within it work.[11]

The search for a science of pedagogy was directed primarily by the emergence of the new academic discipline of psychology. Perhaps the most influential and proactive voice for American educational psychology was Edward L. Thorndike, who maintained that learning could be understood through the examination of stimulus and response connections, which comprised the outwardly behaviors of organisms.[12] From the results of his experimentation with animals, Thorndike fashioned four laws of learning: learning is quicker and more permanent when complex tasks are broken down into simple stimulus and response connections and then arranged in a proper sequence of difficulty building up to the complex behavior; learning is strengthened by isolated practice of these connections; the connections become stronger when the organism is rewarded; and training in each specific skill is needed because training in one skill does not transfer easily to other needed skills.

The most prominent example of the combination of business, science, and psychology for social betterment is found in scientific management, a method to increase worker productivity and to promote industrial harmony.[13] Scientific management required analyses of the labor activities of the most able workers so that the best models could become standard practice for all. Able workers' techniques were studied to determine which method was most productive; that method was broken down into its parts, each part being timed in order to eliminate nonessential movements; these streamlined parts were then reassembled into a series of routines performed by groups of workers. The new procedures were learned step-by-step, each worker practicing his or her part while being timed, and financial incentives were offered to those who worked according to the approved procedures.

In this general milieu, the philosophy and radical changes needed to implement progressive reading instruction seemed inefficient, sentimental, and overly optimistic concerning both human nature and learning. By 1910, scientific management was front page news. In 1911, the National Society for the Study of Education appointed the Committee on the Economy of Time in Education (with William S. Gray chairing the subcommittee concerned with reading); and in 1914, Rice published his second book, *The Scientific Management in Education.*[14]

The Committee on the Economy of Time in Education was charged with the job of making recommendations to eliminate nonessentials from the elementary school curriculum, to improve teaching methods, and to set minimum standards for each school subject. The committee's primary method of investigation was a simple adaptation of industrial scientific management: examine learning environments to identify instructional methods; measure the effects of various methods with specifically designed tests, and then identify the methods that yield the highest test scores. With these results, elementary school officials could establish legitimacy within their communities by insisting that teachers use the scientifically validated methods to help students achieve high test scores. The public was expected to interpret high test scores as the profits of scientific instruction. In their first three reports, the committee surveyed the teaching methods and time spent on various subjects in elementary schools in fifty cities around the United States, they presented research-based arguments in favor of standardized text construction and use, new curricular content, and textbook reorganization, and they identified the reading textbooks in use across the country.[15]

The fourth report with its emphasis on instruction was the most widely distributed and read of the committee's reports.[16] Its purpose was "to put its recommendations in simple, direct language, that its report may constitute a handbook and guide for the use of teachers and supervisors who are interested in planning classroom procedures with due regard for both economy and efficiency in teaching and learning."[17] William S. Gray's contribution to the report, "Principles of Method in Teaching Reading, as Derived from Scientific Investigation," offered forty-eight principles concerning norms for student progress across grade levels, directives for oral and silent reading instruction, and even specifications for the printing of books to maximize the economy of reading. Gray's essay emphasized experiments showing that effective reading instruction was more a matter of what teachers did with reading textbooks rather than an effect of particular textbooks. And although he used some of the rhetoric of progressive reading instruction (e.g., "emphasize the content of what is read"), his intention to improve the traditional methods of teaching reading was clear from his words and tone (e.g., "knowledge that the materials are to be reproduced improves the quality of reading"). In sum, teachers were to use Gray's forty-eight maxims to redirect their formal reading lessons in order to make them more scientific.

However, the committee's reports were silent concerning how Gray's modest but numerous suggestions were to penetrate teachers' "mechanical" classroom routines during reading lessons. Since many teachers were poorly educated, knowledgeable superintendents and supervisors in short supply, and teachers already heavily dependent on textbooks, one means for change was the alteration of reading materials. Although minor revisions were suggested in the committee's reports, by far the greatest change—the advent of the teacher's guidebook—was only made possible by the scientific tone and content of Gray's report. His report enables schools to allay public concern by transferring the authority for reading instruction from the subjective opinion of the teacher to the objective facts of science incorporated in the teacher's guidebook of the basal reader. With scientific directives for the standard use of scientifically constructed materials, reading experts and school administrators expected basal series to provide the same technological standardization for reading lessons that had proved so successful in industry. In a sense then, school officials could now calculate how to improve teachers' productivity concerning students' test scores through the manipulation of teachers' use of basal materials.

During the 1920s, "every author of new reading textbooks furnished generous instructions for the use of his materials. Furthermore, authors of texts which had appeared during the preceding period without detailed instructions now came forth with manuals . . . to furnish rather definitely prescribed instruction."[18] This attempt to redirect teachers' instructional actions scientifically marked the beginning of basal readers.

The logic behind the teacher's guidebook makes perfect sense within the context of the times. It was an expression of educators' faith in the powers of science to sort out pedagogical problems and the belief that scientific generalizations were preferable to teachers' and students' idiosyncratic behaviors and beliefs. Guidebooks also incorporated principles from business: they attempted to standardize practice according to methods found to be most productive and economical during experimentation; they separated the planning of goals and instruction from teachers' daily practice; and they supplied supervisors with a norm against which to evaluate teachers' instruction. And if the crisis in school literacy is considered a problem in provoking more scientific reading instruction from teachers, then the teacher's guidebook is a direct application of Thorndike's psychology. It was the correct stimulus to evoke the correct response from teachers, who in turn would use basal materials as the correct stimuli to evoke the desired responses from their students.

In summary, basal reading materials met the expectations of a public and educational community enthralled with business, science, and psychology as they tried to find a remedy for the legitimacy crisis in reading instruction at the turn of the century and ways to prepare students for the changes of an industrialized America. Moreover, basal materials required little additional tax expenditures, bypassed or effectively bolstered weak supervision by providing the criteria and materials for scientific reading instruction, and directed poorly educated teachers to provide that instruction. Basal reader publishers promised school personnel that all children would learn to read if teachers and students would simply follow the directions supplied in the teacher's guidebook. Although the contents of basal reader technology would change modestly in the next sixty years, the rationale for and the format of basal readers were set by the spirit of the first two decades of the twentieth century.

READING INSTRUCTION WITH BASAL READERS

During the last sixty years, the success of basal readers has been almost complete. For at least the last twenty-five years, over 90 percent of elementary school teachers use basals over 90 percent of the time during reading instruction.[19] This success was no accident since publishers, reading experts, state education officials, and professional organizations have promoted their use among teachers.[20] Moreover, the connection between basal readers and scientific management is still very strong, as demonstrated in the National Institute of Education's *Becoming a Nation of Readers,* which promotes basal readers as the primary technology of American reading instruction and states that "America will become a nation of readers when verified practices of the best teachers in the best schools can be introduced throughout the country."[21] Standardized reading tests are to offer the objective means to determine which teachers and which schools are best. Together these positions, championed in *Becoming a Nation of Readers,* restate the equation concerning legitimate reading programs set back in the 1920s: basal readers + scientific management = high test scores.

State Intervention

State departments of education have enthusiastically accepted the validity of this equation and are attempting to realize it through legislation and policy. In many states, officials attempt to tighten the coupling between state identified goals for student competence and classroom reading instruction through the expected (and sometimes enforced) use of basal materials. In this way state officials and local administrators can impress their careful management of reading programs upon critics who charge that schools are not meeting the literacy needs of individuals or society. For example, Florida's Educational Accountability Act of 1976 required "effective, meaningful, and relevant educational experience designed to give students at least the minimum skills necessary to function and survive in today's society."[22] The method for providing this experience was not left to teacher discretion or to the school district because the Florida legislature passed a law requiring basal reader publishers to provide "written proof of the use of learner-verification and revision during preparation, development, and post-publication revision of the materials . . . themselves, revision of the teacher's manuals, and revision of the teacher's skill through retraining."[23] That is, publishers must supply reports that they have tested their product in Florida classrooms and made adjustments in the textbook content, in the directives to teachers in the guidebooks, before the readers can be considered for the state's textbook list.

Clearly the intent of this legislation was to promote the development of better textbooks and basals, but in effect this law established basal materials as the only legal means for providing reading instruction, made basic skills the primary objective of reading instruction, and set up basal reader publishers as the instructional monitors of teachers' effectiveness. Moreover, the criterion for success is reduced to the matter of a passing score on the state's minimum competence test.

Other state legislatures also offer new versions of how scientific management can improve traditional basal reader use in order to improve students' test scores. For example, Maryland's School Improvement Through Instruction Process Program, Missouri's Instructional Management System, and Arkansas' Program for Effective Teaching supply overarching directions on use of the teacher's guidebook and other basal materials. Each of these programs require closer supervision of all teachers' instructional efforts and link reading instruction more closely with students' test scores on state minimum competence and other standardized reading tests. At present, all but four states have such tests in place requiring students to demonstrate appropriate reading competence at regular intervals.

Government, then, not only makes basal readers available through funding, but it sets limits concerning how, when, and for what purpose they will be used. As a result of this legislated learning, a formal system of accountability makes the school district more responsible to the state than to its public, which effectively centralizes the control over reading instruction in the hands of state departments of education.[24] The pressure on districts to meet standard goals as represented in competence tests, to use the standardized basal materials, and to teach reading within specified times is in turn translated by district administrators into expectations for standard performance from schools and individual teachers.

District Administrative Policy

In virtually all school districts, a textbook adoption committee is convened periodically to select one or, less oten, more than one set of basals to be used in elementary classrooms until the next adoption committee meets in five to seven years. This practice is found in the twenty-two states where districts pick from state-approved textbook lists and in non-adoption states where districts work directly with the fifteen to eighteen basal reader publishers. Most studies of this process are not laudatory in their descriptions of committee procedures.[25] They suggest that little time is devoted to actual examination of the materials, that committee members work from checklists that emphasize presence rather than evaluation of quality, that committee members are often unduly influenced by publishing company representatives, and that few teachers are directly involved in the selection process beyond a cursory inspection of sample materials. Attempts to help textbook adoption committees make more rational decisions have met with mixed results.[26]

Regardless of how they are selected, in most cases the selection of a basal reader is "tantamount to selecting the reading curriculum."[27] The basal's scope and sequence of skills determines the reading goals for the district, the teacher's manual becomes the instructional outline for all lessons, the workbooks and worksheets the practice activities that account for up to 70 percent of students' time during reading lessons, and the criterion-referenced tests the means for the evaluation of student progress.[28] Once they are in place, basal readers become the focus of district accountability systems for reading programs. Most often these systems are organized around straightforward administrative directives concerning how the basal readers should be used.[29] However, many school districts find that categorical basal use is insufficient to solve their problem of teaching all their students to read, and they seek to develop even greater control of teachers' use of these materials. That is, some districts are unable to balance the legitimacy equation. Because reading test scores remain low despite basal use, district administrators attempt to strengthen the scientific management of teachers' use of the materials. Perhaps three examples will make this point clearer.

In a district that served as the Right to Read model for its state, administrators insisted that teachers use one basal reading series according to the teacher's guidebook in order to assure students' mastery of skills and to maintain continuity in the reading program during a period of rapid expansion and of high transience among the student body.[30] To be sure that teachers followed this directive, administrators and their surrogates maintained a biweekly review of students' scores on basal criterion-referenced tests. Because success on these tests is dependent on students' knowledge of the specific vocabulary and questioning patterns of the basal anthology and workbooks, administrators could monitor teachers' use of materials as well as student progress through frequent test score checks. Should students make slow progress, teachers or even entire schools could be coached concerning how to follow the basals more closely. As a result of this system, test scores increased and the district gained significant notoriety in its community.

During the late 1970s and early 1980s, Chicago school administrators sought to implement mastery learning through a district-developed basal series.[31] They were frank about the need for such a program: "each summer Chicago girds itself for its two regularly scheduled disasters, the Chicago Cubs and the newspaper publication of reading test scores."[32]

Commercially published basal readers did not provide enough direction for Chicago teachers who "had constant problems in preparing, storing, grading, and organizing the diversity of appropriate materials each day"[33] and who provided traditional basal-directed instruction, placing students in reading groups that "primarily spent time reading—there is no real instruction in reading."[34]

To remedy this situation, the Chicago Mastery Learning Reading Program offered centrally developed packages of lessons wherein "no prior grouping is required on the part of teachers, instruction is laid out in detail, identification of pupils who need remediation and what skills they need help on is done by objective testing, and the amount of remediation and materials for the remediation are provided."[35] However, because "students were not making appropriate progress through the matrix of objective and tests," after several years of using the program "a system of administratively imposed expectations or goals and accompanying monitoring procedures were instituted."[36] Despite Chicago administrators marketing the program nationally, expansion of it to high school programs, and repeated claims of success, and independent study found that few graduating seniors from inner city schools could read at grade level after they had successfully completed the CMLR program.[37] The school district abandoned the program in 1986.

A third example comes from a district that rewarded school personnel if their students scored higher on the state competence tests.[38] In the program, teachers and other elementary school personnel were offered 5 percent of a starting teacher's salary and the school could fly a flag of recognition if the collective reading scores for the school met a quota set mathematically by central administrators. To assist schools in reaching these quotas, central administrators devised a five-step procedure for how to use the teacher's guidebooks for a single basal series.

Principals were to monitor teachers' reading instruction closely to assure that they were following district policy, and according to one director of the program, principals were given added incentive beyond the merit pay to fulfill their role. "Let's say the scores are down in a school. That principal is brought in for a meeting where we discuss methods to remedy the situation. It's all very informal. Principals are evaluated on their school's reading scores, and if the scores are not high next year, they are put on a growth plan, just like their teachers will be. It's like the domino theory." As a result of the merit pay program, districtwide scores rose dramatically in a short time; the district gained nationwide acclaim for its efforts, but it has been unable to maintain its initial success.

These examples may seem extreme, but they suggest the managerial lengths to which some districts are willing to go in order to comply with state legislation and to garner community support for their programs. The tendency toward greater control seems to be growing.[39] However, as the second and third examples and research on textbook selection attest, the relationship between basal readers and scientific management, on the one hand, and students' literacy development, on the other, is not always straightforward. Despite the near universal employment of basal readers and the practice of scientific management, schools again face a literacy crisis that reportedly puts the nation at risk. Estimates of illiteracy in America range as high as one-third of the population (and it is likely that most illiterates used basal readers during whatever elementary schooling they had).[40] Moreover, aliteracy, the ability to read but the infrequent use of that ability, is much higher in the United States than it is in other industrialized nations.[41]

Although some test scores are up, these scores represent students' abilities only to recognize the words of a text and to answer multiple choice questions on what the text is about (the skills emphasized in basal series). However, few American students are sophisticated readers who can comprehend the sense, feeling, tone, and intention of a text and express their understanding of the text sensibly.[42] The statistics are appallingly low for all, but the figures are much worse for poor and minority students than for white upper- and middle-class Americans.

Attempts to explain the failure of the legitimacy equation have typically taken two forms. First, many reading researchers argue that basal readers are not based on the latest scientific evidence. Even supporters of the legitimacy equation suggest that "currently there would appear to be a lag as long as 15 – 20 years in getting research findings into practice" because basals change so slowly in order to preserve their share of the textbook market.[43] As teachers, state departments, and school districts demand more up-to-date scientific materials, publishers will be forced to incorporate the latest research findings into their guidebooks.[44] These new directives based on research determining the most productive methods of generating high test scores will solve the literacy crisis at school by ensuring once again that all teachers are using the most efficient and effective technology for reading instruction—a scientific basal reader.

Second, reading researchers suggest that the tests are to blame for American students' inability to read in a sophisticated manner. Advocates of the legitimacy equation argue that current tests are inadequate for the task of evaluating students' reading abilities because "the strength of a standardized test is not that it can provide a deep assessment of reading proficiencies but rather that it can provide a fairly reliable, partial assessment cheaply and quickly."[45] Since these tests are used as the criterion to evaluate student, teacher, and school performance and typically feature isolated word recognition and multiple-choice questions, reading curriculum and basal materials reduce reading to primarily these nontypical reading skills.[46] The solution, according to this group, is to change the test content and format to bring them more into line with current reading research and theory. The administrative system to monitor teachers' and students' work based on these new scientific tests will then redirect reading curricula and force teachers to provide more effective instruction.[47]

These two explanations suggest a continuation and extension of the legitimacy equation as the solution for the problem of teaching all Americans to read. However, it may be that basal readers, tests, and scientific management are the causes and not the cures of American illiteracy and aliteracy. A third possible explanation for the failure of the legitimacy equation — often overlooked by reading researchers, state officials, and school personnel — is that the rise in authority of basal readers and criterion-referenced and competence tests has diminished teachers' abilities to provide appropriate instruction, particularly for poor and minority students.[48] Let me be clear about this — it is not that teachers lack the potential ability to provide such instruction that would help all students learn to read in a sophisticated manner but simply that under the present conditions in reading programs, they have lost the capacity to do so. Increasingly, over the past sixty years, basal publishers, basal authors, and state officials have usurped many of these skills, reducing today's college-educated teachers to managers of students and the basal technology.

Because of this process of "deskilling," teachers may see little need to improve their professional knowledge.[49] Since nearly every part of their lessons, but the management of materials, is predetermined, teachers have little need to reconsider the goals of their instruction, to reflect upon the meaning of their work, or to interact with one another concerning curricular or instructional matters. Teachers become dependent on basal definitions of reading and instruction, on basal directives concerning how to use the materials, and on the materials to supply the content of reading lessons. This reduction of literacy to the basal skills confines students' consideration of text to the reproduction of explicit content through a series of specified questions and prescribed answers. After participating in this type of reading instruction for even a short time, students learn that reading means not to question the authority of teachers or text. In basal directed lessons, virtually no one, including the teacher, is asked to tackle the sense, feeling, truth, or intention of an author or to develop his or her ability to express understanding of a text — what it does and might mean to one's life. In short, under the legitimacy equation, no one is asked to be truly literate by any criterion beyond a standardized test.

The management skills that reading experts, administrators, and basal publishers offer as replacement for the lost skills direct teachers' attention primarily to the precision with which they apply basal materials and toward tested skills, both of which have proved inadequate for the last sixty years to lead students to a sophisticated ability to read. So here we have the Catch-22 that elementary teachers and all others interested in reading education face—teachers are required to use basal and testing technology in the name of universal literacy, but the technology prevents students from becoming fully literate.

Although I do not have any quick or ready-made answers to solve this dilemma, I think it may be time to reconsider the policies developed to suit the 1920s that keep the legitimacy equation in place and to consider returning the authority concerning reading instruction back to teachers and students. With the time teachers and supervisors spend in college and in-service courses, it would appear that we have the opportunity to make this move without undue problems — provided that time is spent wisely. Governmental departments of education in other countries have already begun to take the initiative to remove the business principles and technological ideology from reading programs — most notably in New Zealand, now considered the most literate and reading country in the world.[50] School administrators can also support teachers' development by helping the community to acknowledge the possible legitimacy of teacher-initiated instruction, by providing time for teachers to talk about their work and to watch each other teach, and by relinquishing the control over the reading program. I am not suggesting that teachers be given license to do whatever they wish during reading lessons, rather I suggest that they be given the freedom to construct reading programs based on child-centered approaches and trade books that meet the needs of their local communities. Only then can schools encourage students to develop their literate abilities beyond basic skills and to recognize the power of literacy in helping them to understand their lives and their relationships to the larger social structure.[51]

Collectively, teachers have not exercised such freedom in at least sixty years, and they may seem unable to cope at first. But there are several American models to begin this work that they might consider: Donald Graves and Jane Hansen's teacher development project in New Hampshire, Shirley Brice Heath's work in the piedmont area of the Carolinas, and Gay Sue Pinnel's Reading Recovery Project at Ohio State University.[52] There are other models that should help teachers move students' improving literacy beyond self-discovery to critical reflection upon one's life and one's social circumstances.[53] Primary policies at each of these projects are to develop teachers as reflective practitioners who can make thoughtful decisions about the goals, instruction, and materials of their work, to celebrate the human essence of reading, to reject the legitimacy equation as a means for the organization and conduct of reading programs, and to expose the illusion of technological solutions to America's literacy problems. Given the history of American reading instruction during the twentieth century, I think these are sound policies.

NOTES

1. All arguments presented in this essay are extended in Patrick Shannon, *Broken Promises: Reading Instruction in 20th Century America* (South Hadley, Mass.: Bergin & Garvey, 1988).

2. The Massachusetts Bay Colony's legislature required masters to attend to their apprentices' literacy instruction in 1642 and required towns of fifty households to hire a primary teacher in 1647. Elwood P. Cubberly, *Public Education in the United States* (Boston: Houghton Mifflin, 1934).

3. Richard Venezky, ''A History of the American Reading Textbook,'' *Elementary School Journal* 87 (January 1987): 247–265.

4. Barbara Finkelstein, ''Governing the Young: Teachers' Behaviors in American Public Primary Schools, 1820–1880, A Documentary History'' (Ph.D. diss., Teachers College, Columbia University, 1970).

5. Joseph Mayer Rice, *The Public School System of the United States* (New York: The Century Co., 1893).

6. Rice, *The Public School System*, p. 26.

7. Ibid., p. 223.

8. Lawrence Cremin, *The Transformation of the School: Progressivism in American Education, 1876–1957* (New York: Vintage, 1961).

9. See the ''vulnerability thesis'' in Raymond Callahan, *Education and the Cult of Efficiency* (Chicago: University of Chicago, 1962).

10. Callahan, *Education and the Cult of Efficiency.*

11. Harold Rugg, *That Men May Understand* (New York: Harpers, 1941), p. 143.

12. Edward L. Thorndike, *The Principles of Teaching Based on Psychology* (New York: Seiler, 1906).

13. Herbert Kliebard, *The Struggle for the American Curriculum, 1873–1958* (Boston: Routledge and Kegan Paul, 1986).

14. Joseph Mayer Rice, *The Scientific Management in Education* (New York: Hines, Noble & Elridge, 1914).

15. H. B. Wilson, ed., *Minimum Essentials in Elementary School Subjects: Standards and Current Practices,* Fourteenth Yearbook of the National Society for the Study of Education (NSSE), part 1 (Bloomington, Ill.: Public School Publishing, 1915); *Second Report of the Committee on Minimum Essentials in Elementary School Subjects,* Sixteenth Yearbook of the NSSE, part 1 (Bloomington, Ill.: Public School Publishing, 1917); and *Third Report of the Committee on Economy of Time in Education,* Seventeenth Yearbook of the NSSE, part 1 (Bloomington, Ill.: Public School Publishing, 1918).

16. Ernest Horn, ed., *Fourth Report of the Committee on Economy of Time in Education,* Eighteenth Yearbook of the NSSE, part 2 (Bloomington, Ill.: Public School Publishing, 1919).

17. H. B. Wilson, Forward in *Fourth Report of the Committee on Economy of Time in Education,* p. 7.

18. Nila B. Smith, *American Reading Instruction* (Newark, Del.: International Reading Association, 1965).

19. Mary Austin and Coleman Morrison, *The First R* (New York: Wiley, 1963); Educational Products Information Exchange, *Report on a National Survey of the Nature and the Quality of Instructional Materials Most Used by Teachers and Learners,* Tec. Rep. No. 76 (New York: EPIE Institute).

20. Richard Anderson et al., *Becoming a Nation of Readers: The Report of the Commission on Reading* (Washington, D.C.: National Institute of Education, 1985).

21. Anderson, *Becoming a Nation of Readers,* p. 120.

22. As quoted in Arthur Wise, *Legislated Learning: The Bureaucratization of the American Classroom* (Berkeley, Calif.: University of California Press, 1979), p. 25.

23. As quoted in Wise, *Legislated Learning,* pp. 22–23.

24. Jack Frymier, "Legislating Centralization," *Phi Delta Kappan* 67 (April 1985): 646–648.

25. Roger Farr, Michael Tulley, and Deborah Powell, "The Evaluation and Selection of Basal Readers," *Elementary School Journal* 87 (January 1987): 267–281.

26. Janice Dole, Teresa Rogers, and Jean Osborn, "Improving the Selection of Basal Programs: A Report of the Textbook Adoption Guidelines Project," *Elementary School Journal* 87 (January 1987): 283–298.

27. Farr, Tulley, and Powell, "The Evaluation and Selection of Basal Readers."

28. Dolores Durkin, "What Classroom Observation Reveals about Reading Comprehension Instruction," *Reading Research Quarterly* 14 (Summer 1978): 481–533.

29. Gerald Duffy, Laura Roehler, and Ruth Wesselman, "Disentangling the Complexities of Instructional Effectiveness: A Line of Research on Classroom Reading Instruction," in *Issues in Literacy,* ed. Jerome Niles and Rosary Lalik (Rochester, N.Y.: National Reading Conference, 1985), pp. 248–261.

30. Patrick Shannon, "The Use of Commercial Reading Materials in American Elementary Schools," *Reading Research Quarterly* 19 (Fall 1983): 68–85.

31. Patrick Shannon, "Mastery Learning in Reading and the Control of Teachers and Students," *Language Arts* 61 (September 1984): 484–493.

32. James Smith and Michael Katims, "Reading in the City: The Chicago Mastery Learning Reading Program," *Phi Delta Kappan* 59 (November 1979): 199.

33. Michael Katims and Beau Fly Jones, "Chicago Mastery Learning: Theory, Research, and Assessment in the Inner City" (A paper presented at an annual meeting of the International Reading Association, May 1981), p. 6.

34. Michael Katims, "An Interview," in *Mastery Learning, Theory, Research, and Implementation,* ed. Doris Ryan and Martha Schmit (Toronto: Ontario Ministry of Education, 1979), p. 32.

35. Smith and Katims, "Reading in the City," p. 201.

36. Katims and Jones, "Chicago Mastery Learning," p. 3.

37. Designs for Change, *The Bottom Line* (Chicago: Designs for Change, 1985).

38. Patrick Shannon, "Teachers' and Administrators' Thoughts on Changes in Reading Instruction within a Merit Pay Program Based on Test Scores," *Reading Research Quarterly* 21 (Fall 1986): 20–35.

39. Linda Darling-Hammond and Arthur Wise, "Beyond Standardized Teaching: State Standards and School Improvement," *Elementary School Journal* 85 (February 1985): 315–336.

40. Jonathan Kozol, *Illiterate America* (Garden City, N.J.: Anchor, 1985).

41. Neil Postman, *Teaching as a Conserving Activity* (New York: Delta, 1979).

42. Allan Purves, "The Challenge to Educators to Produce Literate Citizens," in *Becoming Readers in a Complex Society,* Eighty-third Yearbook of

NSSE, part 1, ed. Allan Purves and Olive Niles (Chicago: University of Chicago Press, 1984), pp. 1–15.

43. Richard Anderson, Jean Osborn, and Robert Tierney, *Learning to Read in American Schools: Basal Readers and Content Texts* (Hillsdale, N.J.: Lawrence Erlbaum, 1984), p. x.

44. P. David Pearson, "Guided Reading," in *Learning to Read in American Schools,* pp. 21–29.

45. Anderson, *Becoming a Nation of Readers,* p. 98.

46. Purves, "The Challenge to Educators to Produce Literate Citizens."

47. P. David Pearson and Sheila Valencia, "Reading Assessment: Time for a Change," *Reading Teacher* 40 (April 1987): 726–739; Charles Peters et al., "New Directions in Statewide Reading Assessment," *Reading Teacher* 40 (April 1987): 749–760.

48. See Anthony Barton and David Wilder, "Research and Practice in the Teaching of Reading," in *Innovation in Education,* ed. Mathew Miles (New York: Teachers College Press, 1964), pp. 361–398; Patrick Shannon, "Reading Instruction and Social Class," *Language Arts* 62 (October 1985): 604–613.

49. Patrick Shannon, "Commercial Reading Materials, a Technological Ideology, and the Deskilling of Teachers," *Elementary School Journal* 87 (January 1987): 307–332.

50. John Guthrie, "Reading in New Zealand: Achievement and Volume," *Reading Research Quarterly* 17 (Fall 1981): 6–27.

51. Paulo Freire and Donaldo Macedo, *Literacy: Reading the Word and the World* (South Hadley, Mass.: Bergin & Garvey, 1987); Shannon, *Broken Promises.*

52. Donald Graves, *A Researcher Learns to Write* (Exeter, N.H.: Heinemann, 1984); Jane Hansen, *When Writers Read* (Exeter, N.H.: Heinemann, 1987); Shirley Brice Heath, *Ways With Words* (Cambridge: Cambridge University Press, 1983); Gay Sue Pinnell, *Report on the Ohio Reading Recovery Project* (Columbus, Ohio: Ohio State University Press, 1987).

53. Alex McLeod, "Critical Literacy: Taking Control of Our Own Lives," *Language Arts* 63 (January 1986): 37–50; Ira Shor, ed., *Freire for the Classroom: A Sourcebook for Liberatory Teaching* (Exeter, N.H.: Boynton/Cook, 1987); Sara Zimet, "Teaching Children to Detect Social Bias in Books," *Reading Teacher* 36 (February 1978): 418–421.

Part 5

International Perspectives

PHILIP G. ALTBACH

Chapter Fourteen

The Unchanging Variable: Textbooks in Comparative Perspective

---

Textbooks, without question, are among the most important components of any educational system. Research in many countries and in different contexts has shown that textbooks have an important influence on teaching and learning.[1] Textbooks exist at virtually all levels of the educational system, in most fields of study, and in all of the world's educational systems. Textbooks have been a key element in schooling for centuries, although their form has changed over time. Since the printing press has come into widespread use, texts have been used in schools. And despite the growing importance of computers and other means of knowledge transmission in recent years, textbooks are likely to retain their preeminent position in education. They are the least expensive, most reliable means of transmitting knowledge and providing coherence to the curriculum. Unlike computers, they are never "down" and do not require much expertise to use. And in educational systems that remain in many ways conservative, textbooks are tried and true.

While textbooks are educational artifacts, they are also commodities. There is an important economic dimension to textbooks—who pays for them and how are they distributed? Textbooks are political. Who

---

Acknowledgement: I am indebted to Gail P. Kelly, Hugh G. Petrie, and Lois Weis for their comments on an earlier version of this essay and to Lalita Subramanyan for her assistance with editing.

chooses them and what is their content? How do economics, politics, and pedagogy impact the production, content, and distribution of textbooks? These issues have aroused a great deal of controversy and contention in many countries.[2] Indeed, textbooks are frequently flashpoints of controversy in debates about education. In the United States, textbooks have recently been attacked for poor quality. Textbooks are visible and easy to point out. They are, in a sense, a proxy for the ills of the educational system — since textbooks after all mirror the ideas, methods, and orientations of the educational systems that they serve.[3] At the same time that texts reflect educational ideas, they can also provide guidelines for teaching and learning. They help to shape the curriculum since they are often the main element that shapes how knowledge is presented in the classroom.[4] Textbooks are sometimes seen as a means of educational improvement and reform.

Few discussions of textbooks have dealt with the growing internationalization of publishing and of the knowledge system. This essay is concerned with some of the international dimensions of textbooks and with bringing an international focus to key issues in textbook debates in most countries — issues of how textbooks are created and distributed, questions of who should pay for textbooks, and speculations concerning the future of textbooks in a changing educational environment worldwide. The purpose here is to raise issues and focus on points of controversy and debate rather than offer definitive answers.[5] This discussion begins with a consideration of the international dimension of textbooks, as this provides a context for later analysis of such questions of textbook production and distribution and some key policy issues.

INTERNATIONALIZATION

Textbooks are an increasingly international commodity. Due in part to the growing impact of multinational publishers and in part to the fact that educational research is increasingly used worldwide, there are more and more international connections in textbooks. Textbook concerns differ from country to country. For many parts of the Third World, the problem is simply to provide a sufficient number of books to school children.[6] In the United States, while some urban school districts are undersupplied, issues tend to cluster around policymaking and quality. In Eastern Europe, questions of efficiency and cost in textbook production and articulating content to rapidly changing political circumstances are widely debated.

The control and ownership of the publishing enterprise has an impact on textbooks. For the industrialized nations, the dramatic increase in the role of large multinational publishers is without question the most important development in publishing in the past several decades. This "multinationalization" of publishing has had an impact on textbooks since some of the largest publishers of texts in countries like the United States have come under the ownership of multinational firms. Maxwell/Pergamon of Britain has recently gained control of Macmillan in the United States and is now one of the largest textbook publishers. Bertelsmann of West Germany is also among the largest American publishers. Longmans (Britain), Kluwer and Elsevier (Netherlands), and Hachette (France) have entered the American publishing market.[7] Harcourt Brace Jovanovich, long an industry leader in the American textbook market, has yielded its dominance in the aftermath of a damaging takeover battle in which the firm went deeply into debt to maintain its independence from foreign control.

At the same time, major American firms have long been an important international publishing influence. With European economic integration in 1992, there will be an increase in the role of multinational corporations of all kinds, including in the field of publishing and textbooks in Western Europe. It is possible that as Eastern Europe becomes integrated into a broader European economic order, this region will, for the first time, become involved in international publishing. However, even with the greatly expanded role of the multinational publishers in the industrialized nations, textbooks have generally remained essentially national in scope and content. Markets are sufficiently large and wealthy to support books designed specifically for a single country. For the most part, policymakers and educators insist that textbooks be designed with specific national, or in federal systems such as the United States, Australia, and West Germany, state, concerns and there is strong resistance in these markets to books that are not embedded in the specific culture of the country in which the book is used.

In the Third World, international influences are in many cases much more significant. In countries which were under colonial domination, publishers from the colonial power entrenched themselves in the local market and often remain powerful today. In many instances, particularly in small countries, it has been beyond the ability of local educational authorities and publishers to develop and publish textbooks, and foreign books are used. The situation is most serious in Africa, where textbook markets are often small and bifurcated and the infrastructures of both education and publishing are relatively weak.[8] Books intended for use in African primary schools are frequently designed and written by experts working at the headquarters of the multinational firm in London or Paris. They use African examples, but they cannot reflect specific national circumstances. Books produced in this way can often be used in several countries at the same time. The books may not be entirely relevant for local conditions and may not meet the needs of the local market, but they are economical to produce and yield significant profits for the Western publisher. Perhaps more important, they may be written with assumptions about both the curriculum and the learning process that are not well suited to the country in which the books are used. And in such contexts, research shows that the book will be a significant influence on the nature of the curriculum, instruction, and the knowledge imparted to pupils because teachers are usually poorly trained and there is a lack of carefully designed curriculum materials, guides, and nontext materials.[9]

In Asia and Latin America, with better developed publishing and educational systems for the most part, the situation is not so desperate and textbooks, at least at the level of primary education, tend to be specifically designed for local needs and most frequently printed in the country in which the books are used. The trend in many Third World nations has been to give the responsibility for producing school textbooks to governmental agencies with the idea that books should be produced inexpensively and widely distributed to pupils free or at very low cost. Governments also wish to maintain control over the content and design of textbooks.

Public sector textbook production has had many implications. For one thing, it has made the development of general (nontext) publishing in the Third World more difficult since textbooks are often a mainstay of private sector publishers, who find it difficult to survive without this segment of the market. It is also the case that public agencies are sometimes less efficient than private firms in developing and printing books. Nonetheless, the public sector has in general ensured that books have been produced and distributed. For languages with relatively few speakers and for regional markets, governmental initiative is frequently the only means of providing textbooks. The debate concerning whether textbook publishing is better handled by public or private interests continues in many Third World nations.[10]

Textbooks are part of an international knowledge system which is characterized by inequalities. The impact of this knowledge system is significant and, as the means of communication become easier and there is more contact among researchers and educators worldwide, it is likely to increase. The increasing multinationalization of publishing also contributes to the role of the international knowledge system.[11] The major industrialized nations dominate the world knowledge system. This is not surprising since the major publishers are located in these countries, the major universities and research centers are located there, and the major international languages (especially English) used for science and research are centered there. For example, more than 60 percent of the world's research and development is done is a single country — the United States. English is the major language of scholarly and research communication, with a large majority of the world's scientific journals being published in English. The new database research networks are centered in the industrialized nations. And more than one million postsecondary students (mostly from the Third World) are studying abroad—the large majority of them in the industrialized nations. These and other factors contribute to the inequalities evident in the international knowledge system.

The implications of the international knowledge system are significant. The increased use of research to inform decisions about educational practice and about textbooks in particular reinforces the system. Increasingly the preparation of textbooks has become more professional, with care being taken to ensure that textbook writers take into account the latest knowledge about learning theory, tests and measurement, and the like. The bulk of the world's educational research is produced in a few countries—and especially in the United States. This research generally uses American designs and is focused on topics of relevance to American educators. The paradigms are related to the realities of the United States.

Yet the research is used worldwide, often in countries with far different circumstances than the United States. The textbooks that have been developed in the industrialized nations reflect the latest research and are sophisticated in their design and integrated into curriculum packages. It is not surprising that these books are often used in Third World countries, particularly when policymakers want to have the "latest knowledge," often neglecting to ask if this knowledge is relevant to local circumstances.

Textbook development and production are affected by the international knowledge system in many ways. New technologies, such as computer-aided instruction, generally emerge from the metropolitan centers and, in part because they have the legitimacy of key scholars and institutions, are disseminated widely. These technologies have an impact on thinking about textbooks and, ultimately, on the ways that textbooks are used. New curricular ideas emerge from the center and are gradually diffused to the peripheries. The very concept of the textbook is affected by international factors. The use of glossy paper, illustrations, and hard covers for most textbooks is related to the conditions of the schools of the affluent center countries and to the policies of adoption agencies in those countries.[12] While poorer countries often produce less elaborate books, everyone is affected by what is considered the "gold standard" of textbook production.

The international knowledge system is a powerful combination of forces which dominates in many ways the development and dissemination of new ideas. The links between resources, expertise, the size of academic systems, and infrastructures means that ideas and knowledge products are to a significant degree centralized in a small number of countries and academic systems.

The example of Canada illustrates well the role of the international knowledge system. Canada, of course, is not a poor nation—it has one of the world's highest standards of living, a very high literacy rate, and an active publishing system. Yet, Canadians have worried about maintaining their cultural and educational independence in the face of tremendous market forces from the United States. Special programs have been set up to ensure that Canadian cultural and educational products can compete with foreign books.[13] Despite such efforts, Canadian textbooks reflect many influences from abroad — from the United States and Britain for Anglophone Canada and from France for Quebec. Canadian textbook publishers and authors rely largely on U.S. research to inform their work. In some cases, foreign (American, British, or French generally) books are adapted to meet Canadian needs—but the basic assumptions in those books remain, whether or not they are relevant to Canadian realities. Because Canada is a relatively small market and because it lacks the complex research infrastructures of its larger neighbors, it remains to some extent dependent on knowledge from abroad. The kind of dependency and reliance on foreign models that has characterized developing countries also plays a role in industrialized nations which are small, and may not have the necessary research or curricular infrastructures.

There are without question a range of external influences which affect the development and publication of textbooks. In recent years, the World Bank has been concerned about the textbook "famine" in the Third World and has devoted resources to the development and publication of texts. These programs have involved both the creation and the publication and distribution of textbooks. Sometimes, publishing infrastructures had to be created and relevant expertise obtained to develop books. While World Bank planners took local realities into consideration and used local expertise as much as possible, significant external influences were also evident at all levels of the programs.[14]

In the industrialized nations, the impact is less direct and more subtle. But it is clear that the increasing internationalization of knowledge, the role of expertise, and especially the increasing impact of the multinational publishers will ensure that international factors will play an expanding role in determining the nature, publication, and distribution of textbooks in the future.

THE POLITICS OF TEXTBOOKS

Textbooks are among the most political of commodities.[15] In a sense, textbooks define the nature of education. They embody legitimate knowledge. They are perceived as a powerful teaching tool and their content as one of the key determinants of what gets taught in schools. The content of textbooks is thus highly political and often a terrain for battles over the nature of education, and sometimes over important social issues or even how the nation, religion, or other very sensitive issues are interpreted. Textbook wars have been fought in many parts of the world. In the United States, textbooks have been one of the major battlegrounds for such issues as church-state relations, the nature of pluralism in American society, and other highly contentious questions. Much of the "creationism" debate was played out in textbook battles, and textbook controversies have occasionally flared into violence, as occurred in West Virginia in the 1970s.[16] In these instances, religious fundamentalism and conservative politics lay behind the campaigns.

In Japan, the interpretation of Japan's role in World War II has been played out in a series of controversies concerning the ways in which the war is portrayed in Japanese schoolbooks.[17] The vehemence of the textbook conflicts in Japan (which have involved the powerful teachers union and segments of the academic community on the side of a "revisionist" view of Japan's role in the war and a recognition of the very harsh domestic and foreign policies of the period against the official doctrines of the Education Ministry), reflects significant divisions in Japanese opinion. The Ministry of Education, which has so far prevailed, has ensured that Japanese schoolbooks treat wartime Japanese activities relatively gently. Textbook battles have even spilled over into foreign policy. Several years ago, the Chinese government protested the treatment of the Japanese occupation of China during the war in new Japanese textbooks.

The current political change sweeping Eastern Europe will quickly be reflected in the content of textbooks. School books almost always reflect the official view of history, society, and economy. When basic assumptions are questioned, textbook controversy and often change is an inevitable result. In the Soviet Union, for example, when the political position of the government was dramatically altered, textbooks were quickly changed. Current Eastern European realities will require that the orthodox Communist interpretations in textbooks be changed. One problem for the textbook writers is that there is much controversy about fundamental issues in these societies and there is, at present, no accepted orthodoxy to reflect. It is not only the East Bloc which has textbook orthodoxy.

In the Third World, textbooks are the subject of considerable attention and sometimes controversy because their interpretation of national history often shapes consciousness of the nation. An initial problem is to create indigenous textbooks in situations where colonial-era books were the only ones available. Newly independent states must create a sense of their own history and interpetations of that history, and textbooks are frequently a flashpoint of controversy about such issues. The interpretation of the colonial experience, of national liberation movements, and of the role of religious and ethnic movements are among the issues which create debate and conflict. For these reasons, and others, the content of textbooks becomes a matter of concern not only for educators and the ministry of education, but also for the educated public and the political system.[18]

In the United States, as in other countries, the question of who makes decisions about the content, orientation, publication, and distribution of textbooks is embedded in politics.[19] Such decisions have significant economic implications, since textbook publishing is a major segment of the publishing enterprise in any country. Moreover, it is potentially lucrative because textbook publishing is relatively predictable and the costs of distribution are low since publishers can sell in large quantities directly to school districts. Thus, publishing interests often struggle over access to textbook markets. The content of textbooks is also a matter of political controversy in the United States, and these conflicts have spilled over into the political and sometimes the legal arena, with court controversies relating to textbook treatment of such issues as race, religion, and evolution. Many observers have pointed out that in the United States the states which have centralized adoption policies—large states such as California, Texas, and Florida—have immense power in the American textbook market.[20]

Textbooks are politically divisive precisely because they are perceived to be important. Their economic impact makes them worth fighting over. A contract to produce and distribute texts for a particular subject area may be worth a considerable amount of money for a publisher, even in a relatively small market. Major decisions in some countries concerning whether texts should be published in the private or public sectors are, of course, subject to intense political pressure. Textbook content also arouses political controversy because what is taught in textbooks is seen, in a sense, as defining the national experience and putting specific interpretations on key social issues. Because textbooks are read by large numbers of school children and have a captive audience, their content is taken very seriously. Textbooks, even when they are published by private sector companies, are in a way the "official" interpretation of reality.[21]

Textbooks are politically controversial precisely because they are so important, so visible, and so crucial to the educational enterprise. Where the preparation of textbooks is professionalized or where there are few opportunities for political struggle, textbook politics may be relatively limited. For example, the sort of open political warfare and frequent recourse to the courts that is evident in the United States seems less common in Britain. In Singapore, the existence of the Curriculum Development Institute of Singapore (CDIS), which prepares many of the country's textbooks, and a rather bureaucratized and authoritarian political system limits textbook controversy. Nonetheless, textbooks remain the flashpoint of political controversy in many places.

TEXTBOOK CHOICES

At the present time, education issues are hotly debated in many countries in an effort to improve the schools, provide more opportunities to all segments of the population, and to save money in a difficult economic environment. Issues relating to textbooks have been discussed as well, often as part of broader debates about the direction, nature, and scope of education. It is useful to focus on some of the points of discussion relating to textbooks as these debates may well affect the nature of textbook production and distribution.

Public vs. Private

There has been a great deal of discussion of the most effective means of delivering textbooks to pupils and, in line with widespread criticism of public enterprise everywhere, a growing stress on the use of the private sector to publish textbooks. In the United States and most Western capitalist nations, the private sector is the main publisher of textbooks and this issue is not important. But in many other parts of the world textbooks are produced and distributed by public agencies — government ministries, semi-autonomous boards responsible to the government, school systems, and the like. In the Third World, most newly independent nations took the responsibility for textbook development and publication from expatriate publishers and gave it to the public sector. It was felt that public agencies would be able to get newly designed (non-colonial) books to students cheaply and efficiently. China, after the Communists achieved power in 1949, immediately nationalized the textbook industry, rewrote existing texts, and printed large numbers of books. This massive publically funded textbook campaign was an important element in rapidly improving China's literacy rate.

There are many different models of public sector Third World textbook development and the results have been mixed.[22] In some instances, such as the experience of the semi-autonomous government-funded *Dewan Bahasa dan Pustaka* (National Book Agency) in Malaysia, books have been effectively developed and distributed. In India, results in terms of producing books efficiently has been mixed. In some Indian states, state textbook agencies have provided efficient and relatively inexpensive book development, mostly in India's many regional languages. In others, state boards have been riddled with corruption and have not provided needed textbooks.

In recent years, the World Bank and other foreign aid agencies have attempted to place greater stress on the use of private sector publishers for textbook development and publication. In many countries, public-private cooperation in textbooks has worked well. In Singapore, for example, the CDIS creates textbooks and hands them over to private publishers for printing and distribution. With the massive infusion of World Bank loan funds into Third World textbook projects, the private sector publishers have gotten a significant boost.[23]

In Eastern Europe and the Soviet Union, textbooks have traditionally been published by state agencies and distributed to students free of charge. Indeed, the basic concept of book publishing differed from established Western ideas. In the socialist countries, books are seen as a means of education, political development, and cultural enlightenment. Books were not expected to necessarily earn a profit. As a result, many books were priced without regard to the cost of production. At the same time, government authorities placed significant restrictions on what could be published — ensuring political and ideological reliability.[24] Recent political changes in Eastern Europe have created an entirely new situation for publishing, and it is not clear how the development and provision of school textbooks will be affected. However, in countries such as Poland, Hungary, and Czechoslovakia, a private sector publishing industry is developing, with considerable freedom from governmental ideological restraints.[25] The influence of the Catholic church, never absent in Poland, will likely increase and there are signs that multinational publishers will enter these markets. British publishing baron Robert Maxwell has already invested in newspapers in Hungary. Investments in book publishing are no doubt coming.

Although American textbook publishing is in private hands, there has been increasing criticism of the "centralized adoption" states for exercising too much control over textbooks and not permitting a sufficient role for the free market to operate in textbook selection. Some have argued that this system has diminished the quality of textbooks by insisting that selected volumes be written at the lowest common denominator. Throughout the world there is a growing debate about how textbooks can be most effectively and efficiently produced and marketed. There has been a growing trend toward relying on the private sector and criticizing public initiative in textbook development and publication. It is, in a sense, interesting that at the same time that American private sector publishers have been under unprecedented attack for lowering the standard of texts —and by implication the educational system—other countries are turning to the private sector as a means of improving the efficiency of the textbook system and possibly lowering the cost of books.

Who Should Pay?

Textbooks in fact constitute only a small part of the total educational budget in any country or school system. In the industrialized nations, schools spend under $300 per year per student on classroom materials (including textbooks and other nontext materials)—a small percentage of the $2,200 (measured in constant 1980 dollars) spent on each student in primary and secondary education annually. In contrast, the very poorest countries spend about $1 on classroom materials while medium-income Third World countries allocate less than $10 for such materials.[26] While there are immense inequalities in the provision of education among nations—inequalities that are matched when one examines the provision of educational materials — textbooks and related items constitute only a small part of the education budget in any educational system. Indeed, it is very likely that textbooks are the most cost-effective part of expenditures on education!

Regardless of the relatively low cost of textbooks, there has been increasing discussion of who should pay for books. In the United States, the common, indeed virtually universal, practice is for most books to be lent to students without charge. This is not the practice worldwide. Indeed, it is possible that the poorer the country, the more likely it is for students to have to pay for their textbooks. In many countries, students pay for their books and keep them. In poorer countries, books tend to be produced more cheaply and lack lavish illustrations, high quality paper, and durable binding. While such textbooks do not have the visual appeal of their Western counterparts and it is possible that they are quite as effective as learning tools, they are much less expensive to purchase, whether the buyers are individual pupils or school authorities.[27]

In the past decade, there has been increasing debate concerning who should pay for textbooks in the light of severe shortages of money for education throughout the world, and especially in the Third World. Policymakers have sought ways of reducing the cost of education—drawing back from a commitment to universal literacy, increasing the size of classes, and shifting more of the burden for the financing of education on those going to school (and their families) are among the cost-saving efforts. In this atmosphere, the already existing practice of having students pay for their own books is being widened and expanded to countries where books have been provided without cost.

The implications of the "who should pay?" issue are significant for educational systems, the textbook industry, and for educational policy. In many cases, it is very difficult financially for students (and their families) to assume greater responsibility for education. Increased costs to the individual may result in the lowest income students dropping out of school. There are also questions of whether it is advisable for books to be loaned to students versus selling them. A related issue is the nature of the books to be produced—relatively more expensive books with illustrations and better design may be more effective in stimulating learning. For the Third World, the most serious problem is simply to provide sufficient numbers of books to students—many students have no books at all. At the present time, there is pressure to shift more of the burden for paying for education onto the "users." This trend is related not only to the worldwide fiscal crisis of education but also to the ideology of agencies like the World Bank and to the dominant economic thinking in many countries, which has stressed "privatization" and decreased public spending in all areas. At least for textbooks, the implications of key decisions about funding are very significant for all of the groups involved in the design, production, and use of school books.

Publishing Infrastructures

Producing and distributing textbooks is a highly complex undertaking. While money is a necessary element, just as important are expertise—concerning curriculum and learning as well as the highly specialized nuances of publishing. The process of publishing is one of coordinating a variety of elements—authors, editors, compositors, printers, and distributors, among others.[28] Textbooks are, in a sense, even more difficult to publish since there must also be coordination with the educational authorities and sometimes political policymakers who determine the nature of the books. The complexity of the nature of publishing is frequently ignored in discussions about textbooks.

Raw materials—mainly paper—are an important part of textbook publishing. The choice of paper has a significant impact on the nature and, of course, on the cost of a textbook. In the West, textbooks generally use the most expensive papers in order for the books to last and so that highly sophisticated artwork and graphics can be used. In the Third World, less expensive paper is frequently used. Paper tends to constitute a large proportion of the total cost of a book in the Third World, where paper costs are high (as a greater proportion is imported) and labor costs low.[29] Such choices must be made with appropriate expertise and experience. The choice of production techniques is also a matter of considerable importance. The latest composing and computer-assisted design arrangements produce very well-designed books which can have excellent graphics, color presentation and the like. In the industrialized nations, it is often no more expensive to use sophisticated design and production techniques than it is to use others. In the Third World, however, the choices in design and composition dramatically affect the cost of production. The publisher must have the knowledge and experience to make appropriate choices.

Textbooks must be written. The author (or authors) are the most important ingredient of textbook quality and it is surprising that little attention is paid to the nature of textbook authorship in debates about textbook quality and development. Regardless of the quality of production or number of pictures in a book, if it is written poorly it will not be an effective learning tool. The preparation of a primary or secondary school textbook is a highly complex undertaking—the book must not only be written, but it must coordinate with other related books in its area or related fields. It must satisfy the curricular guidelines set forth by educational authorities. It must be written in a way that will be understandable to the intended audience but at the same time the style should appeal to the audience. A textbook is written with many constraints and many participants. Curricular authorities and governmental officials are concerned with the content and sometimes the writing style of the books and wish to ensure that the book is relevant for the prescribed curriculum. Sometimes teachers are also involved in the process, providing input and "testing" text materials.

More and more frequently, in the United States and increasingly in other industrialized nations, textbooks are written by teams of people rather than by a single author.[30] Frequently, much of the actual writing is done by writers hired by the publisher with supervision from recognized experts in the field. These "managed texts" are increasingly widespread at all levels of the educational system. With such books, it is possible for a publisher to tailor a textbook to meet the specific requirements of adoption agencies in the powerful states. However, managed texts have been criticized for removing any sense of clarity of thinking or imagination from textbooks since they are written according to preset formulas, with more attention to using language that will be understandable to the lowest common denominator than with a sense of style. The concept of authorship changes under these circumstances—authors become agents of publishers, often working for a preset fee rather than for royalties, and having little autonomy.

Few other countries have moved as far as the United States in the direction of the corporate authorship of textbooks. In the Third World, the problem is simply to locate authors with the needed qualifications to write textbooks. The situation is even more difficult because there is an immediate need for relevant books in a range of subjects and for most grade levels all at once. At the same time, there are fewer norms established concerning the content of textbooks and even the scope of the curriculum. The content of textbooks is contested everywhere, but disputes are perhaps even more serious in the Third World, where there are often disagreements about the very nature of the polity, the role of ethnic and religious groups, and the like.

As the economic climate for education and also for textbooks worsens, the challenges to those responsible for textbook publishing increase. Fiscal constraints increase, the market becomes more competitive, and publishers try to cut corners in order to make a profit. Decisions concerning the use of paper, graphics, authorship, and the like become not only matters of curricular and aesthetic concern, but also of economics and the costing of books. Too often those making basic decisions about textbooks have little understanding of the details of textbook publishing and the nuances of a highly complex set of arrangements and infrastructures. In the United States, recent consolidation in the publishing industry has increased the pressure on textbook publishers to earn substantial profits as corporate management has become more powerful in the publishing industry. In general, publishers who deal with textbooks have an increasingly difficult task in a period of great pressures—and also a great need for high quality textbooks. At the same time that technology permits an improvement in the technical quality of books at the same or even reduced cost, economic and curricular pressures are greater.

THE FUTURE OF TEXTBOOKS IN A COMPLEX WORLD

Textbooks are among the most important elements of contemporary educational systems. They define the curriculum and are among the most important determinants of school success. Despite rapid technological change and considerable debate about the nature of education and the most effective means of delivering schooling, textbooks remain a primary element in the educational process. They will, without any question, remain at the center of the educational enterprise.

Yet, textbooks face major challenges. In the United States, education has been widely criticized for low quality. Textbooks have also been attacked by critics with little understanding of the nature of textbook adoption and publishing in the American context. Overseas, although textbooks are one of the least expensive educational "inputs" and have proved to be highly effective in producing positive results, nonetheless, they have been criticized for being too costly and ways have been sought to reduce expenditures on school books. By any objective measure, such economies would seem to be misplaced.

Pressures for privatization may have an impact on textbook production in the Third World and in Eastern Europe, although it is not clear that the new arrangements will produce better or cheaper products. In the West, the impact of the multinational publishers is just now beginning to be felt but there will be an inevitable internationalization of textbooks in the 1990s. In Western Europe especially, textbooks will be affected by the various moves toward European economic integration in 1992. There are likely to be greater pressures for textbooks to produce good profits for increasingly "bottom line" oriented multinational publishers. At the same time, there may be some homogenization of the content of books as publishers seek to spread increasingly high textbook development costs to a number of countries.

The entire textbook infrastructure has become more international. Expertise, produced largely in the major universities of the industrialized countries, is increasingly used on a worldwise basis. New databases communicate research findings quickly to an international audience. There is a growing awareness worldwide of educational research and research findings have an impact on the development of textbooks. The international knowledge network which produces and disseminates research and provides expertise remains highly unequal — knowledge is created in the West and is used worldwide. The newly dominant multinational publishers are also centered in the major Western countries. New publishing technologies will also become more prevalent worldwide. These technologies are also products of Western technology and spread from the centers to the peripheries. Thus, the growing internationalization of textbooks maintains the dominant role of the industrialized nations. Within the industrialized world, struggles among multinational publishers, technological changes, and the needs of educational systems will continue.

At the same time, consciousness of the importance of textbooks in education, the development of publishing capability and research expertise in many countries, and continuing stress on education may mean that countries which have heretofore been peripheral and dependent in education and in the development and production of textbooks, may move in more independent directions. At the very least, it is commonly agreed that the provision of textbooks to school children is a top priority. And it is widely known that the content of textbooks makes a difference. The 1990s brings a period of uncertainty. Textbooks will continue to be a key element in education at all levels and in all countries. It is less clear how texts will be created, published, and distributed. In a difficult economic climate, issues of who will pay for books and the role of education in rapidly changing economic and political environments remain in question.

NOTES

1. The most important comparative study on this issue is S. Heyneman, J. Farrell, and M. Sepulveda-Stuardo, *Textbooks and Achievement: What We Know* (Washington, D.C.: The World Bank, 1978).

2. In the United States, for example, issues of religion and education have frequently been played out in relation to textbooks. See, for example, Edward J. Larson, "Constitutional Challenges to Textbooks," in this volume, chap. 5. See also Raymond English, "The Politics of Textbook Adoption," *Phi Delta Kappan* (December 1980): 275–278, for an overview of the political elements of American textbook adoption.

3. For a critique of American textbooks by a key policymaker, see Bill Honig, "California's Experience with Textbook Improvements," in this volume, chap. 7.

4. See Michael W. Apple, *Teachers and Texts* (New York: Routledge and Kegan Paul, 1986).

5. It should be pointed out that the research on textbooks is uneven. There is a considerable body of knowledge — mostly generated in the United States — concerning the detailed pedagogical aspects of textbooks, but hardly any research on the nature of textbook publishing or on the international implications of textbooks.

6. The World Bank, which has financed perhaps $1 billion in loans for textbook development to developing countries, has stressed textbooks as a key means of educational improvement. See B. Paxman, C. Denning, and A. Read, *Analysis of Research on Textbook Availability and Quality in Developing Countries* (Washington, D.C.: Education and Employment Division, The World Bank, 1989).

7. This issue is discussed in Gilbert Sewall and Peter Cannon, "The New World of Textbooks, Industry Consolidation and Its Consequences," in this volume, chap. 4.

8. See Keith Smith, "Who Controls Book Publishing in Anglophone Middle Africa?" *Annals of the American Academy of Political and Social Science* 421 (September 1975): 140–150. For continuing coverage of African publishing, see the *African Book Publishing Record.*

9. See Philip G. Altbach, "The Oldest Technology: Textbooks in Comparative Context," *Compare* 17, no. 2 (1987): 93–106, for further discussion of these themes.

10. For an overview of Third World publishing issues, see Datus Smith, Jr., *A Guide to Book Publishing*, rev. ed., (Seattle: University of Washington Press, 1989).

11. Philip G. Altbach, *The Knowledge Context: Comparative Perspectives on the Distribution of Knowledge* (Albany, N.Y.: SUNY Press, 1987), considers these themes in greater detail.

12. Harriet T. Bernstein, "The New Politics of Textbook Adoption," *Phi Delta Kappan* (March 1985): 463–466, for a consideration of the recent American experience.

13. S. J. Totton, "The Marketing of Educational Books in Canada," in *Royal Commission on Book Publishing: Background Papers* (Toronto: Queen's Printer and Publisher, Province of Ontario, 1972), pp. 270–310.

14. Pacifico N. Aprieto, "The Philippine Textbook Project," *Prospects* 13, no. 3 (1983): 352–359. See also Stephen P. Heyneman, Dean T. Jamison, and Xenia Montenegro, "Textbooks in the Philippines: Evaluation of the Pedagogical Impact of a Nationwide Investment," *Educational Evaluation and Policy Analysis* 6, no. 2 (1984): 139–150.

15. Michael W. Apple, "The Political Economy of Text Publishing," *Educational Theory* 34, no. 4 (1984): 307–319.

16. D. Nelkin, *The Creation Controversy: Science or Scripture in the Schools* (New York: Norton, 1982). For an overview, see M. R. Kline, "Social Influence in Textbook Publishing," *Educational Forum* 48 (1984): 223–234.

17. Teruhisa Horio, *Educational Thought and Idelogy in Modern Japan* (Tokyo: University of Tokyo Press, 1988).

18. See Krishna Kumar, *Social Character of Learning* (New Delhi: Sage, 1989) for a broader discussion of the role of texts in developing countries.

19. For an excellent general discussion concerning the American situation see Paul Goldstein, *Changing the American Schoolbook* (Lexington, Mass.: Lexington Books, 1978).

20. Harriet Tyson-Bernstein, "Textbook Development in the United States: How Good Ideas Become Bad Textbooks," in *Textbooks in the Developing World,* ed. Joseph P. Farrell and Stephen P. Heyneman, (Washington, D.C.: The World Bank, 1989), pp. 72–87.

21. Francis FitzGerald, *America Revised: History Schoolbooks in the Twentieth Century* (Boston: Little Brown, 1979).

22. For different national examples, see "Provision of Textbooks: Developed Systems and Infant Industries," in *Textbooks in the Developing World,* pp. 113–194.

23. Barbara Searle, "The Provision of Textbooks by the World Bank," in *Textbooks in the Third World,* pp. 36–51.

24. Edward E. Booher, "Publishing in the USSR and Yugoslavia," in *Perspectives on Publishing,* ed. Philip G. Altbach and Sheila McVey (Lexington, Mass.: Lexington Books, 1976), pp. 173–186. See also Gregory Walker, *Soviet Book Publishing Policy* (Cambridge, England: Cambridge University Press, 1978).

25. Thomas Weyr, "Porn, Politics and Paper," *Publishers Weekly* 237 (January 12, 1990): 21–28.

26. Joseph P. Farrell and Stephen P. Heyneman, Introduction in *Textbooks in the Developing World,* pp. 2, 4.

27. While it is beyond the scope of this essay, it should nonetheless be noted that the inequalities in educational expenditure are growing and Third World nations are actually spending less per pupil when inflation is taken into account than they were a decade ago. The implications of this crisis in educational finance are immense. See *Education in Sub-Saharan Africa: Policies for Adjustment, Revitalization and Expansion* (Washington, D.C.: The World Bank, 1988).

28. Smith, *A Guide to Book Publishing.*

29. See Jorg Becker, "The Geopolitics of Cultural Paper: International Dimensions of Paper Production, Consumption and Import-Export Structures" (Background study in preparation for the UNESCO World Congress on Books, London, 1982).

30. For a discussion of this process at the postsecondary level in the United States, see Philip Whitten, "The Changing World of College Textbook Publishing," in *Perspectives on Publishing,* pp. 247–259.

Contributors

Philip G. Altbach is professor and director, Comparative Education Center, Graduate School of Education, State University of New York at Buffalo. He is co-editor of *Educational Policy* and author of *The Knowledge Context* and other books.

Michael W. Apple is professor in the Department of Curriculum and Instruction, University of Wisconsin-Madison. He is author of *Teachers and Texts* and other books.

Peter Cannon is associate editor of the *Social Studies Review.* He has been an editor at Crown Publishers.

Bill Honig is superintendent of Public Instruction, California State Department of Education.

Sherry Keith is associate professor of social sciences at California State University, San Francisco.

Gail P. Kelly is professor and chair of the Department of Educational Organization, Administration and Policy, State University of New York at Buffalo. She is co-editor of *Educational Policy.*

Edward Larson is in the Department of History, University of Georgia. He is author of *Trial and Error: The American Controversy Over Creation and Evolution*.

Tom Loveless is a doctoral student in curriculum and instruction in the Department of Education, University of Chicago.

Allan Luke is senior lecturer and deputy dean of the Faculty of Education, James Cook University of North Queensland, Townsville, Australia. He is author of *Literacy, Textbooks and Ideology.*

J. Dan Marshall is assistant professor in the Department of Curriculum and Instruction, National College of Education, Evanston, Illinois.

Howard Mehlinger is professor and dean of the School of Education, Indiana University, Bloomington.

Hugh G. Petrie is dean of the Graduate School of Education, State University of New York at Buffalo. He is co-editor of *Educational Policy.*

Gilbert Sewall is director of the American Textbook Council, New York. He is author of *American History Textbooks: An Assessment of Quality.*

Patrick Shannon is professor of education at the University of Minnesota at Duluth. He is author of *Broken Promises: Reading Instruction in 20th Century America*.

Naomi Silverman is senior editor at Longman Publishers, New York.

Joel Spring is professor of education at the University of Cincinnati.

Harriet Tyson-Bernstein is a consultant on textbooks in Washington, D.C. She is author of *A Conspiracy of Good Intentions: America's Textbook Fiasco*.

Lois Weis is professor and associate dean of the Graduate School of Education, State University of New York at Buffalo. She is co-editor of *Educational Policy.*

Kenneth Wong is assistant professor in the Department of Education, University of Chicago.

Arthur Woodward is director of the Norman Howard Demonstration School Project, Rochester, New York. He is co-author of *Textbooks in School and Society*.

Index